Memories of

2009.

Enid.

My Early Years

by Ernest John Greaves

Edited by Enid Moulder

La Choix Publishing
Stewkley

First Published in Great Britain in 2007 by La Choix Publishing
PO Box 6302
Stewkley
LU7 0GX

Paperback published in Great Britain, 2008, by La Choix Publishing

Printed and bound in Great Britain by
CPI Antony Rowe Ltd., Eastbourne, East Sussex

Book Cover: Profile Marketing Services www.profilemarketing.co.uk

2008 Paperback ISBN 978 0 9557563 1 3
2007 Hard Back ISBN 978 0 9557563 0 6

To my father who captured some of his most cherished memories on paper and then entrusted me to edit and publish them. A shared labour of love which has answered some of the many questions I now wish I had asked whilst I had the opportunity.

EDITOR'S NOTES

The times in which my father lived his youth had different values and perceptions to our world today, and some of the language and behaviour he accepted as normal in his childhood and during his time at sea would not be considered appropriate today. Some of the comments and views expressed therefore need to be read in the context of their time.

Dates may also be slightly awry as my father kept no diary, relying on dated photographs and his memory, where possible I have checked and sought to clarify. However, as I wished to change as little as possible of the text, I am conscious that anomalies remain.

Chapters 5, 6 and 7 were originally written as two chapters covering five years, with multiple cross references which made it difficult to understand the chronological sequence. I have rearranged and divided the two chapters into three; consequently any anomalies in these chapters are mine.

Photographs have been inserted at the earliest point of relevance in the story, although not necessarily in the order they were taken.

For those readers who are interested in reading more about the Northumberland colliery villages, there are a number of other books of interest, including 'Memories of Burnopfield' by Dorothy Rand and George Nairn (ISBN 1-897585-54-5), and 'Around Burnopfield' compiled by John Uren. (ISBN 0-7524-1514-X)

ACKNOWLEDGMENTS

23th September 2007
Stewkley

I promised my father that I would publish his memoirs, although it has taken me over three years to do so. During that time I have had the encouragement and support of my husband, Bruce, our two daughters, Suzanne and Christina, and Suzanne's partner, Tony.

I particularly appreciated Bruce's support when I have been stuck or have lost patience with the computer technology, which is not my area of expertise

However, this book would have been another year or two in production had it not been for the help of Erin Laporte, who endeared herself to me entirely by her eagerness to proof-read at the mid-way point when I was flagging, and her avid interest in the story-teller and his history.

Erin was particularly anxious to know more about my father's life after 4 October 1940. However that is where he left his story, apart from the briefest of epilogues which remains as the final page of the last chapter.

Therefore for readers who may be similarly interested I have added an epilogue in the form of the address which the family wrote for my father's funeral. This does, to some extent, provide a brief resume of the next fifty-six years.

Thanks are due to my cousin John Noble who read that address. His delivery of this and his own additional words of farewell spoken in a soft Geordie accent, provided the best possible send-off for my father.

I really wanted the book cover to reflect the different facets of my father's story, so thanks are also due to Sally and Duncan of Profile Marketing who worked so patiently and diligently to develop the book cover from a very sketchy sow's ear into a silk purse.

Thank you too to Rob Towsey and Stacy Killon of CPI Anthony Rowe Printing Services for being a fount of information, for their unfailing patience with my many questions and with the length of time it has taken me to edit the book.

My biggest thanks have to go to my father. For simply being himself, for his love, and for writing an engaging and unusual record of historical interest combined with an international adventure and a love story.

I am particularly grateful that he very specifically gave me the freedom to amend and change the text in any way that I thought would make the book more readable.

When I have wrestled with whether to change a word here or move a phrase there, which has been often, I have been reassured by his permission; but I have always tried to maintain the integrity of his experiences and the expression in his words. If nothing else I hope I have achieved that.

23 August 2008 - Stewkley

Since I published my father's memoirs in 2007 I have received feedback from friends and family that his book is engaging and full of fascinating insights into social and shipping history, and therefore warrants a wider audience.

Girding my loins, I prepared for the up-hill struggle of making the many changes I knew to be necessary if I were to republish his book.

Once again I have been incredibly lucky to find a willing proof reader. This time in my cousin, Amanda Louise Matthews, the daughter of my father's sister Win. Mandy's career has included eight years as a sub-editor and proof reader, and I am truly impressed by her skill in correcting the details, whilst still following the story.

The improvements in this second edition, therefore, are largely due to Mandy. However, I have on occasion, decided to leave the original text, particularly where it seemed to reflect my father's own way of talking. Any anomalies, odd sentences and phrases are therefore down to me.

In their capacity as song writers/singers Mandy and her partner, Derek, have written a song in honour of my father entitled Angel of the North. I particularly like the third verse, which is provided on the final page.

One of my regrets is that my father never met his new grandson, Callum, who was born to Suzanne and Tony on the 9 May 2006. My father would have adored him, as we do.

Enid Moulder - Editor

CONTENTS

EDITORS NOTES
ACKNOWLEDGEMENTS
LIST OF PHOTOGRAPHS

1.	Setting the Scene	1
2.	Early School Days 1922 – 1925	17
3.	School Days 1926 -1929	43
4.	Tanfield Lea 1929 – 1931	61
5.	And so to Gateshead 1931 – 1934	87
6.	From Sanderson Brothers to Clark Chapman & Company 1934 – Easter 1938	131
7.	Cycling and Romance June 1938 - March 1939	170
8.	Preparing for Sea - March 1939	207
9.	Liverpool to Auckland April– May 1939	235
10.	Auckland to Penang May – August 1939	255

11.   Penang to Hong Kong   297
          August – December 1939

12   Hong Kong to Home   337
          January - March 1940

13.   Liverpool to New Zealand   357
          March – June 1940

14.   Australia to Home at Last   393
          June - October 1940

          Epilogue   435
          October 1940 – July 2004

LIST OF PHOTOGRAPHS

1. St James Choir
2. A family picnic
3. Me and Mick, Lowfell
4. Win, Enid, Mam and Dad, South Shields
5. Win, me, Enid and Mick at number 2 Beaconsfield Avenue
6. Enid, Gwen, Win and Lil, Whitely Bay
7. Gwen
8. Lil
9. Enid
10. Winifred
11. Tommy Jobe
12. Myself and Alan Mathews
13. Me, Gilmore Tenant and Bob Porteous, at camp, Low Fell 1937
14. Bert Moderate, Syd Robinson, Sid Porteous and me, at camp, Low Fell 1937
15. Myself and motor bike
16. Sincerely Edith
17. *SS City of Kimberley*
18. The Engineers, from left to right, 2nd Engineer, Chief, 4th and 3rd, 1939
19. Washing day
20. At work
21. More work
22. Taking a break
23. Manhattan skyline 1939
24. A day out in Sidney harbour – the apprentices in the rowing boat

25. Funeral Cortege, Saigon, 1939
26. Me and a Cadet, Saigon 1939
27. Boston skyline, 1940
28. World Fair, New York, 1939
29. *The Killoran*, Auckland, 1939
30. The Repulse Bay Hotel, Christmas 1939
31. Back row left to right, Jack, Cyril, an Aussie Gunner, Wireless Operator, Cadet, me in the front 1939
32. From left to right, 3rd Engineer, Wireless Operator, Jack, the Carpenter
33. One way traffic, Kolambugan, 1940
34. Climbing for coconuts, Kolambugan, 1940
35. Manila, Philippine Islands, 1940
36. Rough weather 1, Pacific Ocean, 1940
37. Rough weather 2, Pacific Ocean, 1940
38. The Wedding Day, Edith and me
39. The Wedding Day, at the back from left to right, Win, me, Edith, Alan, Joan in the front
40. Mrs Edith Greaves, 1941
41. Dad and daughter, Oxford, c.1957

CHAPTER ONE
Setting the Scene

The Lintz was only a small village, just one of scores scattered over the north of the country, old, dirty, but a wonderful place for a child in which to grow. Most of the houses were in terraces, some short, some long, but nothing seemed to be planned. It was as if a giant hand had picked up the rows of houses and put them down in no sort of pattern. Most of the houses were built of stone, although there were a few of brick on the outskirts, and the house in which I was born was the only semi-detached in the village.

There was one public house, the Albion Inn, and one shop in its own right. However enterprising villagers had converted their front rooms, one as a chemist, one as the post office and another became the newsagents and tobacconist. The latter also sold sweets. This was our favourite, with a penny in our hand it was a treasure trove.

The main shop in the village was owned by Dawson's and here we had the old-style grocers with nothing pre-packed. The sugar came in large sacks and was weighed out into blue paper bags; one pound usually, but sometimes in half-pound or even quarter-pound bags. Money was very scarce in those days.

The butter came in large cases and was served, untouched by hand, with the aid of butter-pats which looked like two small wooden paddles. A piece of butter was taken off the huge cube, which stood at the end of the counter, and with the aid of the butter-pats was patted into shape. The butter was then wrapped in greaseproof paper and weighed. It was amazing how the shopkeepers could guess the weight of the piece of butter. Very rarely did they have to add a little or take a little off to make the right weight. I can still see in my mind the large cube of butter standing on a slab of marble, covered by a sheet of muslin to keep the flies off.

There was no butcher's shop in our village. The nearest was in Burnopfield nearly one mile away, but twice a week a butcher came around the village with a horse and cart catering for our day to day needs. A Co-op salesman also called once a week to take orders which were delivered later in the week.

The main shopping was done on Saturdays, by main shopping I mean clothes and suchlike. When anything was needed, apart from everyday needs, Mam and Dad had a trip to town, Newcastle or Stanley. On these occasions they took one of us bairns, clothes had to be tried on so the lucky child had to go along. If on the occasion Newcastle United were playing at home I went along as well, Dad and I watching the football whilst Mam did the shopping with my sister. Afterwards we met at a teashop, had tea, and then did some shopping together.

The shops stayed open until 9:00pm but by about 7:30pm we were at the market to get the Sunday joint. Refrigerators and freezers were few and far between in those days and most of the market butchers couldn't afford them, so the joints of meat were sold off very cheaply at the end of the day. Five shillings would buy a joint of beef to last us for nearly three days.

Before I was born, a long time before I was born, the village boasted a school, but that had been closed in 1893 and converted into the Miners' Institute which offered billiards, dominoes and cards. There was also the bar, and of course the arguments regarding the local football teams. The street opposite the Miners' Institute was however still called School Street.

At the top of School Street was the Wesleyan Chapel, and at the lower end, the pub. The school that we nippers attended was about half a mile down the road towards Burnopfield. This school was much larger than the one it replaced in the village as it had to accommodate the children from Burnopfield and all the small villages around.

The house in which we lived, and in which I was born was number one Office Square, near the south of the village. Two hundred yards further south was a cluster of brick bungalows, which I believe were the original miners' dwellings. There were three terraces of these bungalows, all with a brick outhouse behind for the dry midden and the coalhouse. The unusual thing about these dwellings was the fact that most of the ground about them was paved with red bricks, as was the Office Square.

The Square was bounded by the colliery workings and the machine shop, the forge, the offices, our semi-detached house and the bungalows. I suppose that the paving gave the bungalows their name, as the cluster of dwellings was known locally as the 'Brick Flats'.

The road outside our house ran towards the south, past the Brick Flats to the bottom of the Black Road. Here was the Billy Pit, as we called it; really its name was the South or High Pit, and I believe that it joined the Anna Pit although I'm not sure.

Straight ahead the road led towards Dipton and the Dene Wood, bear left and one took the Black Road to Pickering Nook. Until I was eight this was the nearest bus stop. The Black Road was once a railway line taking coal from the Lintz to White-Le-Head to be transported to Jarrow on the Tanfield railway. There was a tunnel at the top of the Black Road beneath the roadway.

The north end of the village was bordered by the main road from Burnopfield to Hamsterley and Shatley Bridge, and the east by the road to Pickering Nook.

The boundary to the west was the colliery workings and the pit heap, or spoil heap as some people call it. A long rail track stretched downhill from the colliery to the rail yard at Lintz Green and down these tracks thundered forty tons of coal; two twenty-ton wagon loads at a time. The average output of the colliery at one time was ninety-thousand tons of coal and forty-thousand tons of coke annually.

The speed of the wagons was controlled by an operator in a brake house via a wire rope attached to the wagons which ran around a braked drum. The full wagons going down pulled the empty wagons up.

There was also a brakeman who travelled down on the loaded trucks whose job it was to unhitch the trucks when they arrived at their destination. Another brakeman came up with the empty trucks and unhitched the empties when they reached the top. Full and empty wagons were then hitched up to their respective ends and the operation repeated.

There was a large field outside our house and across the field was the eastern border of the village, the road from Pickering Nook to Burnopfield and then Newcastle. Later this road became a bus route so that we didn't have so far to walk when we travelled to Newcastle.

The name of our village was Lintz Colliery, but the village is now called Lintz. The name was probably derived from the name of a rich family who settled in the area prior to the 12th century, the family of *De Lynce* from Linz in Austria. However, the village itself dates back to the opening of the colliery in 1855.

I was born in our semi-detached house on the 15th of October 1917 and my very earliest memory is standing up under the big kitchen table when I was about three years old. Yes, I hurt my head and cried. Mam was feeding the baby but had time to put her down and attend to me. The new baby was Enid, who would have been about three to four months old.

Mother had three boys and six girls, but one girl died of croup a long time before I was born. Hepzibah was about four years old when she died. Tom, or Fred as we called him, was the eldest. Why he got the name Fred I don't know, his full name was Thomas Edward after Dad. Margaret (Maggie) was next, then came Arthur Hugh, Hepzibah, Gweneth and Lilian (twins), me, Ethel Enid (known as Enid), and Winifred Evelyn who was the youngest. All were about two to three years apart. We all had our little chores to do and as we grew older so we grew into our elder siblings' jobs.

As a baby I was given a ball of wool to play with, this kept me quiet for hours, winding it around the chair and table legs. I thought that I was making my own colliery.

Well, that was my explanation when asked, so I have been told. My mother must have had loads of patience stepping over the wool as she walked around the living room, but I suppose that as long as I was safe and quiet my mother didn't worry.

I remember that I used to get excited when told that Gwen would soon be home from school, girls always make a fuss of the baby and I must have enjoyed being made a fuss of.

When the twins Gweneth and Lilian were born Mam was very ill, so ill that her life hung in the balance. Grandma took Lilian and cared for her as her own, and Lilian didn't come back to live with the family for ten or eleven years. Grandma lived not in the village, but in Spennymoor, so we didn't see her or Lilian for long periods. As a result Gwen and I became very close.

Our house, three rooms upstairs, two down, was built of stone with a slate roof and was just a few minutes walk from Dad's office. We had electric lights but no power points, and all the cooking was done over the big fire or in the oven at the side. At the opposite side of the fire was a water heater, but only for washing purposes. The electricity supply was very unreliable and an oil lamp was always kept ready for use.

The kitchen or living room was big and cosy with this big fire, always warm even in the coldest weather. And coal couldn't be cheaper than free, which ours was. The kettle was always on the hob, and if not on the fire it stood at the side, a gentle stream of vapour issuing from the spout ready for making a pot of tea. As the teapot was also at the side, keeping warm, it was tea on tap so to speak.

This kitchen was also our playroom, our dining room and bathroom. The large fire was ideal for its purpose, about eighteen inches wide and fourteen inches from back to front. It burned about a hundredweight of coal a day, but as coal was free, cooking and heating were very inexpensive. The electric light was also free.

The floor of the kitchen cum living room consisted of paving slabs, much like the patios of today, and since some had broken over the years heavy lino had been laid on top of them. Over the lino thick homemade rugs covered the whole floor.

Worn out clothes were used to make the rugs, and throughout the year these were cut into strips about one inch by three inches, stored in old pillow cases and put aside. Then in the winter Mam would borrow the wooden frame, buy the rug canvas and we would start. The canvas was stretched over the frame, and the frame was mounted between the backs of two chairs. Then we all sat around on chairs and made the proggy, or clippy, mats.

The strips of cloth were put in a heap on the canvas. A hole was made in the canvas with the progger (rather like an awl), and a strip of cloth inserted. Another hole was made beside the first one, then the other end of the strip was pushed through and pulled tight until both 'legs' were the same length. The tufts were so close together they kept each other tight in place and made a lovely soft rug. We all participated in the making, telling jokes and stories as we progged away.

Every night we banked up the fire and brought it back to life for breakfast. To do this Dad heaped coal dust on the fire last thing at night, so it smouldered all night and was ready to stoke up next morning. The fire had to be

7

kept alight as it was difficult to start from scratch, and we always needed a cup of hot tea first thing in the morning.

The fire was indispensable, both to cook and to dry clothes on wet days. Spin dryers and tumble dryers were unheard of and if the weather was wet, wash days meant a kitchen which resembled a sauna.

Cold draughts were kept at bay by rugs at the bottom of the doors and heavy curtains drawn over the windows at dusk, and of course the fire kept up to a blaze.

The chimney was quite easy to clean. A sheet of paper was crumpled up, held over the fire, and as the paper caught fire the draught took it up the chimney and set fire to the accumulation of soot. Thick smoke poured from the chimney stack enveloping the village and the adjacent countryside. This was quite common practice in those days but now even coal fires are illegal in some areas.

We had a large tin bath with a high back and we all had the same bath night, Friday, except Mam and Dad that is. We all took our turns with the bath in front of the fire and the high back towards the door The water was boiled in the big kettle and the bigger pans and the water was changed occasionally, but not for everyone. With the doors closed and draught excluders laid along the bottom it was very cosy, until for some reason the door had to be opened.

Mam or Dad held the big bath towel up when we were ready to get out, and we were dried on their knees by the fire. Then night clothes were put on to sit around the fire until everyone was shining pink. After that it was supper with cocoa, and off to bed according to age.

On other nights at bedtime all the kids were lined up by the kitchen table with a big bowl of hot water, soap and towels at the ready. One at a time we were lifted up and told to stick our knees out ready for the scrubbing. Faces and necks were washed, ears cleaned, noses wiped, then all polished off, night clothes on, and ready for bed.

Tom didn't get washed as the young ones did. As he was nine years older than I, he was allowed to wash himself.

And as each baby came along it was an event. They were welcomed into our circle and everyone had a hand in bringing them up. Eventually they ended up on the table to be scrubbed before going to bed like the rest of us.

If the electric light failed and we had to use the oil lamp on the table extra care had to be taken to ensure that no splashing occurred, as if one drop of water touched the lamp glass, it would crack from top to bottom.

During the winter, before we were washed, our beds had been warmed by either a stone hot water bottle or an oven shelf wrapped in an old blanket. The oven shelves were about a quarter of an inch thick and were solid cast iron. These were put in an hour before we were ready for bed and after washing it was bed and straight to sleep, or else.

The kitchen opened on to the back yard, just big enough for a children's game of cricket. At the bottom of the yard there were two doors, one was the door to the coalhouse and the other was the door to the dry midden, or toilet. This was a concrete box with a wooden lift up lid, about five feet wide. In this lid were two holes each with a wooden lid, one larger than the other, and the bigger of the two was for the adults. Down here were emptied all the ashes from our big fire, and this was where we went to the toilet. Every week two men came with a horse and cart, and emptied it out with shovels through a small door at the back which opened onto the street.

On the left hand side of our yard was the door leading into the washhouse, which had a window overlooking the yard. The washhouse held a cast iron boiler built into the corner and under this was a small coal fire. The boiler was for boiling the whites and supplying the hot water.

Earlier on our only cold water tap was also in here to supply water for the whole household. Later, a hole was made in the wall of the walk-in larder adjacent to the wash house, and a further tap and kitchen sink was fitted into the larder, so there was no more walking out into the cold of winter to fill the kettle.

Inside the washhouse stood the dolly tub and poss stick[1], being the main ingredients for a successful washday. Originally only hard soap was used, pared into thin wafers, but later soap powders became more popular as they became cheaper. Before powders were used in the washing, the water became a jelly when it cooled.

As a lad wash day became my bath day as well as having a bath on Fridays. Rather than waste hot water, Mam suggested that I had a bath in the tub, and I must admit that after playing on the pit heap and among the colliery workings I needed a hot bath. Although seeing me come indoors from play it was more than a suggestion, more like, 'Get your clothes off and get in.'

But I didn't mind. It was great fun down in the tub

---

[1] This typically consisted of a long wooden handle with an inverted cup shaped head, often made of copper, which was used to pound the washing as an alternative to rubbing by hand. Editor

there were no draughts, one could practically go to sleep it was so cosy. Later on, when I could be trusted to give myself a good scrub, wash day became my regular bath night.

The winter days and nights were never welcome as life became a continuous battle against the dirt and the cold. Although we were very comfortable at home with a big fire keeping the house nice and warm, the muddy roads made everything dirty, so shoes often had to be scraped clean then washed dried and polished.

Additionally, while indoors was warm having no indoor toilet meant that we had to go outside, and opening the kitchen door let the cold in. It was necessary to wear a warm coat as it wasn't comfortable sitting outside in the cold, but in the cold weather we didn't have the smell. So you can imagine we didn't sit and ponder during the hot weather, nor the freezing winters.

Besides we always had homework to do during winter and Mam made sure it was done properly. Still, who wants to roam the streets in the cold and wet, when there's a nice cosy kitchen in which to read?

During the winter nights, and when the weather was bad we played all the childhood games, ludo, dominoes, draughts, tiddly winks. Dad played too, unless he had brought work home from the colliery, and Mam would often take a well-deserved nap whilst we were playing.

Dad was also a wonderful story teller; sometimes he made them up as he went along, and some were taken from his memories, especially if there was a moral in there. We never wanted him to stop, and often he forgot about time until Mam happened to wake up, then we had to be off to bed.

Summer time was rather different however. The lighter nights prohibited sleep, so we were allowed to stay out a little longer during the good weather to tire ourselves out, which we did quite willingly.

When we were in bed we kept very quiet. If it was still light we lay reading, ready at any time to whip our book under the covers. As the light faded we moved out of bed very quietly towards the window where we managed to read a little longer. Sometimes, if our books were really good, we would hang a spare blanket over the door and window, then put the light on. If I'd fallen asleep over my book when Arthur or Tom came to bed they quite often had difficulty getting into the room because of the blanket over the door, however they never once let on.

We lads slept in the back bedroom, no furniture at all, only the big brass bedstead. On the walls was a big print of Durham Cathedral and another of the 'Monarch of the Glen'.

The girls' room next door had a big brass bedstead and a chest of drawers. On the walls there was a picture of Dad in his Royal Navy uniform, a picture of his ship HMS Tarlair, and a large picture of Little Red Riding Hood. On the chest of drawers was the brass-bound family bible, in the front of which was the record of our family history.

We had a cat and a dog, Puss and Mick, they got on well together, Puss kept the mice at bay and Mick looked after us kids. No one dare approach us with ill intent if Mick was around.

One day a colliery worker spoke to Winifred as she was coming home from the shop. Mick didn't like the look of him, although Win probably knew him quite well, and Mick pounced. The incident cost Dad a new pair of trousers. Mick was a dog unto himself, he'd been told to look after Winnie and he was doing his job. Win was only three at the time. Mam would give her a note and the money, tell her which shop, and then tell Mick to go with her. Mick would see her back home safely.

Mick was always on a short fuse with anyone other than the family. He was a Sealyham terrier from stock trained for badger baiting. Illegal now, in those days it was a country sport. He would fight anything on four legs, and he and the wire-haired fox terrier next door would often go out fighting together. When they went down the village together, dogs they met crossed the road to keep out of their way. Quite often he came home with a rabbit. How he managed to catch a rabbit was beyond me, his legs were only three inches long; unless of course he'd taken it from another dog.

Puss, the only name she ever had, was a great mouser and her kittens were sought after. She was thrown over the yard wall the day Enid was born, someone didn't want her so we gave her a good home. We didn't have many mice in our house. Puss frightened them so much that they fled next door. However Mr and Mrs Scott, next door, had no cat so they had our share of mice as well as their own. Puss died on Enid's 21st birthday at Low Fell, but she kept our homes mouse-free for twenty one years.

The colliery was almost worked out when I was born. The coke ovens were already broken down and derelict and it only lasted eleven more years before it closed down in 1928. One of the owners of the colliery was Colonel Shield who lived at Leazes Hall, a mansion surrounded by a ten foot wall. It was the oldest house in

Leazes and it is now a private residential nursing home.

I loved the Lintz, as we called it, no other place have I loved or known so well; every nook and cranny, almost every stone and tree, all were as familiar to me as the back of my hand.

That was our village and our home, very rudimentary, but we kids loved that village. Even now, nearly eighty years later, my elder sister, Gwen, and I believe that it was the greatest place for any child in which to grow.

1. The Choir, me bottom right

2. The Picnic - From left to right, Me, Win, Lil, Enid, Dad, Gwen, Arthur, Mam

CHAPTER TWO
Early School Days
1922 – 1925

At five years old, as is the fate of all little ones, I had to attend school which was a three-quarter of a mile walk. At least it seemed that long at the time. Dragged down there by my big sister Gwen who was three years older than myself, I was handed over to my teacher, Miss Leadbitter[2].

I resisted strongly, I felt betrayed. I didn't think that my beloved sister would do this to me, but I was dragged into a classroom nevertheless. When I looked around and saw how many kids the teacher had captured, all on her own, I capitulated and studied the other boys and girls in the room. About thirty altogether, some clean and polished, some dirty and dishevelled - a mixture of the classes.

There was the colliery manager's daughter and the local farmer's sons and daughter, all mixed as one. My first instinct was to stay out of trouble and in this I was quite successful, until I was six and was moved up to the next class.

---

[2] Miss J Leadbitter taught the infants at the Leazes Board School for 43 years. A photograph including her, the Headmaster Mr Abbott, and a class in c1920 is shown in 'Around Burnopfield' by John Uren. Editor

As five-year-olds we learned the alphabet, our tables and to read and write. I had a good start in this sort of thing as in our large family we always played together, and simple words and tables were understood to a degree. My little sister Winifred could play a good game of whist when three years old.

As I said, when I reached the age of six the whole class moved into another room under the eye of a new teacher and, as before, I decided to keep out of trouble. I did try, however the teacher who taught the six-year-olds was very strict, and even though I tried my hardest I was always in trouble. I don't think she liked me; I had more than my share of the cane in her class.

Corporal punishment was commonplace even for six-year-olds. I'm sure that if they'd thought of capital punishment they'd have tried even that. The stick and strap were the order of the day, and discipline was maintained at all times.

It must have been easy for teachers in those days. They only had to have someone out in front of the class, give him or her two strokes of the cane and the rest of the class bent over their books with renewed vigour.

But we all knew our tables, could read and write an essay on a simple subject, and could spell reasonably well. Also the discipline helped later on, as I found a good foundation in the basics made future learning that much easier.

When we reached the age of seven we were moved into the seniors, which was another classroom in another part of the school. I was very disappointed that trying my best in the previous class did not result in less punishment, but I thought it might work out right this time.

Mr Abbott was Head of the school and he too believed in installing discipline into the young mind, sparing the rod and so forth. Unlike our previous teacher however he explained where we'd gone wrong, although the punishment hurt just the same.

He rarely came into the classroom, but if we were late we passed his desk in the hall. All late_comers lined up in front of this desk and here we learned the difference between a reason and an excuse. He could read the difference in the pupil's eyes. If he was in a benevolent mood he didn't pick up his cane, but this was very rare, and his own sons shared the same fate as the other culprits.

As we had been punished this way since we'd started school we took it in our stride. We held no grudges, accepting it as an everyday occurrence. If by any chance we were let off or somehow escaped punishment we accepted that as a gift from heaven.

I wonder what those kids are doing now - Bobby Carr, Jack Turnbull, Mary Rayson, Eddy Murray, Mary Dawson, Marion Braidford, the colliery manager's daughter and Ella Cushion; whose elder sister, I believe, was one of the teachers.

She was the teacher we called Dainty Dinah, after the lady pictured on the toffee tin lids. She was so like that petite lady, small, slim, and with her very high heeled shoes. She taught the eleven-year-olds and never had any trouble, not with the boys any way, as they were all in love with her.

When I was six I can faintly remember the time that Win was born. In those days almost all babies were born at home, the mothers lying in bed for two weeks afterwards. During this time she and the children were looked after by one of the older girls of the village.

The boys usually found jobs at the mine, or the mines in the next village but there were few opportunities for employment in the village for girls. Consequently many girls were willing to look after the children for five shillings a week. Such a young lady looked after we kids while Mam was in bed.

She was there to give us our breakfast, tidy the house and see that Mam was comfortable. She looked after Mam during the afternoon, and was there when we came in from school with dinner ready. As soon as Dad came in from work he took over, however Dad was only working around the corner and so popped in now and again during the day to make sure that everything was all right. The district nurse, Nurse Buckley, called every day to ensure that her patient was comfortable and well-looked after.

Everybody was interested in the new baby, especially my sisters and the neighbours, but my Mam wasn't too keen about the neighbours popping in and out. However, when Mam was up and about again the pram was cleaned, oiled and polished, and then the neighbours could admire the latest.

Mam was very ill when the twins were born and Grandma came over from Spennymoor. I don't know whether she came to look after Mam or because Mam was so ill that there were fears that she may not live.

Nurse Buckley was afraid for Mam and both babies were christened right away. Even now, no one knows who the eldest is or even who is who, no one can say for certain, although Gwen has always been considered the elder.

The nurse said Mam was too weak to look after both babies, so it was talked through and Grandma took the weaker of the two, Lilian, and looked after her, although no one expected her to live.

Lilian was brought up by Grandma at Spennymoor and she regarded the baby as hers. One can see why. She'd looked after Lil since the babe was a few days old and probably saved her life. She grew so fond of Lil that she couldn't bear to part with her. Lilian grew up in a tougher world than the rest of us. She had to fight her corner in a small town instead of our little village where Dad was held in high esteem. Lil finally rejoined our family eleven years later when Gran was seriously ill. Then she attended Leazes School with us and we fought side by side, she was a match for any of the village kids.

Bullying was endemic in those days, it did no good to complain to the teachers, they told us to go out and fight. Everyone had to hold their own, one had to be a good runner or a good fighter, preferably both, and one had to use one's loaf. If the bully was much bigger than me, I ran and if he was smaller or the same size, I fought. Usually the bullies wouldn't fight; instead they'd frighten some other kid and persuade him or them to attack someone.

But eventually I worked it out. I was watching a football match in the village; it was wet, cold and muddy, very muddy. I was playing out dressed in my oldest clothes, when I saw this bully across the field in his Sunday best. Sure, I started the fight, and I preferred wrestling to boxing. He looked a sorry mess after rolling about in the mud. I was often covered in mud when I came in after play, but I wouldn't have liked to be in my opponent's shoes when he arrived home in his best suit.

He avoided me like the plague for a long time afterwards, he didn't want a repeat. I never told anyone, but the word got around. It gave me a great deal of satisfaction to be free of the bullying.

When I was seven I decided to join the church choir. This meant three members of the family were in the choir of the church of St James, a lovely small church just down the road from the school. The Reverend Mr Madill was the vicar, and Mr Davis the organist and choirmaster.

This decision opened new interests, not entirely appreciated at the time. No free-roaming child wished to be tied to choir practice every Thursday night and for service every Sunday morning from 10:30am to 12:00noon, with Sunday school during the afternoon, then evensong from 6:30pm to 8:00pm.

Still, choir boys don't have to be angels and a sweet or two during the sermon helped the voice; besides, being in the church choir also helped one's standing in the community. Additionally all the women, with the exception of Mam, thought the little choir boys were angels.

Bob Bell, the colliery blacksmith, and my hero as a seven-year-old, was a front seat extrovert, sporting three watches, one on each wrist and a pocket watch with a gold albert[3] across the front of his waist_coat. He also

---

[3] I believe this was the name of a chain to which the watch was attached. This hung across the waistcoat, the chain secured on one side with the watch resting in the pocket on the other side. A security device but also for show. Editor

wore a couple of rings on his fingers. I was always welcome at his forge, just around the corner from where we lived.

Every Saturday morning, after I'd finished my jobs at home, I made my way there to blow the bellows, as and when I was told. The bellows in those days were all blown by hand. Bob was also the farrier and shod the farm horses and the pit ponies, as well as putting new steel tyres on the cart wheels and dozens of other jobs besides.

Every Monday morning he went down the mine to inspect the ponies' hooves and make sure the shoes were OK. He said he'd take me down one day but insisted that I asked Mam first. I asked, but Mam blew her top - no way was any child of hers going down a pit, and Dad was ordered to have a word with Bob. He probably did, but it would have been a friendly chat. My visit was never mentioned again, by either party, but it was quite plain that I would never go down the Anna Pit. However I still blew the furnace on Saturday mornings, and continued until the colliery closed down and we moved away from the village.

Years later Bob was awarded a medal[4] by the Royal Humane Society when, during a fire at a neighbouring colliery, he forced his way into a burning stable and led out all the horses. He was badly burned in the process but recovered to carry on at his job.

Next door to the smithy was the machine shop, this was another exciting place, and here I learned all the

[4] The Royal Humane Society do not award medals for rescuing animals and I have been unable to discover anything to suggest that Bob received a medal for his bravery. Editor

drilling techniques. What to do and what to look for whilst drilling wood, steel, cast iron, brass and aluminium, all good fun for an inquisitive seven-year-old.

I learned the cutting speeds of the different materials, when to use water or oil and when not to use any lubricant, how to sharpen a drill, and most important how to do all this safely. Seven years later all this came in very handy when, at fourteen, I started work as an apprentice engineer in Gateshead.

The roads in the village were mainly dirt roads and only suitable for horse-drawn traffic, they were almost impassable for motor transport during the winter. I recollect that when I was seven year old the only cars that I'd seen in the village were the Doctor's car and a model 'T' Ford that took my dad to collect the colliery wages.

Dad went to Anfield Plain every Thursday to collect the wages, ready to be paid out the next day. I remember being allowed to go with him once during the holidays. About 8:00am the car drew up at the door and Dad and I got in. This was my very first journey by car and I sat in the front, with the two bodyguards and Dad in the back. It was out of this world for me. With the other lads in the village I played cowboys and indians, but this was real life, and my classmates would be dead jealous. I was in the same car with bodyguards with real guns in shoulder holsters.

At the bank Dad got out with his attendants, went inside and within ten minutes was out again. Dad in the back, a bodyguard on each side, sitting back, jacket open and guns exposed. Oh yes, this was something to talk about when I got back to school.

Parts of the village roads had stones rolled into the top surface which were then covered with cinders. The local doctor, Dr Boland, visited the sick in his car but during the winter he had to leave it on the firmer ground and call at the patient's house on foot. The district nurse, Nurse Buckley, did her rounds on her cycle. She it was who delivered me and all my brothers and sisters.

Bicycles were quite common but not everyone could afford a new one. The cycles usually seen were old and rusted. There was very little cash in our village, but I managed to get a bike together. It was rusty, and there were no tyres on it, no brakes, no ball bearings in the wheels, and no pedals, except for the spindles. It had a chain and handlebars, but no saddle except for a couple of sacks folded up two or three times and tied on with string. I loved that bike and learned to ride on it.

Wherever we went we had to walk, at least to the bus stop or station. The nearest bus stop was half a mile away and the railway station two or three times that, so we naturally developed strong legs.

When I was five or six the buses had solid tyres and the upholstered seats were stuffed with horse hair. Wearing short trousers, as we did at that age, left the back of our knees to the mercy of the horse hair in the seats. It was awfully painful. The girls suffered just as much as they wore short socks, but their dresses, if long enough, saved them much agony.

Until I was ten or twelve I wore strong hobnailed boots that took a long time to wear out and, wherever possible, the younger ones grew into their elder's clothes, until the clothes were ready for the clippy mats. During the winter, and we had some hard winters in the northeast in those days, I also wore leather leggings while the girls had long boots that buttoned up past the knees. For the wet journeys to and from school we wore sou'westers and oilskins. There was no plastic then nor Wellington boots, which would have been a great advantage.

There were small lorries on the roads outside the village, but with speed limits of ten and fifteen mph by today's standards they travelled very slowly. However this allowed the lads to hang on the back for a lift along the road and although the drivers often stopped to chase us off they were always too slow to catch us.

Other pastimes included sliding down the pit heap on sheets of metal, or trying to reach the top of the heap whilst other kids rolled stones down to stop you. We learned to be very nimble.

We pushed derelict railway bogies up the rail on the pit heap and rode down, there were no brakes and we changed the points to ensure that we had a long ride. There was always the chance that some other kid would come along, see us, and change the points as we neared the bottom, sending us on to another line.

Tom, my eldest brother, had a very large and heavy leather trunk, filled with books and all his gear, and usually when he was returning to college we walked to the station with the trunk on a sack barrow. I was there to push the sack barrow home while Tom sat in the train to college. It was a long way from the station.

One term, being late to get the train, Dad, Tom, the brakeman and I rode down the incline on one of these trucks. On the buffers of the wagons were footplates about twelve by eighteen inches and a handrail to hang on to. Dad and I climbed on one plate, Tom and the brakeman on the other, and with the trunk and sack barrow on top of the loaded wagon we hurtled down that incline.

Tom caught the train, while Dad and I walked back home. I would have liked to have come back up with the empties, but Dad said we weren't going to push our luck. The only fly in the ointment was that I couldn't tell any of the lads at school. We would have been in all sorts of trouble as even in those days there were safety rules and regulations.

The pit pond, from which the water was taken for the colliery boilers, was also a great attraction, newts, frogs and minnows abounded. Most of my playmates had aquariums in which we kept minnows and pondweed. I'd feed mine on ant's eggs for a week then Mam insisted that they were returned to the pond. So we caught some more and gave them a week's holiday with good food at home, but they only had one week each.

None of my friends could swim, but as none intended to fall in, swimming wasn't essential. Such was the confidence of youth. However, whilst I lived at the Lintz I cannot recall anyone falling in the pit pond despite the steep sides.

It was a grand place to sail our boats, carved out of wood with our knives and fitted with paper sails. We sailed the seven seas, we raced at Cowes and sailed the Broads. We travelled the world with our youthful imagination. Sometimes we had a long wait until our ships came home as they sailed quite slowly and the sea was half the size of our local football pitch, it was also all of nine feet deep. The pond was fed by a clear spring flowing in at one corner and only once can I remember this spring drying up.

The pit workings were also a great attraction. Colliery workings are now railed off and closed to the public, but in the nineteen twenties they were places of adventure to the village lads.

The old coke ovens had long been derelict, but most still stood, although broken down in places. The flues, running the length of the rows were good places to hide, that is if one remembered the holes down into the oven. A drop of ten feet on to a pile of broken bricks was not a nice prospect.

The rows of ovens were about one hundred and fifty feet long with a cinder track running the whole length. It could be that the cinder track was once a narrow gauge rail track when the coke ovens were in production, but now the ovens weren't used, the rail tracks had been taken up and used elsewhere. These cinder tracks were used to race the miners' whippets and for sprint races between the younger miners. A number of the miners were semi-professionals and ran for money at sports meetings throughout the north east. A lot of money was wagered on these races, and also of course on the whippets.

Over the field, outside our back door, was the Plantation, which provided a short cut to Burnopfield, the picture hall and the allotment. The Plantation was almost half a mile long and a quarter of a mile across and from here, on a clear day, one could see the Cheviot Hills, almost fifty miles away over the Derwent and Tyne valleys. The Plantation was covered with fine grass and gorse and small stunted trees were scattered about, a sign of the poor soil and being open to the strong north winds.

The gorse and broom were a beautiful sight when in full bloom and picnics were very popular here.

The bushes were there for hide-and-seek and the stunted trees and the slope of the land were handy for our aerial ride. This was a rope tied between two trees, one higher than the other, and using a pail handle or a bent stick over the rope we hung on sliding down the rope.

All our picnics were for the whole family, including the dog, wherever the kids were he was there. Mam sat and knitted, at teatime dispensing home-made brown bread sandwiches, tea cakes, biscuits, fruit, and ginger beer. Dad, as usual, played with us and saw the little ones came to no harm.

If we continued through the Plantation the allotment came into view, this was our second garden and helped to feed the family. Here we grew raspberries, strawberries and the usual vegetables, peas, potatoes, cabbage, carrots and turnips. I say 'we', because at times everyone helped to work the soil except Mam. Mam had enough to do in the house, with none of the aids like vacuum cleaners and washing machines which now everyone regards as necessities.

After working in the allotment with Dad and my brothers it wasn't unusual for me to be wheeled back home in the wheelbarrow, on top of the tools, fast asleep. This was of course when I was small. When I grew a little I had to walk, nothing came free.

Another beauty spot where we often picnicked was the Derwent valley at Lintz Ford, this was a deep gorge with a lovely clean river running through. The sides of the gorge were covered with large trees and in the autumn the leaves lay over a foot deep. It was wonderful running through them, kicking as we ran, stopping now and again to pick and eat wild raspberries. Down by the riverside we made Mam comfortable, and then took our socks and shoes off to paddle in the shallower areas, with Dad in as well keeping his eyes on us. We also kept an eye on Mick here, he only had three-inch legs and the current was quick in places.

After a spell of getting our feet wet and feeling hungry, what better than sitting down with Mam who had everything in the way of sustenance, before running back to the river?

Oddly enough, in those far-off days, one could arrange a picnic a week or more ahead and be certain that the day chosen would be nice and sunny, or is that just my imagination? The only draw_back with this location was getting there and back; it was a long walk, two to three miles, and we only had little legs. Dad always had the job of carrying the smallest back as it was hard work walking home after paddling all afternoon.

The other favourite places for our picnics were the Barque Wood and the Dene Wood, both were near at hand, a walk of twenty minutes or so. The Barque Wood, so named I was told because here they cut the timber years ago to build the old wooden barques at Gateshead on Tyne. This wood was less dense than the dene, more grass and less trees but still a good and safe place to play.

The Dene Wood was a shallow 'v' shape, it was also the nearest place, and I think our favourite. At the top end it was being filled in with rubbish, an early landfill one would say, but further down was a grand wood. There were big trees for climbing, trees with straight shoots coming from the roots, ideal for our bows and arrows.

Here we did our bird-nesting and bird-watching. We were cowboys, indians, pioneers of North America, and anybody else one could think of, including amateur Tarzans.

One game, very popular when there were a number of kids there, consisted of three of us starting from the bottom of the wood and three from the top and each had to reach the opposite end without being caught, very few succeeded.

At the bottom of the dene was a spring of very cold water which never dried up, and all around was marsh, abounding with newts and frogs. The water was clean and pure and when the water supply to the village was cut for any reason, this was where we obtained our water for domestic purposes.

Villagers carried buckets and queued to get them filled ready to carry home, this was where our little bogies, or carts, came in handy. Women in the village were always ready to pay a few coppers to us lads for bringing a couple of buckets up for them. If Mam's ginger beer bottles were empty I borrowed these as they held a gallon each. Three at one time on my bogie was quite handy, and with the corks in I didn't spill any either.

But the Dene Wood was more than a wood and a playground; it was a school. It was full of life. There were bluebells, foxgloves and all the wild flowers in season, blackberries, hazel nuts, wild raspberries and strawberries, birds in profusion, corncrakes, larks and plovers. Birds one rarely sees nowadays as well as all the usual birds of today. I enjoyed finding a nest, climbing a nearby tree and watching the parent birds feeding their young ones. There was always something to do, always

31

something to learn.

We carried ropes around our waists, to help us reach the first branch of the trees, and of course our clothes were of the oldest, covered in patches, almost disposable. In fact nowadays they would have been disposed of long ago, but at least we had no worries about getting dirty.

My sisters were equally keen on the freedom of the wood. They all climbed trees but preferred to pick flowers, skipping and so on; however they could all scrap. I've seen them seeing a lad off twice their size, it was all girls in together, and when they fought there was no such thing as Queensberry rules. Girls were more like lads in those far-off days than they are now. They played football and cricket as well as any boy, holding their own in every way. As my sister, Gwen, says, 'We weren't children, we were young animals.'

During the cricket season everyone turned out to support the village team. All the colliery villages had cricket teams and competition was intense. We knew every member of the team, and being a small village they knew us.

When the team was playing away from home our whole family walked to attend, so we could cheer them on. We had to walk as these small villages were not always on bus routes. We took our packed sandwiches to sustain us, just like any other picnic, which I suppose it was. A five-mile walk each way would be too much now, seventy five years later.

The team's captain was Mr Sam Hickman who had two sons playing; George, the batsman, who subsequently played for his county and Joe, the fast bowler. Both of my elder brothers had trials for the team but unfortunately didn't make the grade; 'unfortunately' because it was deemed a great honour in the village.

Dad was on the committee so I suppose we were favoured. He occasionally brought home a ball that was no longer fit for match play, or an old cricket bat which he would cut down to size. Being a big family we could have a game among ourselves in the backyard. We often played in the field outside our house, just across the other side of the road, and the girls were as good a playmate as any boy.

I had no trouble getting my cricket gear together. I had a set of stumps and a bail that the colliery carpenter had made for me, they were square ones admittedly, but they worked. The old carpenter was a good friend of mine. I'd stood and watched him working, asking questions, just to show him that I was interested, and I was. The handling of tools fascinated me. He also knew Dad well, so when a little lad of seven looked up and said, 'Can you make stumps?' Well what could he do? You get nothing if you don't ask.

Bob Bell the blacksmith was persuaded in the same way, nothing was impossible if one went the right way about things. The little devil always won, the rough miners loved him.

After school, even in winter, one of my jobs was to take the milk can and get the milk from the farm. On the way to the farm I had to pass the Brick Flats and had a standing arrangement to call and pick up a couple more cans from two old ladies and collect their milk as well, for this service I picked up a penny or two.

We had three farms round about, two at Burnopfield and one quarter of a mile away. The latter was the one we

33

patronised, owned by Mr Dunn. He was tubby with a red face, and he wore jodhpurs and leather gaiters. He didn't like little kids playing in his fields so we had to keep our eyes peeled, but as the kids could run faster than he could we weren't troubled too much.

However his wife liked children and when we paid for the milk at the week_end we often received a penny back for our pocket.

As well as the milk I often picked up a big swede, these were scattered over the fields for the cattle during the winter. If I was served with milk by the farmer's wife I'd look up with eyes wide and ask if I could pick up a swede as I crossed the field. 'Course you can love, do you like swede?'

'Love it,' I'd say. So on the way back I'd keep my eyes open for a really big one. The cows wouldn't miss one swede. I liked swede, and anyway the cows could eat grass, I thought.

On fine nights though, there were opportunities for getting into mischief. A drainpipe, loosely stuffed with newspaper and set on fire makes a lovely noise and had the occupants outdoors in no time at all. This wouldn't do nowadays though; the plastic pipes wouldn't stand it.

We would tie two knockers together on adjacent doors with black thread through the middle of them, with a length of thread long enough to hold when hiding. If one used black thread it was rarely rumbled. The idea was to get both doors open together as this snapped the thread and left no trace, but one had to know when to stop if you didn't want a good thumping. We must have been very lucky or very artful as I was never caught. I believe I've always been lucky.

Every year we had a choir trip with the church choir, and more often than not everyone voted to go to Redcar. Everything was laid out ready the night before, and at four in the morning the alarm clock went off. It made a terrific noise. The first time this happened I was unaware we had an alarm clock, as at other times the knocker-up from the colliery tapped on the window with a long pole and woke us up, so we'd never needed an alarm before.

When the alarm started ringing like the clappers it was all systems go. Getting dressed, too excited to eat breakfast; then making sure that nothing was forgotten and just sitting, heart pounding, waiting for the charabanc while still getting over the shock of that alarm clock.

At last it arrived at the door, a bus with a soft top. Hop in, make sure your best pal had kept a seat near him, and then we were off. Mam had been generous and had given me half a crown, a fortune in those days. So singing our heads off we headed for the seaside.

We always stopped at Stockton, first to attend to the call of nature, secondly to buy a pound of cherries in the market. These cherries served two purposes, both equally important. These were firstly to eat, and secondly to hit pedestrians as we passed and also of course the choirmaster who traditionally sat in the front seat.

Cricket on the beach was a tradition, everyone took part and we tried to keep the same sides year after year. After our game of cricket we all went our own way around town. Some to watch the automatic rock-making machine in the rock shop window on the sea front, trying to find out how they got the letters to go right through. Others went to find a small present for their parents, after all they'd supplied the funding and I don't think that I could have spent half a crown on myself. Sweets were two pence a quarter pound, and the cherries at that time cost four pence a pound, so Mam had a present for about one and sixpence.

Usually the driver had raised the canvas hood during the day ready for the journey home. When it was time to come home most of the little ones were tottering on their feet and glad of a rest in the coach. Most were fast asleep after the first half hour, me included, and when we reached home I was carried off the coach by my elder brothers and put to bed.

Our choir trip always took place on Saturdays and the following day no lover of good singing attended the church to hear the hoarse voices of the choir.

I liked the harvest festival in September, when the church was decorated it was a wonderful sight. We always had a full congregation. Mr Davis, organist and choirmaster, always chose the most popular hymns so that everyone could let go and sing because they all knew the tunes and words.

Christmas, Easter and the harvest festival were all processional and recessional; that is, the choristers walked from the vestry, through the churchyard and entered the church through the main door, singing the first hymn as they came down the aisle to the choir stalls. We did the same, in reverse, after the service.

On these occasions one had to shine, to be really polished, hair brushed, and washed behind the ears with a whiter than white surplice, remembering all the time that one was on show.

On special occasions my elder brother, Arthur, sang the solos. He had a really fine soprano voice, my voice couldn't compare with Arthur's, no way. Although once only, I sang solo the first verse of 'Abide with me' at a funeral.

Christmas time was the season for our choir social. This took the form of a sit down meal in the church hall, and to make up the numbers all choir members and church staff could take a friend of the opposite sex.

I was only seven when I attended my first social. I had no girl friends so I attended with the sister of my friend in the choir, Auria Dixon. Her father was a farmer in Burnopfield and she became my first girl-friend. She was my guest to subsequent socials, while Arthur took my sister Gwen. The hall was decorated with flowers and the usual Christmas things and lights, with balloons for the little ones, and we had a band in attendance.

From 7:00pm until 9:00pm the youngsters had the floor, playing the usual children's games, but the older generation joined in and enjoyed them as much as the kids. At 9:00pm or 10:00pm we all sat down to eat, with all the goodies of Christmas fare. There was plenty of jelly and custard for the young, ham salads and pork pies for the elders, all in festive mood. After the meal the floor was cleared and for the rest of the night, until 12:00 midnight or 12:30am, we danced the night away.

Younger members who couldn't last the distance fell asleep and were laid out on the stage. They were made comfortable and covered with jackets and overcoats until the end of the proceedings. Then they were picked up and carried off by older brothers, sisters or friends, and put to bed probably not to wake up till morning.

Mr Davis did his best to create and keep the choir interested in music. During the winter months he organised musical evenings in the vestry, it was very cosy with a big coke fire and well attended by the older members. He would bring his record player and suitable records, classical and jazz, but the elders and youngsters didn't mix and the young ones soon gave the meetings a miss. One can say he tried. We, the little devils, were quite happy with hymns and psalms but we preferred to stay at home and waste our time.

Around the end of August, in 1924 I believe, scarlet fever struck the area. Me, always in trouble, was the first to be taken to the fever hospital at Tanfield in a horse-drawn ambulance. But I don't think that I started the epidemic, which was very contagious, the hospital was overcrowded when I arrived. The patients were sleeping two and three to a bed, two at the top and one at the bottom. I can't remember feeling ill although I must have been as I can't remember running about a lot at the time; later on was a different story however.

For the first few weeks we were really knocked out, just lying still in bed, while others who had got over the worst were running around enjoying themselves.

Due to the shortage of beds when I arrived I had to sleep in a cot, suitable for a five-year-old, but when the sister saw that I couldn't straighten my legs she found a bed for me. The only medicine I received was a draught of black liquorice to keep the bowels open and later two teaspoons of Virol per day. I think that was all the medicine any of us had.

While we lacked medicines, when we began to get better we didn't go short of food. There was roast beef, Yorkshire puddings, thick creamy rice pudding and seconds whenever one asked. The kids ran wild as soon as they felt better, the poor nurses couldn't cope, and the older children helped the nurses with the little ones.

Visiting days, Saturdays and Wednesdays, were looked forward to. The parents looked through the nearest window, trying to get a glimpse of their child or children. No one was allowed in so we learned to lip read, and they sent in books, pencils, paper and so forth. I think the nurses did well to get across to the little ones why their Mam or Dad couldn't give them a cuddle.

The funniest part of all the treatment was the fact that, lying in bed so long, we forgot how to walk. We all had to learn to walk again when we were allowed out of bed. In this the children helped each other and all of us made a joke of it, I made a lot of friends in that hospital. It was a children's hospital and there was more laughter than crying during the seven weeks that I was in there.

After seven weeks in the hospital if one passed the test, an inspection by the doctor, one had the soles of one's feet painted with iodine, and parents were informed that their little one was all right to come home.

Arrangements were then made, and in my case my big brother came to take me home on his bike. It was my birthday, 15th October. He pushed me home on the crossbar, jumping on and freewheeling down the hills. For dinner that day, Saturday, we had an old favourite, sheep's head broth. After a week at home I was back at school, although I suffered for months with an ear infection.

After I came out of hospital most of the village kids went in, one after the other. Back at school classmates asked me what it was like in hospital. Some I must have frightened telling them it was better they didn't know, it was gruesome, but overall I enjoyed the experience. Of the family Gwen and Arthur went into hospital, the rest escaped. Lilian was at Spennymoor with Grandma, Margaret was at Benwell School for the blind, but I suppose that four-year-old Enid and the baby Winifred were just lucky.

As I grew older so my jobs around the house changed. The yard still had to be scrubbed with the bass broom and the hose pipe every Saturday. But now I was growing bigger I also had to give my elder brother a helping hand to shovel the coal from where it was delivered into the coalhouse by way of the little square door in the back wall. At first I couldn't throw a shovel of coal that far. The door, two feet by two feet and five to six feet from the ground, was too high so I threw the bigger pieces in whilst my brother used the shovel. As my muscles became bigger and stronger I managed quite well, and three months later was able to do it by myself.

Once I found a brown cylinder in the load of coal, picked it up and put it to one side until I'd finished the job. I though at first that it was five bob's worth of half-pennies, so I took it indoors and handed it to Dad.

I'd never seen Dad turn white before. He didn't say anything, just put his coat on and went out. He came back an hour later and told me that it was a stick of gelignite. Living in a pit village I knew what that was. I also knew that if my find got to the ears of the management, the Pit Deputy would be in trouble.

The Deputy was the man in charge of the shot firing at the pit face. He it was who counted every shot placed and every shot fired, and the two had to tally. He'd really be in trouble as he must have counted a shot as fired when it hadn't. However as I know now the gelignite would only have burned in the fire, not exploded. I never found out if the half crown I later received came from Dad or the Deputy.

Another skill that I acquired at eight years old was the plucking of chickens, geese and ducks and preparing them for the oven. Skinning and preparing rabbits was carried out in the wash house, and was a speciality of mine. Feathers get all over the place and make such a mess, but they were washed and used to stuff pillows.

Rabbits cost one and six pence from the travelling butcher who came around, I think, when he felt like it. I was always ready to try a new job, or I should say, something different. Probably that was why I was asked to do these jobs. It saved my Mam having to do it, but I was always pleased when these things turned out all right. After all, job satisfaction is important.

When all my jobs were done on Saturday mornings I was free to go round the corner to my favourite place, the machine shop and forge, where I watched, listened, helped and learned, asking questions all the time.

I suppose at first I was tolerated as my father was cashier and paymaster for the pit and so very well known. He was very popular too, as he was always willing to help anyone in any way. Any shortages in the pay packets were sorted out on the spot. If any of the workers needed a few extra bob, wife ill or bairns needing something, or if a young miner was saving to get married, Dad was like the local job centre. He'd find little jobs for their spare time like digging gardens, and he enquired if there were extra shifts going at any of the other pits in the area. The pits were all the same company and these things could be arranged in those days, as there was not so much red tape and restrictions as now.

Dad was very disappointed when the colliery closed down in 1928. He loved the village and its people and would miss them, as we all would, except Mam. She hated the fight against the dirt.

CHAPTER THREE
School days
1926 - 1929

As coal mining was becoming uneconomic, the pit owners wanted to cut the miners' wages; the miners objected and came out on strike. The unions became involved and the strike spread across the whole country. At the time of the general strike in 1926 I was eight years old, coming up to nine.

At eight years old I knew nothing of politics, all we knew was what happened in our village. But we did understand that if the colliery closed Dad would not have a job, and we'd not have any coal or electric light. After a while things turned really nasty. The bus taking the secondary kids to school was stoned, including my sister. All the windows were broken because the driver should have been on strike.

The pit owners brought in other miners from out of the district to try and force the local miners back to work. They had police to escort these so called blacklegs down through the village, eight strike breakers with an escort of a dozen police. But the people of the village were ready. As the miners and police passed down School Street, the upstairs windows opened and all sorts of filth was thrown over them, not excluding the contents of the previous night's chamber pots.

We were sitting on the fence around the field only a few yards away and the children of the village thought it great entertainment. Really it was the beginning of the end for the colliery as it closed a couple of years later, and that was really the end of the Lintz village as it was.

Dad was unemployed during the strike. There was no work, no pay, and of course no coal so no heating. As we relied on our coal fire for heating and cooking, coal had to be found, so foraging was the order of the day. Playing as we did all around the village, we kids could find anything. The Black Road used to be the line to Tanfield, although the rails had been pulled up years ago, and down both sides under the hedges and under the surface there was enough coal to fuel the fires of number one, Office Square. I supplied the coal, or most of it.

All the coal that had fallen off the wagons scores of years ago lay waiting and with the help of a large box on my bogie and my half sized pick and shovel, hundredweights of coal found their way into our coal house. This was good quality coal, so to make sure no one saw me coming or going up the Black Road the coal was always covered on my truck. I even went out at night to hide the source. Some people collected coal from the pit heap, but that wasn't such good quality.

There was plenty of wood about in the form of sleepers and pit props, but Mam and Dad had made it plain that these were to be left alone. Tons of sleepers however disappeared during the strike, as well as other timber left lying about.

Dad got a little job. The miners started a drift mine on Dipton Fell and needed someone they could trust to watch over it during the night. They also needed someone the miners knew and who knew the miners, just to see fair play. After all everyone could be tempted to try and get a bit extra. For this Dad shared in the output.

Mam took Dad's supper up every night at midnight and kept him company for an hour or so, then walked back on her own. This was about three quarters of a mile over the fell each way in the dark, with only a small torch. When asked later why Dad didn't take a few sandwiches she replied that he needed something hot, and besides she was in the strike as well and was willing to do her bit. Dad had a brazier to keep him warm, but it must have been a lonely job all night on the fell.

Other miners travelled to the coast and borrowed boats. They fished for mackerel or whatever took their bait, brought it back to the Lintz and sold it cheaply. All the money went into the strike fund.

Boilers were set up in the school yards, fires lit and soup made. This was doled out at dinner time, with a slice or two of bread to any of the children who had no dinner to go home to. There were no school meals then as there are now, and it was quite common for some children to come to school without breakfast. Often the teachers who brought their lunch to school would give their lunches to poor kids who didn't get enough to eat at home.

A good thing about the strike, in the children's eyes, was that we had an excuse for not doing our homework as we were all out at night picking coal. This was the reason not an excuse. It was a full-time job for some children outside of school, and coppers could be earned picking coal for people who couldn't go themselves.

The garden had to produce food and Dad was kept busy, each day after his sleep he was in the garden. We kept chickens at the top of the garden, thirty six in all, with a few ducks and at one time two geese fattening up for Christmas. Arthur used to look after the chickens until he hurt his leg playing football. I remember him once going to the shops before feeding the chickens, the chickens saw him and flew the fence following him to the shops and back.

On a piece of common ground opposite our house we kept a goat, Polly. Polly was handy when we cleared the garden of potato haulms and the remains of the sprouts and the tomato plants. She'd eat anything. She was a bad-tempered goat but we were heavy enough to hang onto her horns and when she'd calmed down a little we let go and ran as fast as we could. Polly would chase us until her chain tightened up.

Mother was the only one to milk the goat, but even then Polly had to be restricted and was always kept on the chain. Gwen and I often took Polly down the wood where she enjoyed herself stripping the trees. She preferred the trees to the poor grass around her shed. The only trouble taking her down the woods was that she liked it so much we had great difficulty dragging her back home again.

We fed the hens, cleaned out their living quarters and the goat's, put down clean bedding and saw that they had plenty of clean water. We weeded and helped plant the garden and allotment and helped Dad in his greenhouse with his prize tomatoes. We always had enough to do, no reason to be bored. There's always help and companionship with a large family, although we had plenty of quarrels as well they were all friendly ones.

During the strike the pit pond for some reason or other had dried up. This revealed all sorts of rubbish, old prams, cycles, tins and glass bottles of all kinds, and skeletons of dead cats and dogs. Oddly enough, we didn't know why, some of these bones were fluorescent. Sid Bunn and myself were fascinated and seeing that the pond was surrounded by fence posts strung with wire we put a skull on top of each post, some of them glowing a ghostly green.

Everyone going to and from the bus stop had to pass them, but Sid and I were disappointed as it didn't create much of a fuss. In fact people regarded it as a joke. We never claimed any responsibility for it; I don't think my parents would have appreciated it.

The drying up of the pond gave the younger miners something to do. They set to and cleaned out all the rubbish, every bit, even taking the mud down to clean earth. When the rains came and the spring began to run again, the pond filled, and when the water cleared they had a swimming gala. I remember clearly standing at the side of the pond cheering the winners.

The strike ended after about eleven months. The miners were starved into going back and had to accept a large wage cut. After that the writing was on the wall for the colliery, and things were never the same in the village.

We had a picture hall in Burnopfield, in fact we had two, The Grand and The Pavillion; the latter was the nearer of the two so that was the one we patronised. The penny matinee started at 5:30pm, every Saturday afternoon. We had special shows with a serial, a cartoon and a main feature, usually a comedy or a western. We kids attended as a group.

When I was younger I was taken there by my sisters

Gwen and Maggie, with Maggie in charge. Later as we grew older, we went by ourselves. On each occasion we called at the sweet shop run by two old maiden ladies, always referred to as the Misses Pallisters. There we spent our pocket money, all one penny of it, usually on Edinburgh rock. Looking back I wonder why. We must all have had a sweet tooth then.

As all the pictures were silent and black and white, the pianist played his or her heart out to give the effects, very necessary when the goodies were chasing the bad guys. Sometimes on special occasions we received a free comic, back numbers of course, sometimes an apple or an orange. Naturally the apple became a core and oranges had to be peeled and the pianist became the target of over a hundred juveniles.

Since then I have tried in my imagination, without any success, to put myself in the position of that lady or gent playing the piano.

It only cost a penny to get into the picture hall, so for four pence Mam and Dad had an afternoon of peace and quiet, quite cheap. On Sundays peace and quiet were even cheaper, we all went to Sunday school which cost nothing.

On fine summer nights after church we would all go on a family walk, sometimes two or three miles, sometimes further. Dad always carried some dolly mixtures or similar sweets in his pocket. He would wait until we were well in front and couldn't see what he was doing, and then in passing he would impale the little sweets on the thorns of a hawthorn bush. After a few yards he would say to one of us, 'I'm sure I saw a sweet tree back there.'

Then when we ran back to find it, he would press a few more on to a nearby bush; while we were picking the sweets he'd shout, 'Here's another one,' and we would have another crop to pick.

The youngest believed as they believed in Santa Claus, and their elders kept quiet just as they did at Christmas. I wonder how many hours we spent looking for sweet trees when we were tiny tots?

On wet Sunday evenings during the cold winter months, when it was too cold or miserable to go walking, we all sat around the big table playing cards. We could all play whist from the age of about three. Or we would have a big fire in the sitting room or parlour. Mother played the piano and we all sang our heads off, mostly Sankey hymns with a rousing chorus. We sounded like the Salvation Army and if they heard us from over the road they must have been exceedingly jealous.

The Salvation Army had a corrugated iron hut on the waste ground by the hut in which we kept our goat. The roof of the hut was also corrugated iron so that if it rained heavily during the service they really had to 'raise the roof' to be heard. But as I said before, our favourite times were spent down the woods, picnicking with our parents during the summer holidays.

We were down the dene on one occasion when a great bull approached us. We didn't like the look of him one little bit, and I don't think he liked us either. As he came towards us he was between us and the fence, and the nearest thing to us was the tree. This was no trouble to me but Win and Enid had to have help from Fred. We sat up in that tree for what seemed hours; both the little ones were crying, probably thinking that they weren't going to see their Mam and Dad again. But even bulls run out of patience in time and as soon as it was safe we dropped down and ran for the fence. Oddly enough, we never seemed to have trouble when our parents were with us.

As kids we never had much pocket money, but there was always fruit at home and sweets at the week end. Occasionally we were given a halfpenny to spend on our way to school. One halfpenny doesn't sound a lot these days, but then we could purchase ten aniseed balls and we could make one of those last for half an hour. If we were fortunate enough to find a halfpenny we were in clover. Fairy soap also held a bonus.

On every packet of Fairy soap was printed the picture of two fairies, these could be exchanged for a farthing each, another source of aniseed balls. As they do today the shops stocked special lines of sweets for the children, small imitation pork chops, green peas and potatoes, Barrett's sherbet dabs and coconut mushrooms.

Christmas time, as today, was the kids' time so we were up early. I lit the fire and when it was going well, everyone up and about, we were allowed to open some of our presents. They were all laid out in the sitting room, a train set and Meccano set for me, a doll's pram for one of the girls, books and boxes of chocolates. We didn't get many toys during the rest of the year, but we had it good at Christmas, even though no chocs were allowed to be eaten before breakfast or dinner. During the afternoon, after dinner and the washing-up, Mam and Dad had a snooze in the kitchen while we kids played with our presents in the sitting room.

If Christmas fell on a Sunday we had church to attend. Tom, Arthur and I attended St James' church for evening service from 6:00pm to 8:00pm. Arthur would sing the anthem for which he'd been practising and driving us crazy for the previous three weeks. Then after church we'd have the party, playing all the old traditional games. Dad, as Master of Ceremonies, kept order and acted as referee. All the family took part, as well as our guest, John Scott, who lived next door.

He was an only child and often joined in our jollifications. It's no fun by oneself on Christmas evening, especially when he could hear the noise from our house.

It must have been about Christmas time when Arthur hurt his leg playing football, receiving a kick on his ankle. It swelled up despite attention from Dad, and the local doctor was called in. The swelling grew worse and the doctor lanced the leg, but Arthur became very ill and he was moved to hospital.

In the ordinary course of events this would have been easy, but during the night a heavy snow storm deposited four to five feet of snow over the village and when the back door was opened we were met by a solid wall of snow. Dad left from the front door which was only partially blocked and managed somehow to get a shovel from the outhouse. However there was no way that the ambulance could get through the snow to the house.

Seeing the ambulance at the bottom of the village, some miners enquired of the driver why it was required. The miners of the village got to work and cleared a path from the ambulance to our back door through the six foot drifts of snow, and my brother was carried down the village on a stretcher by the two attendants.

For two years he was in and out of the infirmary and

after a number of operations he graduated to a wheelchair, then crutches and finally two sticks. During all his trials he still carried on with his studies and finally got back to the High School, then to Nottingham University where he eventually obtained a first-class honours degree in economics.

In 1928 my eleven plus exam came along. Three years earlier my sister Gweneth had passed the intermediate exams for the Central School, although the following year she had moved up to the Alderman Wood High School. Now it was my turn. I preferred exams to class work. I didn't like being asked questions in front of the class, I liked time to think and this one could do when sitting an exam.

It was an odd situation. I didn't want to pass this exam, I didn't wish to leave this school, I didn't wish to study as my older siblings did, and yet I wanted to do as well as they or anyone in my class did. My mother and father had, I think, already decided that they couldn't afford any additional expense at the moment, so no pressure was put on me to pass. I believe, and I think rightly, that I was more practically minded as I was never far away from the workshops at the colliery. My own thoughts? Well, I had to do my best. After all I had my pride, but I hoped that like Mr Micawber something would turn up.

I passed the preliminary exam, and a few weeks later, the intermediate for the Central School. I was happy with that. It was as far as my elder sister progressed so I too could attend the intermediate school, but I was still hoping that something would turn up. The next letter to arrive was to give me instructions to attend the High School for an exam and interview. There were only so many places to fill at the High so the number of passes was whittled down by the exam. If I passed this hurdle I would be offered a place there; if I failed I would be offered a place at the Central School, which Gwen had attended, or I could stay where I was.

I set off to walk to Tanfield Lea, best clothes, polished shoes and face. There were three of us from the same school, although their names escape me at the moment. We sat in a classroom, about forty of us, with the examiner out front complete with mortar board. Within twenty minutes I felt a lot easier in my mind.

I had no idea that we were expected to know so much about Shakespearean plays, Latin or the French language. These questions were far beyond my comprehension, and as the time passed, the happier I felt. I could still try my best and fail to qualify, a wonderful thought. And so it was, Mr Micawber had turned up trumps. I'd failed with great relief, and even better, with no recriminations from anyone.

I learned much later that Dad had a feeling that I'd be much happier in a workshop as an apprentice, I agreed with him. So when the kids at school asked if I cared I could tell them that I didn't want to pass anyway, quite truthfully with a smile on my face. Somehow due to my lack of concern I went up in their estimation. I hadn't passed so I was one of them, but no one was more thankful than I was. On the other hand when I think again, Mam and Dad may have been thankful too.

As I said before, the strike was the beginning of the end for the colliery, and the village, as it was, and the pit closed down not long after my eleven plus exams.

The closing of the pit was catastrophic compared with

the strike of 1926. There was no hope of the colliery opening up again, and there was little chance of alternative employment in the area.

Every one was out of a job, including Dad, everyone in the village was affected. Some of the miners were given jobs at Doncaster, so I lost some of my friends, but the other people in the village had a hard time. Dad was on the dole, looking for a job, but there were no jobs going around the village.

There was a vast difference then in the rate of unemployment benefit. Mother and Father were worried, this rubbed off on the children so we worried too. Admittedly the children were less concerned than the parents as they had such a lot going on around them.

The soup kitchens opened up in the school yard again and the miners' children were fitted with boots or shoes. Our Headmaster took me aside one day and quietly told me to inform my parents that he wanted all the family to visit the school at 7:30pm, he would see that we were fitted with a new pair of boots or shoes. They were issued to all the miners' children but as the Headmaster said, 'Your dad wasn't a miner but he worked at the colliery, and I can't see why his children shouldn't benefit.' We all received new footwear, which in the circumstances was a boon.

When the colliery shut down the first thing we missed of course was the electric light, but it was only a short while before we had a new supply. Coming home from school one day we saw workmen putting in new poles, but what intrigued me was how the electrician climbed the poles to rig the cables. What a wonderful way to climb trees. I could have a great time down the Dene

Wood with spikes on my feet. I wondered at the time how to get a pair.

The new electric supply was for lights only, as it was before, so we didn't really benefit from it and now it had to be paid for. The houses were too old to be rewired with power plugs, besides, who was going to pay for this to be done? The houses belonged to the colliery and it was out of business.

However fuel for heating and cooking was no problem. Houses were becoming empty daily, people moving away leaving garden sheds behind, and railway sleepers by the ton lay all over the old workings. Most of the young miners had gone to other pit villages. Gardens were neglected, friends from school disappeared and there was no one left except the old folk. The village began to look like a ghost town. So once again we had to tighten our belts to survive.

There was plenty of wood around to fuel our fires, although that meant the old colliery workings were pulled to pieces. The sleepers were dug up and sold for five pence each, but even five pence was hard to find, buying wood to burn was burning money. I even dug for coal again and the garden was tended as was the allotment.

The big chimneys were toppled by the simple means of pulling some bricks out, propping them up with pit props, pulling more bricks out then setting fire to the timbers. When the props were almost burnt through the chimney fell.

The best day of all to remember was the day the pit ponies were brought to the surface. This was the first job at the closure. They were brought up one at a time in a net slung beneath the cage. The cage was taken above ground level and the net and pony swung from under the cage on to the flat in front. This was a common practice as the ponies had a holiday every six months in the fields by Friarside Colliery, and there was no other way to get them out. It was common sense to stand back for a while until they got over their fright, although it was surprising how quickly they recovered with their drivers talking to them.

After they were fully recovered they were to go to the fields at Friarside and that was a job for the village kids. I don't know whose idea it was that the lads of the village take them down, it would have been better if the putters[5] had taken them, but probably they were already on the dole.

Friarside was about a mile and a half through the village and down the steep hill. As each pony came up it was petted and led around by its rope bridle, most of the lads had a piece of apple or a sugar lump. The idea was to lead the ponies down to the fields, but who was to complain if the animal would allow one to ride? After the pony had been calmed down a volunteer would come forward, grasp the bridle and lead it away, walking it for a hundred yards or so, and then try to ride it.

Well, some would and some wouldn't, and some couldn't, but the village folk had a hilarious time watching the antics of the would-be cowboys. They were thrown right and left all down the village then getting up to chase their mounts, which had had enough of captivity and only wanted to be left alone. The same villagers had

---

[5] Putters were the younger miners who led the ponies when they were working down the mine. Editor

a different laugh on their faces when the ponies found out that the cabbages in the gardens were very tasty and better grub than they'd been getting down the mine.

When all the ponies were up and enjoying their freedom, the winding house and the big wheels had to come down. I saw the winding house come down after they had removed the machinery, and I remember that some years before one of my nine lives went with it.

The pit winding house, about three storeys high, housed the winding gear to lift and lower the cage, it was solidly built and the side faced the colliery yard. On the wall were chalked wickets for cricket, so we didn't need a wicket keeper, and the goalposts for football. The ground about was compressed cinders and gave us a level playing field. The roof was being repaired at the time and the workmen had left a ladder in place overnight, apparently to save them the trouble of taking it away and bringing it back again. It looked a heavy ladder.

I saw a bird fly into a hole near the top of the ladder and started up to investigate. I reached the top, looked down, half turned and slipped. Down I came on my bottom. Bump, bump, bump! My bottom was sore for a long time. Sid and I kept quiet, if my parents had found out my bottom would have been even sorer.

If my feet had caught in the rungs of the ladder or I'd slipped sideways, falling from three storeys I would have been dead.

During this time on the evening of May 17th 1929 I was bringing the milk home from the farm, as I always did after school, when I felt the earth shake and heard a dull rumble. Although I'd never heard anything like it before I knew its significance, I knew that it was a colliery explosion. I also knew that as it wasn't at our pit, it must be Friarside. All the local pits were in the South Garesfield group.

The Anna's steam hooter was now blaring out continuously as I ran home as fast as I could. There was nothing I could do, but I had old school pals[6] in that mine and I now understood my mother's objection to me going down the mine even for a visit.

Coming home one day Mam was more like her old self, Dad had a job at last. However it was not in this area, and as it was going to be difficult travelling from the Lintz, we'd have to move. These were exciting times.

I would have to leave my school, but there again I'd lost so many classmates and pals from the village even school didn't seem the same. I would certainly miss the woods and the colliery workings, but my blacksmith friend, the carpenter and fitters who tolerated me were all gone. They had been my Saturday companions for nearly five years and I was going to miss them all.

Some little time later Mother announced that we had a new house to go to at Tanfield Lea, which was only about five miles away, and it was on a bus route. It would be easier for Dad to get to work and was just a short walk down the road near Gwen's school. Brother Tom was at Culham College, and Arthur at Nottingham University. This move was only temporary, it was pointed out, we'd

---

[6] A newspaper cutting on the accident was included with my father's original manuscript. A hero of the day was a young lad, John Baker, who was just six years older than Dad and had started in the pits at fourteen after leaving the same school Dad attended. John Baker was seventeen at the time of the accident, and was awarded the Edward Medal, later replaced by the George Medal, for his part in the rescue operation. Editor

soon be moving on in twelve month's time.

I think that this move had been thought of even before the colliery closed down. Our parents were worried about job opportunities for the children, and they would also need a bigger house as we grew, but for the time being, as Tom and Arthur were away from home, there had been enough room.

CHAPTER FOUR
Tanfield Lea
1929 - 1931

The day we moved turned out to be fine, no one likes moving house when it is raining, and we treated it as a carnival. I cannot for the life of me remember if we had a van or a horse-drawn cart with a canvas top.

We knew the people who were moving into our house, they had bought our goat and Dad's beloved green-house, where he grew his prize tomatoes, and we also left the old wringer for their use.

Having said goodbye to our friends and neighbours we set off with heavy hearts, at least I did. Dad and I loved this old place and the people, but it wasn't the same place that it had been. There was no turning back, we were leaving my birthplace and moving to Tanfield Lea and number twenty four, The Crescent.

It was a three-bedroom council house with, wonders of wonders, a flush toilet and, wait for it, a bathroom with a big white bath and hot and cold water. The water was heated by the boiler behind the kitchen or living room fire, so my first instinct was to get the fire going. Everyone wanted a bath that first night, but that was denied us, so we drew lots.

Coming to civilization took some of the heartache off leaving the Lintz, it was dirty and uncomfortable and about time it was blotted out. But there was no heartache for Mam, she had had enough of the dirt, she could plan a new home for us all. There was a garden for Dad at the back and a small one for Mam at the front for her flowers.

The house was on the main road from Pickering Nook to Stanley and everything was different here. We had to act as if we were civilised, it was going to be difficult. We had new friends, a new school, a different lifestyle altogether and running around in our oldest clothes wasn't the thing here. Tanfield Lea was much too upmarket.

We soon got used to a civilised way of life. The bathroom was still a delight. One could sit a long time on the toilet, there was no smell very unlike the one at the Lintz. There it was straight in and out, as quick as possible.

I recall the first time that I used a water toilet. Mam had taken us on holiday in Sunderland, well, not a holiday. Mam was visiting a relation and it was easier to take the little ones than leave them at home. There was a water closet at the bottom of the back yard of this terraced house. When I first used it I was afraid that the water wasn't going to stop, so I pulled the chain and fled. It was a long time before I could stand in there while the water kept running.

Most of the houses at Tanfield Lea were brick-built semis, although there were a few terraces. There was a small shopping centre, a chapel and church hall, the school and on the outskirts, a small colliery. Near the pit was the cricket field which we knew from visiting here on the occasions of the Lintz v Tanfield Lea matches. Stanley was our nearest town, only a mile up the hill and here we did most of our shopping. A market on Saturdays was an added attraction.

There was a huge field adjoining our back garden which no one appeared to have any use for. A stream ran through and being flat the stream meandered all over and made a large area of marshland. The field stretched for over half a mile or so, a wonderful outlook.

Ten minutes away there was a wood of hardwood trees, with less character than the Dene Wood, but a lovely place for all that and there were rumours of wild cats being there. We never saw any even though it was called Cat Wood. Over to the east was the small colliery, very old but still working, employing a dozen or so miners, and here it was that I had my first experience of smoking.

The lads next door showed me a perimeter wall which had a lot of loose bricks; this was the place where the miners hid their fags before going down the mine as they weren't allowed to have matches underground. We took one fag and passed it around the three of us, two puffs and I felt ill. I didn't have another puff for five years.

As the road passed our house it carried on up the hill to Stanley. There was a penny bazaar here, reputedly the beginning of Marks and Spencers, but I don't know if that is true or not. Nothing cost over one penny, it was surprising what one could get for a penny in those days. There were also two picture halls, an ice cream parlour, and a huge market with naked flares to light the place up at night. The stalls had canvas covers to keep the rain off, and as the flares were hung on the corner posts I was always waiting for the canvas roofs to catch fire, but never one did I see.

Stanley was the biggest town in the area, with many

big shops and here we did most of the shopping. There was no reason to go to Newcastle now so we missed our trip to the football match, but instead I could go up to Stanley by myself. There was also a boxing stadium, I don't know if it still exists.

We didn't have far to walk to school which had a large sports field for football and cricket. We even had coaching for cricket and were encouraged to call at the master's house and borrow the cricket gear for use on the field after school. The Head thought it would keep some of us out of trouble. We made good use of the sports field as we had no other site to display our sporting abilities, apart from the field outside our house and that wasn't suitable for cricket.

Another plus, the Headmaster knew Dad. They had played football for the same village team in the old days before either was married.[7] As was usual on my first day at my new school I had an interview with the Head. The Head recognised the name and asked questions which led him to understand that he and Dad had played together for Trimdon football team. I was greatly embarrassed but not displeased when he introduced me to the class and mentioned the fact. I was happy there. Arthur was at university and Tom was at college or doing courses all over the country, so I had a bedroom all to myself, admittedly the smallest bedroom, but my own.

The road to and from Stanley had a number of 's' bends leading down to Tanfield and on a winter's night, when the windows misted up, I used my finger to draw

---

[7] Dad mentioned that his father had had the opportunity to play as a professional, but my grandmother had insisted he gave playing football up when they married. Editor

the outline of a small car in the condensation. When the traffic came down and through these 's' bends the headlights shone through the window and my little car appeared to move from one side of the room to the other. I often fell asleep watching that little car.

Whilst we lived at the Lintz one of the great events of the year was the Burnopfield annual flower show. Dad took a great interest in the show, as did we all. He was the local tomato growing champion and for years had walked away with both the first and second prizes at the show. However, this year, although he was a committee member, he had nothing in the show. We had moved before the growing season and our old house was now occupied by Mr and Mrs Waite who, as I said before, had Polly our goat and the garden and greenhouse.

However we still had to visit the flower show, it was tradition, and of course money was to be made by selling band programmes and handicap cards for the men's races. The funfair along with the tents and marquees were in a huge field, at the end of this field the ground fell away down a steep slope to another smaller field. This lower field was all marked out for the racing.

The bandstand was built halfway down the slope, the slope itself being used for seating by the public. The band, usually the South Shields silver prize band, played twice on Sunday, afternoon and evening, and there was a silver collection at both sessions.

Dad was always in charge of the kids' races, ages four to six, seven to nine, then ten to fourteen, all handicapped of course. The little ones always had a prize as Dad carried two pockets of choc bars during all the kids' races, so there were never any complaints. Dad was always ready to supervise the children's events, he loved the little ones and if any didn't like being beaten or were disappointed he always had a little prize and an encouraging word.

My sister Lilian, who was now living at home with us, won a sewing basket that year in the skipping competition which took place on the Saturday. Anyone who wished to enter gave their name to the steward and turned up in time to do their piece. Everyone skipped as long as they were able, without stopping, they were each timed and at the end of the day whoever skipped the longest was contacted and presented with the prize.

On the top field, in the tents, were all the exhibits - flowers, wines, vegetables, you name it, it was there. Even the local schools were represented, putting forward examples of the pupils' skills. Embroidery, handwriting and water colour painting were all exhibited in different groups, according to age, and all certified by the teacher of the class. The groups ranged from age six to fourteen.

Dad of course was interested in the gardening exhibits, especially the tomatoes, as for years he'd held first and second prizes for his tomatoes at previous shows. While he was looking he ran into Jim Waite, who had a good show of tomatoes and Dad asked him where he had obtained his seed. Dad had always saved his own seed from the previous year.

'Well Tom, remember when you cleared out your garden last year, and you took all the green stuff over to the goat? Well I was attending to the goat when I saw these seedlings pushing through by the animal's hut. These tomatoes are from your last year's seed.'

Jim Waite inherited Dad's championship.

Unfortunately this was the last flower show we attended at Burnopfield, as by the following year we had moved to Gateshead.

At school new friends were made, one special one, Joicey took a shine to my sister Enid who was only eight and six months at the time. He lived at Tantobie, a small village one mile distant where his father had a butchering business, shop and abattoir. His father had a large round with his butcher's cart on Saturdays. Joicey and I often accompanied him on his rounds, just for the ride and to help in any way we could. His full name was Joicey Craven, a nephew of Lord Joicey, the millionaire pit owner.

We roamed around Stanley together. There one could go to the market and exchange comics for one halfpenny, and we could go into the ice cream parlour and have ice cream in a glass, with raspberry or chocolate sauce for two pence. But this particular day there was a good picture showing at the pavilion.

'Come on Ern, we'll go to the pictures.'

'And what do we do for money?' I replied.

'Come on, we don't need money,' he said. 'Follow me and say you're with me.'

Joicey walked into the foyer and as he passed the ticket box he said, 'Hello Sarah, he's with me.' And he pointed a finger at me as we walked through.

Well, we were in, the best seats too. During the ensuing conversation I learned that the picture hall was owned by his uncle. He was a popular pal. It was nice to walk into a cinema as if one owned it.

The chapel at Tanfield had a large hall nearby. This was used for the local dances and other sources of entertainment that could be arranged. Wednesday was the youth night which enabled the kids to get together off the streets. We had slide shows by people from all walks of life, some had spent years at sea, and some were ex-army. We had talks I wouldn't call them lectures, on all manner of subjects, more often than not accompanied by lantern slides. Ice cream was often handed around, free, and usually a good time was had by all.

When I told the family about all the activities, Tom asked what the denomination of the church was. When I told him that it was the Primitive Methodist Church he remarked that that was OK, as they wouldn't find anyone more primitive than me. I thought that was uncalled for, and way below the belt.

I wasn't there long though. One night the person who was to give the talk didn't turn up, mischief brewed and a dozen were given the order of the boot, yours truly being one. So maybe my brother Tom was right in his observation. That was the last regular visit to the hall, although I did attend some of the later shows put on by the visiting concert parties.

One morning at school my teacher informed me that right after lunch the Headmaster wished to see me and for the rest of the morning I worried. I couldn't think of anything I'd done wrong, I just waited and worried.

On returning to school after lunch I made my way to the Headmaster's study, still worried, knocked and was told to enter. He sat behind his desk with a smile on his face and I stopped worrying. He asked me if I knew of Bibby's shop in Burnopfield, the painter and decorators.

'Yes sir,' I said. So I was requested to call at this shop, pick up two wallpaper pattern books and return to school before four. The Headmaster gave me the bus fare and my brain started to work right away, could some of this bus fare stay with me?

Off I went, this was better than school I thought. Then thinking ahead, how could I work this? If I caught the bus outside the school and got off at the top of Hobson bank, I could walk through the Plantation and save a copper or two; although on the way back I'd be carrying the books. A little thought came into my head, no, no, play it straight Ern, something's going to go wrong.

I decided to go straight there and straight back. So I boarded the bus, paid my fare, making sure that I asked for a half, and lay back to enjoy the trip. The buses were now much more comfortable than they had been three or four years previously. They had pneumatic tyres instead of solid ones and the upholstery was soft on the back of one's legs.

Arriving at the shop I gave the letter to the person behind the counter. He read it carefully, and then said he was sorry but one of the pattern books was out on loan, so he could only let me have one. He wrote a reply on the letter I'd given him and handed it back to me, then put the book on the counter. Mr Bibby explained to me that this was one of his new books; the old ones were much smaller and therefore lighter. When I lifted the book off the counter I thought that I was in trouble. When I got outside I knew I was.

Either the book was too long or my arms were too long, or my legs were too short, because after a short while the book was dragging along the ground. I was sure the Headmaster wouldn't like the edges of the book worn away. However, logic came to my rescue; I was always a believer in logic. I'd seen pictures of African women carrying loads on their heads, why not try that?

Up on my head went the book but it wasn't as easy as I thought it was going to be. It was heavy and tended to bend in the middle. As I walked to the end of the road, towards the church, it began to get very heavy indeed, as well as leaving a very sore spot right on top of my head. This needed more thinking about.

I came to the conclusion that my tie wasn't doing any good around my neck, so off came my tie. I looped it through the handle of the book then hung it round my neck, with the book on my back. I carried on like this, looking like an advert for Scott's emulsion or possibly a small Quasimodo.

As I reached the corner, just opposite St James' Church, I saw a figure coming from the church to the gate, and I thought that I recognised the man. I'd been in the choir for five years, and as he walked towards me and came closer I recognised him as the Reverend Mr Pestle. He was the curate of St Margaret's at Tanfield, and was helping out here because of the illness of the resident vicar, the Reverend Mr Madill.

When he reached me he looked down and said, 'Don't I know you, I think you could do with some help?'

Little did he know he was asking for trouble, this thing was heavy. He could carry this back to Tanfield if he wished. He wanted to know if he knew me, so I told him that I was once a member of the choir here at St James and had listened to his sermons on numerous occasions. 'No, no, don't I know you from somewhere else?'

I told him that he'd had supper and breakfast at our

house a number of times and told him my name. He asked about the family, and then enquired why I wasn't at school. So I told him all my troubles. He took the burden from my shoulders and we made our way to the bus stop.

He paid my fare to Tanfield even though I told him that I had my fare in my pocket. He was getting off the bus at Tantobie, the stop before the school, and then walking down to Tanfield to St Margaret's church. I must point out that Tanfield was a separate village to Tanfield Lea, where we lived.

We talked on the bus as we went along. How I was in the choir when he consecrated the new churchyard, he remembered the day very well, he said. And I reminded him of the many times that he had slept on our sofa on Sunday nights after he had officiated at Hill Top church where my brother Tom, on occasions, played the organ. After evening service, as there was no bus to Tanfield, he came home with Tom, had supper, slept on the sofa, then after breakfast caught the bus to Tanfield.

Mam always cooked more vegetables than were needed for Sunday dinner because the leftovers were Sunday's supper. This was always cold meat off the roast, with fried potatoes, peas, turnip, and so forth. The Curate, when there, always had his share. Mam used to say he did two things really well, preaching and eating, if he wasn't preaching he was eating and if he wasn't eating he was preaching, but he really was a good eater. Gwen told me later that he rose to be Dean of Wells cathedral.

Just before he got off the bus at Tantobie he told me that the driver would stop at the school, so that I wouldn't have far to walk with the book. And so it turned out. The bus driver stopped and carried the pattern book to the school door, then off the bus went to Stanley.

I knocked on the Head's door and when I walked in with the book on my back he stood up and took it from me, telling me to sit down while he read the note. He thanked me for getting the book and apologised, he hadn't thought it would have been so heavy. He also told me in future if ever anyone asked me to carry, or even lift anything I thought too heavy I was to refuse or find some other way, but not to strain myself.

I almost told him that I had. I had a shilling left in my pocket, so offered him sixpence back. I couldn't tell him that the curate had paid my fare from Burnopfield. He told me to put it back in my pocket and gave me another one to keep it company, then said that there was no need to go into class, but to come to school next morning. So, I had the rest of the day off and one and sixpence in my pocket. It was a good day's work. Lying in bed that night, a little lad of eleven, the events of the day going through my mind, I wondered how I got that book back.

It was the first time that I'd been on a bus by myself. Could I have taken the bus halfway there, walked through the Plantation and managed to get back to the school on time, and if I had walked through the Plantation would I have met up with the curate?

I remembered my thought as I had started out. I had someone telling me in my subconscious, play it safe Ern, or else something's going to go wrong! And as my thoughts grew hazier and I became sleepier, I wondered how did the curate know that I needed help, who told him to come out of the church just at that time? Maybe God had seen me in the choir? Maybe he had told the Curate to help me? But I'd had a good day, was very tired, and drifting off to sleep in my comfy bed with not a care in the world, I felt I had someone up there looking after me.

After the experience of the pattern book I often thought of luck and coincidences, but a little lad of eleven years doesn't have a great deal of experiences on which to base his conclusions, however, it did make me think of past experiences. Like the time that I fell down the ladder at the colliery, what had prevented me from falling sideways?

Then there were the objects that I found in the pit pond. This was a wooden box, quite small, with compartments which held a dozen small brass tubes, solid at one end. There was another tube which fitted over the end of the brass tubes, to draw them from the box. I showed them to a pal, Walter McKenna, who suggested that we filled one with match heads and hit it with a hammer. At the time this made sense, so that is what we did.

The result was really dramatic. The resulting bang was like a bomb, and since it broke the concrete beneath, we thought it time to make a quick exit. As I lay in bed that night trying to sleep, Tom had came up to bed,

'Still awake?' he'd asked. 'You'd better get to sleep. Mr McKenna has been to see Dad about you.'

We three kids had been running about all day with live detonators in our pockets, ready to go off at any time. Any one of them was capable of killing us, or at least blowing an arm off. Walter McKenna had produced one asking his Dad what it was, his Dad only wanted to know where he got it from. Mr McKenna didn't stop to dress and arrived at our door in his vest, trousers and slippers. He and Dad searched my pockets until they'd found them all, except of course the one we'd exploded. They were returned, or I suppose they were, to the Deputy, who would want to keep things quiet.

So, in my mind, the impression was formed that someone up there was looking after me, and since there have been so many odd things happen in my favour, that impression has stayed with me. Some say it's the luck of the Irish, I have Irish forebears a long way back, some say it's the luck of the Devil. I hope not, but maybe I was a little Devil? Or maybe it's being the seventh child of a seventh child, which I believe I am.

Since my difference of opinion with the Primitive Methodists I was at a loose end on Sundays. So when Joicey suggested that I join the choir at St Margaret's Church I went along with him the following Thursday to choir practice. I sang a hymn followed by a few scales, answered a few questions, and then attended morning service the following Sunday.

It was a long walk, three times a week, but there was a nice atmosphere and the bell tower was an added attraction, if one was interested in bell ringing. Another attraction was that we were paid, not a lot, seven and sixpence a quarter, but it helped.

I managed to get some more customers for the church. I persuaded my brother Tom to join the choir, he was a good tenor and must have thought that I'd reformed, and Lilian and Gwen joined the congregation. Tom only attended while he was at home of course, Gweneth and Lilian I interested by the odd mention of eligible males.

Tom of course was welcomed by the curate, the Reverend Mr Pestle, as was I. As I said, Tom had a good tenor voice and when the following year we moved to

Gateshead he was accepted into the Felling Male Voice Choir. I think Tom's interest was in Joicey Craven's sister, Sylvia,[8] she was very popular with all the eligible bachelors, but he was unlucky. She chose one of the Cheeseman lads from the choir at our old church, St James at Burnopfield, but I couldn't fault Tom's taste, she was a beautiful lady.

Sports day was a great feature at Tanfield. We had a large playing field behind the school, but the sport's meeting took place at Anfield Plain with another school in competition. It was only half an hour away, if one ran. My forte was the eight hundred yards and the four by four relay, third leg.

The only thing about Tanfield that jarred was the fact that we knew that it was only temporary, so there wasn't that feeling of belonging. On sports day for instance we knew that next year we wouldn't be here; it seemed to be unsettling, but we had to make the best of things while we were there.

Our school also had a fully equipped laboratory, this was new and I enjoyed the weekly lesson in there. All the work was basic. We didn't have the complications of foreign languages to worry about, algebra and trigonometry were unknown. So if one listened it wasn't

---

[8] Sylvia Craven and her husband later became caretakers of Gibside Hall chapel, it was owned by one of our local gentry, Bowes Lyon, who made his money from the coal industry. As children we often visited the estate, watching pageants. The hall is gone now, only the chapel remains. Note made by my father. Editor

hard to stay near the back of the class[9] and out of trouble.

I was top of my class and as the monitor, my job was to prepare the classroom for the first lesson after lunch, put the books out and so forth. But coming to school after lunch one day I forgot and was out playing football until the bell sounded, then I remembered, but too late. I was lectured and demoted, but I still retained my seat at the back of the class and that was the important thing.

The cricket field was an attraction during the summer months, as Tanfield was in the same league as the Lintz. This cricket field was the one on which my brother Arthur played when making his only appearance with the Lintz team. Tom's only game for the Lintz took place on the Burnopfield cricket ground, the home ground of the England player Colin Milburn. But after the years of following the Lintz team, living in the same village and knowing the players personally, watching strangers playing wasn't the same in our eyes. However we were there when the Lintz team visited.

At Tanfield I could get close up to water fowl on the marsh, there were sky larks and plovers in profusion. That was where I saw my only cuckoo. If we moved into a large town I was going to miss all this country life. I was going to miss the woods, but again, I realised that if we moved to Gateshead we would only be eight or ten miles from the sea, so it wasn't such a bleak outlook.

---

[9] Those who were perceived as trustworthy and needing less attention were allowed to sit at the back of the class, so the teacher could focus on those in the front. Editor

4. Win, Enid, Mam and Me, at South Shields

3. Me and Mick, Tanfield Lea

5. Win, me, Enid and Mick at 2, Beaconsfield Road

6. Left to right: Enid, Gwen, Win and Lil, at Whitely Bay

7. Gweneth Greaves

8. Lilian Greaves

9. Enid Greaves

10. Winfred Greaves

11. Tommy Jobe

12. Myself and Alan Mathews

14. Bert Moderate, Syd Robinson, Sid Porteous and me, at camp, Low Fell, 1937

13. Me, Gilmore Tenant, and Bob Porteous, at camp, Low Fell, 1937

15. Myself and motor bike

CHAPTER FIVE
And so to Gateshead 1931 - 1934

As forecast, we were moving to Gateshead. It meant change but it was nearer to Dad's workplace, there were good schools and more opportunities for jobs. We had seen the difference moving from the Lintz, so what would this move mean? How would our lives be altered? We were leaving the countryside that we knew so well and going to a big town, a bigger change than from the Lintz to Tanfield.

I liked country life. I liked the fields and woods, the birds and animals. I thought that no more would I be able to watch the birds and animals in their natural habitat. I was wrong in thinking this way, but my only experience of the big towns were the trips to Newcastle with my Mother and Father, frightened of losing them, and being lost. But it wasn't like that after we'd been there a while. Kids are very adaptive, and soon I was making new friends.

We moved to a three-bedroom house, terraced, no garden, with a back yard half the size of the one we had at the Lintz, and which opened onto a cobbled back lane. The front street was also cobbled. I didn't like it.

The main railway line from London to Edinburgh ran past the bottom of the street, and on the banked up track the passing trains were level with our bedroom windows. Our house, number eleven, was seventy yards from the track. The first night that the Flying Scot passed at seventy mph we almost fell out of bed. What must it have been like living in the nearest house only twelve feet away?

The short time we were there we settled in to Gateshead, starting school and making friends locally. But we were soon on the move again far away from the railway and number eleven, Telford Street and into an upstairs flat, a large one. We had been at Telford Street for six months, but this was much better. There were three bedrooms and two attics, and the street outside was cobbled. Most of the streets here had granite cobbles. Once again Mam wasn't happy, we stayed only three months.

Our next move was to Low Fell, a suburb in South Gateshead, a much more pleasant outlook and I think the best part of this town. Our new address was number two, Beaconsfield Avenue, a three-bedroom semi.

As soon as we moved to Gateshead, the three youngest had to be found a new school, this rested on Mam's shoulders. Enid, Winifred and I started attending Kelvin Road School, ten minutes walk away from Telford Street. It wasn't a mixed school, as was our former school, here the girls occupied the ground floor, the boys the upper floor. The school building, which I would say was Victorian, was surrounded by the play area and iron railings and was very impressive.

But Mother wasn't happy, this new house didn't suit. Looking back, I'm sure that Mam wanted a kitchen such as she had at the Lintz but she wanted it here, in Gateshead away from the dirt.

The house was on the main road, but little Mick didn't know this and so became the first casualty. He got out of the house before he was trained to keep off the road, and was run over by a car. I don't think he knew what a car was, if he did he would have attacked it, he'd fight anything. Mam cried her eyes out, even though she never had a good word to say for him while he was alive. We kids loved him, he'd looked after us as children for years and we'd looked after him.

Like the time he was out with Gwen and I when I was about six. He ran off and then we heard all sorts of trouble, with hens squawking their heads off. Gwen grabbed him, pushed him under her coat and we ran home as fast as we could. We got him home, bathed him to get rid of the blood, and then awaited the outcome. We heard nothing then but later heard that Mr Macready had six chickens killed when a fox got into his hen cree.

Tom was teaching at St Cuthbert's school, a church school in Gateshead, and as he was earning full wages Mam expected him to contribute a little more to the family fund. All the moving hadn't been cheap. Tom however was about twenty two years old and wanted to get married to his girlfriend, May Stoker. There was a great upheaval, Mam cried and Tom left home to take lodgings at May's parents' home.

Mam found her house at last. It was only fifty yards away, number forty three, Beaconsfield Road, which had once been the vicarage to the church just behind the house. In the small front garden was a large laburnum tree, and the front of the house was covered with ivy in which the birds nested. It had a cellar with a drain, but as it flooded in heavy rain we couldn't use it. Although Dad converted it into an air raid shelter during the Second World War.

Sometime in the past two downstairs rooms had been taken over for a shop and isolated from the house. So our upstairs drawing room was over the shop, Duncan's grocery store, and our cellar had a trapdoor into the shop.

There were two attics, which became my hideaway, four bedrooms, a bathroom and toilet upstairs and another toilet in the backyard. The upstairs drawing room over the shop was a beautiful room with windows filling two walls, and a coal fire in one corner. Later the coal fire was taken out and replaced by a large gas fire. This room overlooked the crossroads.

On the ground floor were the front parlour and the big living room. So in effect we were back to the big living room of the Lintz, a big coal range, just what Mother ordered, and hot and cold water. With the hot water cylinder in the living room keeping it warm and snug. There was no electric, only gas, but for one pound per week rent who was grumbling?

A coal fire can be very handy. The range never got cold and a stew would stay in the oven and keep warm for a late supper, very useful. The gas lighting was very sophisticated. The hall light had a pilot light with a push-pull switch inside the front door. The front door was solid oak with great stone pillars beside the door frame.

In the right-hand pillar was a large brass knob, pull this and the bell jangled indoors, just like the old horror films. A row of bells, one from each room, was just above the kitchen door and above the door inside the kitchen was the indicator which showed from which room the bell had been rung. I tried to trace the wires from the various rooms, but alterations had covered all traces and the wires must have been covered by new plaster.

At number two, Beaconsfield Avenue I had shared a bedroom with Tom until he went to live at his girl-friend's house, whereas at number forty three I had a bedroom to myself. It was a large room, situated over the storeroom of the shop beneath but as the storeroom was not heated so my bedroom was cold. I had a small gas fire but those things were dangerous then, it only had a rubber tube as a feed from the wall; so a hot water bottle on cold nights was acceptable.

Since I'd been running about on Tom's bike when he wasn't at home I missed it when he left. However when Dad brought a ladies bike home for the girls, I was hopeful, and as none of the girls were keen on cycling I inherited it. It was an old 'sit up and beg' type but it was a bike and capable of being ridden. Actually I had to borrow it at first, but as they were not really interested I stopped asking. I always got the same reply so gradually I regarded it as mine.

When we lived at Telford Street Lilian went to work at our Aunt Ruth's in Eastbourne Avenue as a pastry cook. Aunt Ruth and Aunt Elsie were Mam's sisters. Aunt Ruth had three girls, Elsie, the eldest, Emmy, then Ruth the youngest. Lilian enjoyed the work at first but the money was too little, so when we moved to Low Fell she obtained work fifty yards from home. After twelve months she thought that this sort of work wasn't for her and applied for a post at Stannington Sanatorium looking after sick children.

It was a long way to go to Kelvin School from Low Fell, so Enid and Win moved to the nearest school a few yards down the road. As I had only another year at school

I stayed at Kelvin, although it was a twenty minutes run four times a day. When I think back I must have been really fit.

At school I'd gone into the top class. All the classes in those days were sorted by age so it wasn't my academic ability that counted, not yet. My teacher was a sarcastic old gent by the name of Dent who didn't believe in sparing the rod, so the best bet was to keep ones head down. I'd had a lot of practise.

Oddly enough I can't remember having any lessons on algebra at Kelvin, but when end of term exams came along there were questions on the subject. I'd never heard of algebra but I studied the questions and on the results got one right, how I don't know. But old Dent said he was very disappointed and that I'd better pull my socks up.

Well I thought it over. I wasn't going to get to the back of the class like this, so some homework was in order. For the next couple of months I spent hours in the attic. The attics were filled with boxes of books belonging to Tom, Arthur and Gwen in turn. It was a simple job to find one on algebra, giving questions with answers in the back. When I was up to class standard I was satisfied, and after the next term's exam I was at the back of the classroom again.

I was a big lad for my age and started playing football for the school shortly after I went to Kelvin. Starting out as outside right I found my best position as right back, and played at that position to the end of my school days. There was great kudos in playing for the school team and we always had a good crowd on the touch lines. My brother Tom took charge of his school team and often refereed our matches.

Tom was a very good teacher, but he certainly wasn't a mechanic and I used to overhaul his bike when it needed it. He couldn't fit a new pair of brake blocks, but he could impart knowledge and keep the class interested. I even saw a report of a football match between Kelvin Grove and St Cuthbert's that he had sent into the evening paper, he mentioned a number of the team players by name. Can you imagine the pride of a little lad of thirteen when he saw his name in print? I can, because my name was there.

Our headmaster Mr Sedgwick also took pride in his football team. Every Monday morning at assembly he would ask the Captain who had won the game on the Saturday morning. We were given a word of encouragement if we lost, but if we won, the team often had tickets for the next game at St James' Park.

After playing football one afternoon, coming home on my bike I stopped at a road junction. Along to my left stood a tramcar letting off passengers, and although I thought that I would have time to get across the road before the tram started, this wasn't the case. We set off at the same time, but the tram was a lot faster than me and as my front wheel skidded on the tram line, off I flew. The driver slammed on the brakes and dropped the scoop beneath the front of the tram.

As I lay on the ground I saw the wheel of the tram pass my head six inches away, I remember a close-up view of that wheel. I also saw the tram wheel about to run over the bike wheel and was just in time to pull the bike back so that it missed. When the tram stopped I was up and away leaving the driver shouting curses from his window.

I rode as fast as I could for ten minutes, but when I came to the hill at the end of the road I lost all my energy and decided to walk through the park. I dismounted and began to push, but I started to shake so much that I couldn't walk. I got to the nearest seat and sat, shaking like a leaf. After twenty minutes I was able to walk again and continued home and into a hot bath. I lay there soaking, the tension leaving my body, thinking to myself, there's another of your nine lives gone. Who is looking after you?

About that time Mr Dent had a heart attack and the Headmaster took over his class, so we started to enjoy school again. He was very much an unorthodox teacher. He was very keen on general knowledge and had an easy way with his class. He had a sense of humour and we could talk to him. He often wrote a lot of words on the board, some we had never come across. I suppose that was the purpose of the exercise as we had to find out what they meant and an example of their use.

He also made up questionnaires to test our general knowledge. One day he asked the name of a young salmon and I put forward a 'samlet'. He humorously dismissed this, and the class had a good laugh, but a week later he came into class and announced that he had an apology to make. Samlet was correct. He apologised in front of the class and I gained a point for that test.

After three months Mr Dent returned, and to ease his burden the Head took the top two rows of the class and moved them, desks complete, and set them out in the assembly hall. This was now his class.

The Head's favourite subject was geography and at this he was superb. He and I both liked this subject and when we had geography lessons they sometimes lasted all day. He was a wonderful lecturer. Now and then he would take a lesson sitting in front, this we liked as he would often forget all about time.

On the wall of the hall was hung a model of a ship cut down the centre from stem to stern, and before geography lessons this was lifted down and placed before the class. We'd have a lesson on cargo ships, the parts, the names and their uses.

Our Head had two sons, both deck officers in the Merchant Navy. He used our model ship illustrating the different cargoes from different ports of the world, the different methods of transport, and the different ships for different cargoes. During such lessons he often lost his sense of time or got carried away with his subject. We didn't point this out to him, so often we were still listening at four o'clock.

Other subjects he brought up related to when we lads were to leave school. We had lessons on drawing plans for houses, filling in tax forms, different careers such as engineering, accounting and the Merchant Navy or armed forces. All of this was very interesting and we could see he cared for our welfare. The work situation in the country was serious and anyone who could find a job was very lucky indeed. I stayed at school for a number of weeks after I was fourteen, but the last three months at school I really enjoyed, I didn't want to leave.

During that summer of 1931 one of my school pals invited me down to his place for tea and when I arrived I found him and his younger brothers camping out in a field. The field belonged to his dad, who farmed there. Mind you, the tent was primitive. It was a sheet of lino slung over a piece of rope slung between two trees, with lino and carpet for the ground sheet. We had a good weekend, even though the pig was a bit of a nuisance, waking us up in the middle of the night by walking through the tent. It probably thought it was more comfortable than its sty.

Holidays up to then had always been an odd week at the seaside, South Shields or Whitley Bay. We usually stayed at a boarding house or wooden bungalow in a field, the kids sleeping here there and everywhere. But we appreciated getting down to the seaside, sometimes taking the train to the sea during a bank holiday. I've often thought since that Mam and Dad must have had hearts like lions. The trains were crowded, as were the beaches, and when we were at the Lintz there was a three-mile walk to the station and the same back home.

At Low Fell the nearest place to play any organised or disorganised games was in a large field down by the railway station, about a mile or so away from home, so whenever we wanted a game of football or cricket, we made our way down to this field. There was always a game going on, and almost anyone was welcome to join in. This was how I met the gang, the Robinsons, the Moderates and eventually Alan Mathews.

Although there were fourteen of us we often went together to the pictures, the swimming baths and for our holidays, camping. I was fortunate that some of the lads liked me as a friend, and I got to know them over a long period. We all had bikes to get to the football field and later to carry all our gear to camp during our summer holiday. We also had a cricket team and played various matches with other groups, with a proviso that they provided the cricket gear because we had none. When I think of it now I blush that we had the nerve.

The seaside was still new to me. A popular venue at night was Whitley Bay, and also South Shields for a walk along the beach. There was also my beloved Lintz, where I would call in at Mrs Scott's who used to live next door to us. She always made me welcome to tea or supper, often sending me to the fish and chip van down the village. Other times it was the moors. I was quite happy in my own company, a few slices of bread with some corned beef for a snack. Yes, I was a very happy lad on my two wheels.

When I was fourteen it was time to leave school, and a card from the Labour Exchange arrived by post telling me to apply to Sanderson Brothers of Abbots Road. If I was acceptable they had a job for me in the fitting shop. The interview was on a Saturday morning, timed for 9:00am, half an hour before my last football match for the school. It was a long way from Abbots Road to the football field and I needed a new tyre on the bike, so the tram was the only option. I thought if I went early and the interviewer was early, I might have time to get back for the match.

With my football boots and shirt wrapped up under my arm I caught the tram and arrived there early; the boss turned up at 9:00am. Much to my disgust I wasn't going to have much time, but I must have been suitable as he told me to start on Monday morning at 7:30am. I must have looked as if I'd misheard. I said to myself 7:30am, people don't start work at that time surely, but I had a match to play, and not much time to get there.

I sat in the tram, moving up and down willing it to go

faster, cursing under my breath when it stopped to let anyone on or off. I didn't think I'd make it. I had no watch and as I jumped out the tram I asked the conductor the time. I was half an hour late. But I ran as fast as I could and when I came within sight of the ground I saw that no one was out on the field. I realised that they hadn't started. Mr Lennox had asked the opposition to delay the kick off until I arrived. I ran across the field to the changing room, the kids cheering as I ran. I was crying as they let me lead the team out onto the pitch.

When I look back I was on such a high, I never thought that I was so popular on the football team. I'd never experienced it before, but I would have been bitterly disappointed if I had missed my last game.

As I walked home to tell Mam the good news, that I had landed my first job, my mind was in turmoil wondering what was in store for me. Would I manage?

Sanderson Brothers or Bros., was the name of the firm, but the owners were a couple of friends who'd joined forces and purchased the goodwill with everything else. Mr Logan was the main partner who seemed to run the firm, while Mr Fendley didn't appear to do anything at all. Although, I suppose, both tried to attract work. I think that Mr Fendley was the junior partner, but I maybe wrong. The pattern maker was Bill Fendley, his brother.

On the Monday morning I started work. Like climbing ladders, it was a good place to start, right at the bottom keeping the place clean and tidy, running messages and making the tea at lunch time. The pay was only seven shillings and sixpence for a forty-seven hour week so I hoped that I'd get some satisfaction from it. I'd enjoyed the fitting shop and forge at the colliery when I was a youngster, this was just a continuation of the Lintz.

My old 'sit up and beg' bike was becoming unreliable so I travelled to work by tram. A penny ticket took me to the station and then I walked five minutes to the works, not far from the new Tyne Bridge. Sanderson's was a small company, doing any job that came along and employing one of every trade. That was one turner, one fitter, one blacksmith, one secretary, one electrician, one pattern maker, one draughtsman and one blacksmith's striker. We also had a foreman, but he didn't stay long.

Two things I remember well about the foreman, although I cannot remember his name, one being the very strong smell of bleach when he spoke. It was overpowering and when he spoke I tended to move my head to one side to avoid the smell. I think he must have steeped his false teeth in neat bleach overnight.

The other thing that I remember was that he came from Cullercoats, a fishing village next to Whitley Bay. He had the most wonderful crab sandwiches for his lunch, put up for him by his land lady. I rather think the crab sandwiches were really his breakfast as I often had a sandwich from him at nine in the morning, and I was quite often asked to go out to buy a quarter of pig's cheek for his lunch. A single chap, he lodged in the cottages on the cliff tops.

These were very old cottages occupied by the old ladies who handled and sold the fish. They all dressed in black from head to toe with voluminous skirts and black lace shawls. Sitting outside the cottages, they sorted the catch of the day gutting the fish and boiling the crabs and lobsters. The women also carried the fish in creels on their backs and sold it in the villages, as far as ten miles inland. One of these ladies was Polly Donkin.[10] She visited Lintz Colliery village on a regular basis, and was decorated, for what I can't remember, by King George the Sixth.

But there wasn't enough work to warrant a forema;, no firm could carry passengers in those days, so he was made redundant, without any payment as was customary. I was sorry to see him go, not only on account of the crab sandwiches but he was a nice fellow to talk to, if you avoided his breath.

Mr Race, the draughtsman, took over his duties, and he was someone that I positively disliked. I would have much preferred that he had gone instead.

There was another lad called Jimmy Isdale who was a few months older than me. He'd been in my class at Kelvin but had disappeared; now I knew where he had disappeared to.

If the place was clean and tidy and there were no messages to run I was given a job on one of the machines, only for practice at first with someone watching. I was asked if I'd done anything on a machine before; I said no but I'd done a lot of watching and it wasn't long before I was working a lathe. If he required any assistance I also helped Harry, the electrician, who worked upstairs on the same floor as the pattern maker.

At this time things were moving in the electrical world, the whole country was changing over from direct current to alternating current, so every electric motor in

[10] Polly Donkin was a well known fund-raiser for the Cullercoat's lifeboat. While I found reference to her meeting King George the Sixth, I am not sure that she was actually decorated for her charitable works. Editor

the country had to be replaced. We carried out work wherever it could be found. We - by we I mean Sanderson's - had a contract to service the electrical installations of all Deucher's pubs in the area. Whenever a job came up I was off with my handcart, loaded up with tools and electric cable, helped along by Harry the electrician.

One might think that odd now but then there were very few businesses which ran vans. At Sanderson's my cart was the van and I was the engine. One could put that another way, my cart was the cart and I was the horse, but whenever there was any moving to be done I was the one to do it. Jimmy was working on the machines in the factory, and only occasionally did he get on outside jobs. I thought that I was the fortunate one but I knew one day he would be gone and that I would take his place.

We did jobs at Dunston power station, which was then being built. All the outside bits and pieces had to be galvanised, this was another good job. When the small pieces were ready to be plated they were either threaded onto wire or put into sacks. Then it was my job to sling the sacks on my shoulder and take them down to Jarrow by bus to have them plated with zinc at Parson's works. Once I had delivered them to the foreman I had to wait until they had been pickled in acid then plated by dipping in molten zinc. The first time I watched them through the whole process, but after that I had a stroll around town.

If it was on Wednesday there was always a football match to watch in the park, then pick the stuff up and get back to base for half past four, finish at five with a day's work completed. We also did work for Battersea power station whilst it was being built.

Another job we kids did was to drive the crane which ran on overhead rails from one end of the shop to the other. The crane drivers are professional drivers now, certificated, but at Sanderson's the boys drove the crane. First one up into the cab was the driver. There are regulations now, I don't think there were any then, but I was successfully driving a twenty ton crane at fourteen and two months of age.

Working on a small drilling machine one day I leaned forward to get a better view of what I was doing. A little too far I should think, as my hair caught the spindle, wound round and pulled my head into the machine. Luckily the belt was a shade slack and I was able to pull the handle over and stop the machine. I shouted to Jimmy, he was nearest, and he dashed over. When he saw my plight he promptly pushed the handle over, thereby switching the machine back on.

I did the natural thing, swore at him, grabbed the handle and switched it off again. This time I hung on to the handle, I didn't want anyone else turning it on. He wound the spindle back and freed my hair, but the sudden jerk had freed a patch of hair and skin. We had to go to the office to get the first-aid box and the sore patch was carefully cleaned with surgical spirit. I yelled but no one took any notice. The patch of skin and hair was carefully replaced and held in place with sticking plaster. But it taught me a lesson and for a number of years I wore a cap like everyone else.

A month or two later I was even more fortunate. I was changing the gearing on a bigger machine, a shaper, when the pin which joins the two ends of the belt together caught my hand and pulled it between the belt and pulley. The belt was a big one, five inch by five inch, but instead of dragging me or my arm through a two inch opening it broke. I was still alive with two arms. That was another of my nine lives gone and I was more certain than ever that someone was looking over me.

If I didn't learn to look after myself, I did learn almost every back street in Newcastle. All the business warehouses were in out-of-the way places, little back streets that were difficult to find, but I got to know them all. I would have made a good taxi driver, I had the knowledge and I could take that handcart anywhere. I travelled miles with it, we were great friends collecting electric motors and taking them back.

I remember going to a bakery to pick up a mixer. I undid the screws and lifted it from the bench. The base was in the form of an inverted rice pudding dish and when I lifted the motor and base a perfect rice pudding remained. Only the rice pudding consisted of maggots. I couldn't get out quickly enough, needless to say I never patronised that place again.

I also set the rat traps. These traps were in the form of a cage which could each hold half a dozen rats at a squash, big ones. The secretary gave me two pence to buy the bait, and told me that they liked kippers. I told her that I liked kippers as well. She said that I had to buy them for the rats, one kipper to three cages and left overnight.

I thought that the rats wouldn't get fat on two kippers, and they were not very substantial as a last meal. I didn't catch many, one or two a week or thereabouts, and drowned them in a big tank. I had no compunction in drowning the brown rats, but the black ones were beautiful.

I also made the chaps' tea at lunchtime, and learned the proper way to pack it. Mam nearly had a fit when she first saw me putting up my lunch; she almost laughed herself off her feet. First, one needs a piece of newspaper, eight by eight; in the centre, put a teaspoonful of tea, then on top, half a teaspoon of condensed milk and cover with two teaspoons of sugar. Fold the paper over and over, and one has the makings of a cup of good tea. When it has stood overnight it's ready for use. If made properly it will be quite solid, and when unwrapped it should be in one piece with no sign of sticking to the paper.[11]

But I was in trouble with the blacksmith, I don't know from where he bought his tea, I'd never seen anything like it. It was all stalks, big stalks, and they always floated on the top of the tea in the cup. I took them off with a spoon but more always floated to the surface. He moaned about it every lunch break. I kept out of his way while we were having lunch, the safest thing to do I thought.

I had a good moan to Bob Little, the fitter, and he told me the secret. Make the tea in his cup, he said, leave a little space at the top, let it stand two or three minutes, then hold it under the cold tap and let a little cold water in. I tried this when no one was looking. I didn't know whether Bob was pulling my leg, but it worked. All the floaters had gone, they'd sunk. After I was married Edith could never understand how I got rid of floaters.

Bob and I had a job fitting four electric pumps when

---

[11] I have tried to replicate this recipe without any success. Either modern condensed milk is less thick or the tea then was bulkier! Editor

the Newcastle workhouse was fitted out with a central heating system. Our firm only fitted the pumps so another firm installed the radiators and piping. The workhouse at Tow Law, near Durham, was using large spin dryers with no safety devices. So when legislation was brought in, a device had to be installed to prevent workers from lifting the lid whilst the machine was still running. These devices were made in the works and Jimmy Isdale and I fitted them onto the spin dryers, spending two days there. We were royally greeted and spent two days among a group of old ladies who had been starved of male company, and who all wanted to talk with us.

If there were no outside jobs to do or messages to run, I stayed in the shop and worked on the machines; that is, if there was any work to do. But if work was short, which was often, life became boring and if jobs didn't come in, we were all on short time. Starting work at 9:00am instead of 7:30am we were short of an hour and a half's pay per day, and with no Saturday morning we were ten and a half hours short in our pay per week, but we still had to pay the bills.

At those times all the scrap copper from the electricians, the brass and bronze turnings that had been saved, and anything else of value was collected and sold to provide cash. This gave us the chance to clear the shop floor and make a little more empty space. There was an old lathe that was never used and had been part of the scenery for years they said. On this I learned to swing a seven pound sledge hammer accurately, breaking it up into pieces small enough to be thrown into a lorry.

All the small ends of electric cable were put in a

furnace and the insulation burnt off, the wire was then put into a short cast iron cylinder and pounded into a solid block of copper. Every avenue was explored to raise money. We all had a stake in keeping the place viable, if you lost your job you didn't know where the next one was coming from.

All the steel scrap was taken away on a lorry, that included the cast iron scrap from the old lathe, but the copper and brass scrap was different. That was to go to a scrap merchant at Walkergate, three and a half miles down the river. That was a seven mile trip for my cart, across the Tyne Bridge and down the city road to the shipyards.

It was heavy going over all the cobbled streets and I reached my destination sweating, but happy in the knowledge that the cart would be empty going back. The man and I were talking as he weighed the scrap. He could see that I'd had a hard push, and I was becoming more worldly wise than I used to be. I mentioned that though we'd saved all this scrap up to bring down here I wouldn't get a nickel. I don't know if he felt sorry for me, but he gave me half a crown for myself and the cheque to take back for the boss. I don't know to this day if the cheque was half a crown short of the real value.

After we'd eaten our lunch, if the weather was reasonable, Jimmy and I would make our way to the bottom of the High Street. Here we stood under the railway bridge and watched the cars passing down the High Street and over the Tyne Bridge. This road was the A1, the main road from London to Edinburgh.

Most of the through traffic now goes around Newcastle, but then it went straight through and up by

Morpeth. The traffic now is so congested that it is extremely dangerous to attempt to cross the road. In the early thirties the cars came through in twos and threes, and there were no traffic lights then. Every car was a different shape and it was easy to tell the make of the car one hundred yards away. Now computerised design makes the models so much alike it's no longer possible to do that.

There was one model we both admired, Vale Specials. We only saw two or three, then I saw no more for sixty years when it was a lovely surprise to see two in a motor museum while we were on holiday at Eastbourne,.

Sometimes we didn't stay on the railway bridge long; it depended on the weather and wind direction. On one side of the High Street there was Deuchar's brewery and on the other side, a little way back, was the tannery. On occasions it was an advantage to have a heavy cold or a sinus infection.

A great attraction was the ships on the Tyne, coming and going on the river. Out with my cart I made a practice of crossing over the swing bridge whenever possible. If I had a heavy load it was inadvisable to cross the river this way as it was a steep hill from the low bridge to the factory. With a light load the swing bridge had its advantages as there was always the chance that the bridge would open to allow a ship through. A large ship and I could hear the engines and pumps working as she passed. What a thrill!

How was I to know that seven years later I would be in charge of the engine room in such a ship or that in thirty one years I would be working in the Alfa Romeo car factory in Milan helping to start a new model?

I had no compunction about taking a little time out to wait for a ship to come through the bridge. I was a normal lad, but if I was told to get back as quick as I could I did so. It was hard work pushing the cart with a heavy load and again I remembered the advice of my Headmaster at Tanfield, so on occasions I had to rest for a while.

Well, time passed and I was learning from the fitter and the electrician. Jimmy had left and another new lad had started to run the errands and push the cart, I was going to miss the trips out into town. I was now working on all the machines; drillers, shapers, slotters, millers and planers. I could make my own tools and harden them properly; I could use a file as good as anyone else, and had put weight and muscle on, scaling at ten stone five.

About this time I was having a chat with the secretary, and she asked me why I didn't cycle to work. I told her the truth, that I felt conscious of riding the old 'sit up and beg' bike. It was all right for running about at home but not to come to work on. She told me that she had a bike at home I could have if I wished to pick it up. Although it was a ladies bike it had dropped bars, three speed and celluloid mudguards. We agreed that I would pick it up at the weekend.

This was a turn-up for the books. Bert Moderate - he and I were the best of mates - took my old bike and taking turns to ride and walk we travelled to Whitley Bay. Then we rode the two bikes home. So now I had a good bike and after an overhaul I rode to work and saved a shilling a week, that was an extra shilling for Mam.

But we had fun. There was the occasion when the new lad and I decided to adjust the brake on the crane. The brake was having difficulty holding the load, and it didn't stop quickly enough while lowering. We got the tools together, including grease to lubricate the bearings, and after the adjustments spread a little grease on the open gears to ensure that it ran a little quieter. Then we decided to try it out.

Unfortunately, at that moment, Mr Fendley, his brother Bill and a customer walked out of the office and continued their chat just as we started the crane. A large blob of black grease flew off the exposed gear wheel overhead and landed squarely on the top of Bill's bald head. The boss couldn't hold it back, he laughed his head off, the customer laughed too, a little hesitant no doubt as it could have landed on his grey trilby. The only one who didn't laugh was old Bill himself. But we survived, we were very lucky.

With hindsight, it was really surprising the range of work carried out at Sanderson's. Printing presses were repaired, and with difficulty we made a machine to grade and tar chippings automatically for the roads, very clever our lot. We made a machine for dressing kerb stones - at this time each kerb stone was dressed singly by hand - but the machine was not successful.

We also had a big job at Kelly's, the local printers, which was rather embarrassing really. A connecting rod broke in one of their big presses, and the fitter and I took the side off the press to get the rod out. We got it out, and back at the works it was successfully welded and repaired, and we put it back as well. But when the time came to reassemble the side of the press, well that was something different.

Eventually a firm of printing engineers had to be

brought in to complete the job, but to my knowledge that machine was OK for the rest of its life, the repair was a good one.

The firm also made saw benches, portable ones for timber yards. These, built on three wheels, could be moved around the timber yard by towing, and fitted with an electric plug they were very convenient. We also made refrigerators under the trade name of Superfridge. These were only for commercial use, both single and twin cylinder compressors. I remember one we made for the local butcher started to leak, losing gas, and it had to be topped up.

'Old Bill' had to attend to this emergency and it had to be done on Sunday morning. The butcher's shop was just ten minutes walk away from home and as I lived in the vicinity, I was delegated to help him. I was there on time at 7:30am, and we went in together. We walked into the back room and switched on the light. It was winter time, and dark, but the number of black beetles we saw was astounding. Even more amazing was how quickly they vanished. I thought that we had a lot of black beetles at the Lintz, but here they would have been outnumbered ten or more to one. That was another place that we never patronised again.

But it wasn't all work. I learned to swim at the age of fifteen. I hated cold water and no one could get me into the sea until my parents became friendly with a couple called Sutherland, who offered us their house for a fortnight while they were on holiday. They lived at Seaham Harbour. The offer was made during the school holidays so Mam and Dad took the little ones with them. As I was working I only went there for the weekend.

The girls said that they would teach me to swim, although they couldn't swim themselves. We went down to the harbour on the Sunday morning and after a good deal of horseplay I found myself in the sea. To my astonishment it was warm. This place wasn't actually in the sea, it was in the harbour, three feet deep and as clear as crystal. I decided I'd learn to swim.

So it was serious time in the baths, no playing about, we had to swim. Bert and I visited the baths three times each week, while other activities were put on hold. We learned slowly, but we learned. Every time we attended we tried to swim one length, and then tried to extend it, diving in the deep end and going to the shallows. Even after two months we could only manage one length and no more. One Tuesday night, Bert and I dived in the deep end and this time we were going to swim two lengths of the baths, but once again we only could manage one. The following night we tried again, dived in the deep end and swam to the other end, turned and swam another length. That night Bert and I swam seventy lengths of the baths, when we climbed out we could hardly walk, but we had swum one mile. We had learned to swim!

At sixteen years of age, I was considered old enough to go away with the gang. After that all fourteen of us spent our holidays camping on Mr Boyd's field at Ovingham on the Tyne. Dad couldn't afford to take all the family on holiday together, so I had my own camping equipment, a small tent and a Primus stove. Everything but the kitchen sink was packed into a suitable box and fastened to the bike, grub for a week included, then some pedalling and pushing to Ovingham.

Mr Boyd, once a Heaton Harrier and international

water-polo player, now owned a woodworking business at the Gateshead end of the Tyne Bridge. He was an old bachelor and must have been a good employer as all his apprentices enjoyed a three-week camping holiday in the Lake District every year.

Mr Boyd's bungalow stood on the slope from the road to the river. There was a small, timber-built shop by the roadside, behind which was a narrow belt of trees, then a drop of twelve feet or so to the timber bungalow. In front was a well-trimmed lawn with the flag pole on the edge, with the Union flag flying only when the boss was in residence. This was followed by another drop with a rockery and another lawn, in the centre of which was a double seat. Then a second rockery dropped down to the lawn by the riverside and another bench, from which one had a grand view over the river with the wooded hills, and the village of Prudhoe with its castle behind.

It was a lovely spot. A timber walkway, with hand-rail, ran from the top lawn to the riverside, so one had the choice of walking down the steps or taking the easy route down the walkway.

At first we camped on the field like everyone else, but in later years when he got to know us, he allowed our squad to camp in the private part of his ground, down on the river bank. It was very private and quiet, with no one else allowed and we helped to keep the little estate neat and tidy. He also allowed us to use his swimming pool which he had built himself alongside the river.

About nine feet deep and twelve feet in diameter the water trickled in then out at the opposite side, keeping the pool clean and fresh. We helped to improve it every time we used it, and by diving to the bottom and bringing stones up we deepened and enlarged it.

At the time of our first camping holiday Tom was living away from home, Arthur was at Nottingham University, Gwen was at Kenton College, Enid was attending the secondary school just down the road and Margaret was at home. Winifred was at school, expecting to sit the eleven plus at any time.

The second week in June was Rag Week at Arthur's university. Since his football injury he had always worn a shin pad to protect his ankle. However, he was dressed as a Roman centurion, wearing sandals fastened with leather thongs, which prevented him from wearing the protection on his leg. With his collecting box he jumped on the back of a lorry, hitting his ankle on the tailboard. To hit that one vital spot was devastating, he contracted meningitis and died within a week.

As soon as he was injured Mam and Dad travelled to his bedside and stayed with him all week. We received a letter from Dad on the Friday morning, the day that I finished work for the holidays, informing us of the tragic news. The funeral was to take place in ten days time and we were asked to inform Tom at Mr Stoker's, where he was living. The letter also ordered me to go to camp as arranged with my pals. I think that Arthur's death was such a shock, we were all numbed and we just did as we were told.

I went to camp and I believe that Aunt Hepsibah came over from Spennymoor to look after things at home. When I arrived home from camp my parents were there waiting.

This first camp at Ovingham wasn't as carefree as subsequent years. Arthur's death kept intruding, which I suppose was natural. There were times when I forgot, but it kept coming back.

Later camps were different and I remember one year we had thought of going to Ovingham for Easter but the weather wasn't encouraging. Yet Good Friday came; a beautiful warm morning. Yes! Yes! We dashed around and off for the weekend rejoicing as we cycled there, what a grand time we were going to have.

The following morning was overcast and cold, we sat in the biggest tent playing cards, with the Primus burning near the door doing it's best to keep us warm. No one thought of going for a swim. Next morning we woke to three inches of snow so we stayed in the tent all day. We didn't care to pack our tents and ride home with everything on the back of our bikes in those conditions. On Monday morning we were greeted with three inches of sleet, and after breakfast we packed up and made tracks for home. We never had any thoughts of an Easter camp again.

On later camping trips we got to know Mr Boyd well and visited his bungalow, which stood halfway down the slope to the river, and consisted of one big room. One end, which was stone built, held the big stone fireplace and hearth, and with three easy chairs standing in front of the fire it was very cosy and comfortable. At the back was a large annex, which held the larder, storage area and kitchen.

The opposite end of the large room looked like a western bunkhouse, with two enormous bunks about seven feet by ten, and under the bottom bunk were six enormous drawers. There must have been four double mattresses in those bunks. We were told that at a pinch, they could accommodate sixteen. Trestle tables and folding chairs for sixteen were stored in the storage area beside the kitchen.

On one occasion Bert and I ran out of food and were reduced to eating porridge for breakfast, tea, dinner, and supper. As the Boss, Mr Boyd, often came down, he couldn't fail to see Bert and myself eating the stuff for tea. He remarked that, to him, it was extraordinary that we liked it so much that we ate it even for tea. When we acquainted him of the true facts he was very sympathetic, and invited us all up to the house for breakfast the following morning.

Next morning we presented ourselves at the bungalow. The Boss had gone to work, but his friends stood in as cook and waiter and we all enjoyed a good stuffing of bacon and eggs, sausage and fried tomatoes, tinned fruit and toast, with tea to wash it down.

There was nothing left on our plates, and I don't think there could have been much left in the larder. Fourteen hungry seventeen-year-olds can shift an enormous amount of grub, but that breakfast was greatly appreciated as we cycled home that night.

On another occasion he had two friends staying with him, an old Heaton Harrier friend and his son, and later that night the lad came down with a tin of corned beef, a tin of pineapple chunks, half a pound of butter and a loaf of bread for Bert and me with Mr Boyd's compliments. He had a very good idea of our staple diet.

Food was always important on camps, so the first job in the morning was breakfast, and as Bert, who slept in my tent, was an early riser, he had the dubious honour of making it.

The porridge was first, then the bacon and eggs if we had any. The open air gave us a good appetite and as the food supply was often limited we had an inclination to overeat the first few days. After eating we took a run to Bywell to get the papers, a good excuse for exercise, three miles there and three miles back. Then the first swim of the day, we had four or five according to the weather.

As the river ran past the tents it was eight or nine feet deep and ten feet wide. Twenty feet downstream it narrowed to two feet wide and a foot deep. After this narrow neck it opened out again. We entered the river in the deep channel and turning on our backs steered ourselves feet first towards the narrow gap, hurtling through with the current, then a gentle swim to the pool.

With Mr Boyd's permission we took some turf off the site; on this spot we had the camp fire, and every night weather permitting, we had a sing-song around the fire. A mouth organ, a ukulele and a guitar made the music and the rest of us made the noise. Mr Boyd enjoyed it as well, as we were to find out.

On one occasion he was ill and took to his bed for a while. When we heard of this we cancelled the sing-song but the guest living with him came with a request for us to carry on. He missed the singing as it helped him to go to sleep. We didn't think we were that good, but we carried on.

We kept clean by having a good bath every now and again. During the summer the level of the river dropped, and as the river bed beyond the deep channel was a bed of stones, here and there pools developed, about the size of a big bath and varying between four and ten inches deep. These warmed up in the sun, and equipped with soap and towel we jumped across the narrow neck and had our bath. The water at times became quite hot, the stones around were bone dry, bleached by the sun, and our towels lay drying on them while we sunbathed.

One day in 1934 out of the blue, with no hint at all from me, my mother said to me that she thought I'd earned a new bike, I was almost seventeen and I should have a man's bike. She gave me five bob[12] for the deposit and said that I would have the half a crown[13] weekly rise in my pocket money to pay for it. I knew which model I wanted, and where to get it. Hadn't I rubbed my nose on countless cycle shop windows during the last year or two?

I bought my bike, a Rudge sports, from Eades for five pounds nineteen and sixpence, and later on I equipped it with a Cyclo three speed gear. I called into the shop every week to pay my dues, usually on my way home from work. The shop, owned by Mr Bonar Eades, sold musical instruments as well as bikes, so that when a new record was issued, one that I liked, here was where I bought it. Then they cost the equivalent of seven pence, and by calling in every week I became well acquainted with Doris Melvin and Edith Johnson, the two girls in the shop.

When my bike was almost paid, for I decided I needed new mudguards, cycling shoes and a new cape, although I didn't know how to pay for them. After I'd paid my

---

[12] The pre-decimal 'bob' was a shilling, equivalent to five new pence. Editor

[13] Half a crown was two shillings and sixpence equivalent to twelve and a half new pence. Editor

usual instalment on my bike Doris asked me if there was anything else that I required, 'Yes,' I said, 'but they cost money.'

'Just a minute,' Doris said, 'I'll see Mr Eades.'

Off she went into the back of the shop. When she came back another head appeared round the door and the boss came into the shop. looking me up and down as he came in.

I had seen him and his wife having tea on the moors at Pigdon on my back from Rothbury, and recognised them, so I asked him if he'd enjoyed his picnic on Sunday afternoon. He was pleased that I'd recognised him. He'd wondered who it was that waved, and suggested that next time I should get down and join them. He told me that was one of their favourite spots, and then disappeared back into the office.

Doris told me that I could have credit to the value of the original bill. With this windfall I went home with my new equipment and carried on paying my half crown each week. As the cycle bill came down, which it did very quickly, it was handy getting all the spares and equipment that I needed when I needed them without having to save up. Later, the arrangement came in handy for spares for the tandem.

I loved my bike. It took me off to the coast, the moors and the by-lanes, keeping my legs in trim. The exercise also gave me a great appetite. All the gang had a bike of sorts and the weekends were the times we could get together, visiting the swimming baths and the pictures, playing football or cricket. As I had three nights evening classes through the week I didn't have much time to fit everything in, so weekends were for cycling, winter or summer.

I read the cycling journals and logged all my rides and mileages, even the journeys to work. Now as I look back, I realise that I rode a greater mileage then than I drive now in my car.

I knew a chap at work who was a member of a cycling club, The Clarion, and I paid a visit as a non-member just to see what it was like. They were a nice crowd. I found a few that I knew from work and I got a good welcome from them all. Most of them, even the ladies, were more interested in racing than touring, while I was more interested in the touring side. The Club was well equipped with rollers for training, massage tables, a big coal fire and a kitchen, and this was all paid for from the weekly subscription, which was only coppers.

After the Sunday run there were tea and buns, and next door but one was a cycle shop where members of the club got discount on anything they needed cycle-wise. I was six months with the club and had some good runs with them. I even persuaded some of the purists to change their minds about three-speed gears, as against fixed wheels. I used three-speed gears in summer but in winter a fixed wheel made for better braking. It was safer with tram lines about.

But two events were to change my mind about club riding. One of these incidents occurred descending Blaydon Hill. Riding in pairs down the hill we came, thirty of us, when a rider's brake cable broke. She was at the back and came straight through the middle of the pack, down they fell, half a dozen bikes and riders in one heap. After the riders sorted themselves out, one girl was still on the ground. It was found that a brake lever had pierced her throat. She was carried to a nearby house and from there to the local hospital. She had a very narrow escape, another half inch and they said it would have been fatal.

The other incident happened at Gosforth, north Newcastle, coming back from Belsay, on a dark wet night. Instead of the usual cobbles this stretch of road had a surface of wood blocks, which in these conditions were extremely slippery. One of the leading riders of a group of about thirty skidded whilst crossing the tramlines, and half the club came to grief. Though no one was hurt in this instance it impressed on my mind that if I was to have an accident, I wanted it to be my fault. I came to the conclusion that club riding, however pleasant and sociable, was just a little dangerous.

I preferred the leisurely touring idea and a fast spell when I felt like it, which wasn't too often. However, as so often happened to me, things worked out without any effort on my part when I met Alan Mathews.

The gang were going to play cricket and on the way to meet the team before going to the venue I got a puncture. Alan was there with his bike but we hadn't time to mend the puncture so Alan put my bike in his nearby back yard and took me down to the venue on his tandem. After the match he said he'd take me home and mend my puncture the next day, which I thought was very civil of him.

I thought it curious that instead of taking the most direct route home, Alan steered the tandem down to Saltwell Road in the valley then up the steepest hill in the area. I'd never been on a tandem before, it was a new experience and much easier than the solo bike. We climbed this hill with no trouble at all, and as I thanked him he asked me what I was doing tomorrow. I replied with 'Nothing special, anything in mind?'

We arranged a trip on the tandem, and on the next day we travelled one hundred and forty miles around the Durham Moors.

Two men on a tandem are a team. They must have the same sense of humour, and the same sense of rhythm and riding style. In fact they must have a similar outlook on life and, above all, they must love cycling for cycling's sake. After that Alan joined us on our camping trips.

Alan had bought the tandem with his friend and shared it for seven years as riding partners. Then his friend became his brother-in-law by marrying his sister, and he gave over his half of the tandem to Alan as a good_bye present. He and his wife settled in Whitley Bay. Alan then rode with various other friends, but for some reason or other they didn't end up as permanent companions on the bike.

When we met we got along like a house on fire and within a short time I had a second home at number four, St Alban's Terrace, and Alan had a second home at number forty three. I was adopted as a second son by Mrs Mathews and was always welcome at any time.

Alan was the elder of us two, and knew of all the tea houses in the area. Not only did he know the tea shops, he knew the owners as well. On numerous occasions during the winters we arrived at our destinations wet and cold and hungry. We would be welcomed in, loaned clothes, and sat in front of a big fire drinking tea with a blanket around our shoulders, our riding clothes steaming gently away in front of us.

We usually carried our own food, so that if nothing

untoward happened during our Sunday run our only expense was pots of tea, one and four pence per day.

When we felt fit we rode fast. After work on a Wednesday night we would often have a run out for a paper of fish and chips to Wooler, fifty miles north of Newcastle. This took an hour and three quarters, then a dash home and into a hot bath. I regarded Alan as my brother in every way and to me he was more of a brother than my natural brothers.

There was no speed limit for cyclists, but on more than one occasion we had been flagged down by police cars and told to slow down. They often had a word with us as they drove alongside and were surprised that we could travel at the speeds we did.

Alan and I often went for a short sharp run on the tandem. In the autumn that was often to Ovingham to keep Mr Boyd company for an hour or so, taking something to eat with us in case he had nothing in.

Mr Boyd didn't run a car, going to work by train, and he was always pleased to see us at night after we'd finished work. We'd have a cup of tea, and a small pork pie that we would supply, or something similar, a chat for an hour or so, and then back home for ten. He lived in his bungalow from April till October, depending on the weather and then moved in with his friends at Heaton, a suburb of Newcastle.

After that first run of one hundred and forty miles over the Durham moors, Barnard Castle, Stanhope and Shatley Bridge, Alan Mathews and I were pals as well as partners.

At the time those one hundred and forty miles were my longest on a bike. It was also the easiest, the tandem is not so quick in a sprint, but for long journeys it is ideal. After a long drag up a hill, or a fast sprint, one recovers much quicker when riding a tandem than one would on a solo machine. Most of my weekend cycling was with Alan on the tandem, except of course when one or both of us were indisposed or otherwise engaged.

On one Sunday we'd made plans to visit York, like Dick Turpin, but when the day came Alan was suffering from a heavy cold, so we called it off and I decided to go along on my own.

I set off at 7:15am in the morning mist which was soon to be burned away by the sun. The day turned out to be warm with no wind and I soon settled down to a comfortable rhythm, meeting other cyclists on the way, having a few words while passing, and arriving at York about 2:00pm. The first port of call was the tourist shop to get a postcard which was posted to Alan from York itself, just to prove I'd been there. The next call was the tea shop, to get filled up again. Sweet tea to a cyclist is what petrol is to a car, fuel. Then off for a visit to the Minster.

I had never visited York before. I found it a beautiful city, unlike my home town, Gateshead. I walked around until 4:15pm then decided that it was time to start back. As I settled down I realised that a light breeze was on my back, it would speed up my journey home, my legs felt fine, my breathing easy. I felt fitter than when I'd started out that morning, I was going well.

It seemed that the further I rode the stronger I became, probably the wind behind me was blowing up stronger. I reached Darlington and stopped at one of our favourite tea shops to fill up again with sweet tea, our staple diet, then into the saddle for the last lap.

However when I reached the Durham Road in Low Fell, I was shaking like a leaf. I dare not go home like this, I'd have to wait until my muscles cooled and settled down. The Durham Road was the local 'Bunny' run, and being Sunday all the local lasses and lads were promenading up and down, so I dismounted, sat on a seat and chatted to friends as they passed.

After I'd cooled down I only had another couple of hundred yards to reach home and a hot bath. I reached home at 9:15pm without a puncture or any other trouble. Eighty four miles there and eighty four back, one hundred and sixty eight miles in nine and a half hours. This was an approximate average of seventeen point two mph, not bad at all.

Another Sunday we set off for Jedburgh, ten miles past Carter Bar on the Scottish border, sixty miles from home. We'd started out with three shillings, but having splashed out on a packet of fags costing a shilling we only had two shillings between us. We never had much money. I was just an apprentice and Alan was on the dole. We passed Catcleugh Reservoir on our left, over the border and freewheeled down the twisting road towards the town.

Jedburgh is built on a hill, rather a steep hill, and here it was that disaster struck. As we climbed the hill the rear chain wheel broke. When we put weight on the pedals something has to go, ideally the bike, this time it was the chain wheel.

We tried the police station first, thinking maybe they had a spare from one of the police bikes, but they didn't like the idea. We left there and sat down for a think.

Funny how much easier it is to think sitting down. After a think, we went back to the police station and asked them if they could think of something, as our thinking had not been a success. One bright lad, he may be a sergeant now, suggested that we try the garage down the road, the garage was always open on Sundays.

We freewheeled down the hill as directed and saw a man coming towards us wearing a boiler suit. Our intuition told us that this was our man so we stopped him and explained our predicament. Luckily he came from Geordieland and had been a cyclist himself, so we all went back to the workshop where he welded our chain wheel, warning us not to overload it on the way back. We thanked him and asked him how much we owed him. He only charged us one and sixpence which left us with six whole pennies, at two pence a cup that meant three cups of tea.

We took it easy to Ottermoor, and when we got there it was dark, very dark, pitch black with heavy clouds overhead. But we had no worries - we had our big acetylene lamp, we'd get back without trouble. That was before we hit the brick wall.

Alan was on the front I'm glad to say, and as we approached the Belsay and Rothbury fork out went our big lamp. We were left in the dark, on the moors, and it was black. Alan shouted, 'The light's gone out.' As if I didn't know.

I shouted, 'Then stop.' But I was too late. We hit the wall right between the two roads and I was lying up on Alan's back as he lay over the handlebars.

On examination with the spare lamp, where I'd hit the rear bars I had two lovely bruises, one on each leg, six inches above the knees. Worse than that, the front forks were bent back, and a new pair was going to be expensive. But would the tandem get us home?

Alan was still shaking, so I took the front and very wobbly at first we proceeded to the pub, the lights of which we could see in the distance. There we fixed the gas lamp which only needed water. Pulling two chairs up in front of the blazing wood fire we ordered two cups of tea. Sitting in a corner was a little bloke who looked half starved. Alan asked him if he'd like a cup of tea which is how Alan spent our last two pence. We found that he was cycling to Dundee from Oxford as he'd been laid off by Morris's of Cowley. This was my first contact with the car works.

We got home with me in front. We travelled a lot slower than usual due to the bent forks, with Alan still shaken and quite sorry for himself.

We took the bent forks to Eades, and Doris sent them away to have them copied by a London firm at a cost of fifteen shillings. This was paid off my account at half a crown per week.

On another occasion cycling the country road from Corbridge to Newcastle, Alan on the front, I saw a couple walking side by side a couple of hundred yards ahead. We only had a small lamp on the front and it was a very dark night, with a thick hedge on both sides of the road. I said to Alan, 'There's a couple ahead.'

Alan moved out into the middle of the road. 'It's OK I can see them,' he said. Then suddenly they weren't there, they had simply disappeared.

We dismounted but there was no trace of them, no gaps of any sort in the hedge. Then it struck both of us, there was no sound of footsteps, so we carried on home sharpish.

Later we recounted the incident to our friends in Corbridge. He regaled us with the story of the couple who were killed the previous year by a motorist who hadn't stopped.

Monday night was always spent at Alan's house. This was the night we cleaned the tandem and adjusted anything that needed doing ready for the next outing. With paper on the floor in the living room, we cleaned and polished. Every speck of dirt was religiously searched out. With wax polish, chrome polish for the bright parts, and old tooth brushes to get between the spokes, after a couple of hours we'd be satisfied with it looking as new.

Looking on would be Mrs Mathews from her easy chair in front of the fire, shawl around her shoulders. She was an ex-school mistress and kept a kindly eye on us both.

After we'd cleaned the tandem we would discuss the next outing, the local cycling news and cycling in general. We also thought of ways to make money, like writing up our travels and so forth. We had written numerous stories of trips in the past, but nothing had become of them.

One of our ideas did bear fruit however. The silver foil inside cigarette packets at one time was wrapped around the cigarettes in one piece. We wrote and suggested that if the paper was in two pieces the top part would come away, leaving the lower part of the fags still wrapped, as they are today. They replied to our letter to say that this idea was already under consideration, but to show their appreciation of our interest they were enclosing a carton of a hundred cigarettes. We didn't believe them, but accepted the fags.

Alan had a pal called Tommy Jobes who was a clerk in a shipping office on the quayside in Newcastle and lived nearby. Tommy had a wife and four children, a dart board, tiddley winks, a three-quarter size billiard table and a table tennis table.

So it was the natural thing that Alan, Bert, Albert and myself gathered there on Wednesday nights to have a knockout competition in all the sports with supper afterwards. A cup was presented for each event, always before supper, and held for a week. Everyone brought something, eggs, bread, butter, tinned beans, and anything that could be eaten was welcome. The four children were all under nine so they were off to bed, but first they always received a generous amount of sweets from their 'uncles'.

An insurance agent friend of Tommy's often called, he didn't stay long but always had something interesting to tell. He called in one night to tell us of a client who hung his wallpaper up with drawing pins because no way was he going to leave it behind when he left. Now I know that this idea has gone around as a joke for years, but he swore that this was true.

We didn't believe him, but the next tale he called in to tell us was also a so-called old joke. However this one was true he said and he brought in the newspaper article to prove it.

This client wanted to insure his wife against accidents but he wanted all the details first, when the policy came into effect, and would he get the money if his wife fell downstairs and broke her arm. Yes, he would get the money, and the policy came into effect as soon as the first premium was paid.

Three days later the agent was horrified to receive a claim on this policy; however they paid the client the sum for which his wife was insured. Then the man was arrested when his wife complained that her husband had pushed her downstairs, breaking her arm, but wouldn't give her a share of the insurance money.

It was from our nights at Tommy's that our table tennis team was formed. We arranged games with the local church clubs which had the facilities that we lacked, and the tables and the space. We had some interesting nights and made quite a number of friends at these meetings.

Yes, I have some wonderful memories of those days and of all those grand people. Our last camp was in 1937, I was almost twenty. This camp was at a place called Low Row, not far from Brampton. There was a natural swimming pool there, but we had further to travel, and it did not compare with Ovingham, which was a place we'd grown to love. Over all the years we were together, I cannot recall an argument or disagreement that lasted over fifteen minutes.

CHAPTER SIX
From Sanderson Brothers to
Clark Chapman & Company
1934 – Easter 1938

When I was sixteen, things changed at work. Fourteen year olds were cheaper to employ and I think that Mr Race, the foreman and draughtsman, was looking for an excuse.

For a long time Bobby Little had been telling me to get out of this place and get a job in one of the big engineering works. He told me that this sort of thing happened all the time, a lad reached sixteen and out he would go in favour of a fourteen-year-old. He said there was no future there for me, and to get into a big place where there was room at the top. 'Join the union when you reach twenty. With your ability,' he said, 'you'll get on all right, but get out of here.' The opportunity came quicker than expected.

There was only one toilet in the workshop, and it was occupied by the new apprentice, sitting in there reading the paper. After yelling at him for ten minutes I couldn't wait much longer. The toilet had no roof so I threw a handful of metal turnings over the toilet wall. He came out quick and later told the foreman. Soon after the foreman wanted to see me, he handed me my cards and said, 'I think you know what these are for.'

He'd made his mind up and it was no good saying anything. So I went around and said goodbye to the others. As I left I thought to myself what Mam would say, but at the same time what I did was excusable. I thought that my parents would think so too.

However my good fairy must have been fluttering around for, as I stepped out into the street, Mr Logan was just coming in. 'Here Ernie,' he said. 'Hurry and get me a packet of Craven A and run your legs off. I want to go straight out again.'

I told him that I wasn't coming back, he asked why, and I told him. He put his hand out, took my cards and told me to get moving, giving me a wink as he went in the door.

When I saw the foreman later he never spoke, he was very quiet, and must have had a few hard words from the boss. However I decided to take Bobby Little's advice and find somewhere else, it was going to be very hard for me here. I applied to Birtley Iron Works for a job as a fitter, the company manufactured mining machinery. All of this happened just before I went to camp in 1934.

Shortly after my return from camp I received a letter telling me to present myself to Mr Froud, the foreman. Taking a day off work at Sanderson's I rode to Birtley, three miles south of Low Fell, and had a look around the factory. I'd be working on a lathe for the first week and then I'd be transferred to the fitting shop, so I was told.

I started there the following week on piecework, turning. It certainly was a new experience; I learned the meaning of slavery. The first job was turning gas tight manhole covers. These weighed in at a hundredweight apiece, and every one was turned to fine limits using templates as they had to be exactly alike. After lifting these in and out of the lathe for three days, I felt that I'd earned my money.

The next job was just as bad. This was turning cast iron pipes on a twenty-foot lathe, then turning the end flanges and facing the ends up to length, as well as having to load and unload by myself with the aid of a small crane. I was earning twice as much as I was at Sanderson's but I wondered for how long.

The job after that was turning brass glands for steam engine cylinders on a turret lathe, this was much easier. The tool holder on the turret lathe held four tools for four different operations. Instead of changing the tool for each operation, all that was needed was to loosen a screw and turn the tool holder to use a different tool.

Seeing a chance, I altered a tool to do two operations at the same time and started to make a little more. I finished the batch of castings around me and asked the time setter to have some more sent up.

When he came along he calculated how much I'd earned doing the last batch, and promptly cut the price. He said that I was making too much. We had a row then. I wasn't taking this, the price shouldn't be altered once it had been set. If I was doing them quicker then I should get the benefit.

The next morning I asked the foreman when I was going into the fitting shop, as the price fixer was cutting my rate therefore cutting my earnings. He told me that he wasn't interested, and that I could get on with the job as it was, or I could go back to where I'd bl.... well come from. Well, that got right up my nose. Here I was working my fingers to the bone for three weeks, and they were cutting my piece rates because I was earning too much. I hadn't even found out where the toilets were, and then to be told that in such a manner.

However, as things were, the work was much too heavy for someone of such tender years, sixteen and a half, and it showed. I finished at five every day, rode home, had my tea and then sat at home reading. Too tired to go out to play football or even to go out on my bike, all I wanted to do was sit in front of the fire and sleep.

Then one Friday I came home from work as usual; Mam was out shopping and Dad and I were sitting having tea on the big table. I was really tired and halfway through the meal my head sank lower and lower, finally my head was on the table and I was fast asleep. Dad woke me up and wanted to know all the answers. What was I doing at work?

We talked over the next half-hour. Dad said there was no problem, 'You go to work tomorrow and you tell the foreman that you want your cards and wages next Friday.' So next morning I gave notice and I had to start thinking of a new job.

Dad told me to take my time, not to rush things. I thought a long time about this new job. I had rushed into the last one at Birtley, and didn't want to make the same mistake. I talked to Alan as he was ten years older than I. Not only had he served his time at Clarke Chapman's, his father was Company Secretary. I had a good idea of the kind of work that was done there, making steam and electric winches, deck auxiliaries and so forth. I'd like that I thought, making steam engines! Yes that would suit me.

I wrote to Clarke Chapman's and had a reply and an

interview in quick time. When I told the interviewer what I'd been doing since I left school, he told me that I couldn't be classed as an apprentice, I'd join there as an improver. But a job is a job, so what? I was told to start on the Monday after my notice was served at Birtley.

On the Friday my notice finished at Birtley, Mr Froud, the foreman came up to me and had a few words. He asked me that if I was moved into the fitting shop would I withdraw my notice. I was pleased to tell him that I had another job to go to next week. Then he asked if I minded telling him where I was going to. I felt like telling him 'Where I bl.... well came from.' But I was too much of a gentleman so I told him that I did mind. He didn't like the reply, but there it is, and he stalked off without another word.

And so I started my new job at Clarkies, as it was known locally, it was a job that had a very large influence on my life.

A new place of work is, and always will be, a trial for a seventeen-year-old. It generally means new conditions, new ways of doing things, and above all, new workmates. The latter change is the greatest gamble of all. In most cases I was very fortunate, and when I joined Clarke Chapman and Company I fell in with a great lot of friends.

On my first day I reported to Mr Kirton, the foreman of the winch department. After going through the preliminaries at the office I was taken and introduced to a chap by the name of Murphy. There are no prizes for guessing his nationality, and to go with it the name Pat. He was to be my guide and mentor for the near future, and he taught me how to build a winch.

I think that I was the lucky one for he was gifted with the good Irish humour and the usual gift of the blarney. He was always ready for a joke or a good story, and I soon learned not to believe everything that I heard from him. He had been to sea in one or two ships, was married with three children, of whom he thought the world, and lived in Gibson Street, Newcastle.

In this section there were about thirty spaces for building winches, although it depended on orders as to how many were occupied at any one time.

When I started they were all occupied as the order book was full, but as a fitter and his mate could build a winch in a week a lot of orders were needed to keep everyone busy.

If orders were slow in coming in the workers slowed up, not knowing if they'd get another winch to build right away. But if the order book was full it was full steam ahead. Even so, some teams took longer to build a winch than others, and in some ways it was better to make haste slowly as the performance of each winch had to be approved by the foreman. If the winch didn't pass the test to the satisfaction of the foreman, the person or persons had to put any defects right. I've seen grown men in tears because they couldn't build the winch to the foreman's satisfaction.

When the winch was finished it was lifted and taken to a test bed at the bottom of the section. Here it was hooked up to the steam and exhaust pipes and warmed up by leaving the drain cocks open and allowing a little steam through the valve. When it was sufficiently warm the drain cocks were shut and the winch was run slowly then fast, alternately, for half an hour. Any defects discovered during this time were worked on and corrected.

When a man was satisfied that the winch was working to his satisfaction he called the foreman to check, and the first thing the foreman listened for was knocking.

An experienced engineer would know where to look for this fault, although it is very easy to spot, it was sometimes not so easy to correct. The next thing the foreman looked for was slow, even running. The slower the winch ran without jerking, the better the foreman liked it, as subsequently it would be easier and safer to drive when loading or unloading cargo. All the bearings had to run cool and of course no leaks of steam anywhere.

This write-up doesn't take long, but in fact, oiling and greasing, fixing steam and exhaust pipes, running and adjusting, then running again could take half a shift. That was the part that I liked best, working on and running a steam engine that I had built myself.

When the foreman tested the winch he ran it at all speeds. If he found the machine ran to his satisfaction he'd write it up in his book, naming the builder and signing it. Then he would allocate another winch to the builder. Needless to say, the fitters who did the best jobs got to build the important machines. In those conditions competition tended to creep in.

During my time there I worked on all manner of machines, small, all-bronze winches and capstans for millionaires' yachts. Royal Navy winches had to be built to templates as all parts, right and left hand, had to be interchangeable. Then there were the tiny capstans with four by four[14] cylinders, and in the next bay were the great windlasses for raising the big anchors of the passenger liners.

The biggest winch that I worked on was the twelve by twelve, four cylinder job for the whaling vessel *Balaena*, used for pulling the dead whales up the stern ramp. This winch was twelve-foot high.

Pat and I got on really well together. At first I watched then I copied him, then when I'd found out where everything went I built one side and Pat did the other. Soon I was seeking advice only occasionally and after a fortnight was almost keeping up with him. Pat kept all around him in good spirits with his stories and jokes, and if we got our winch completed within the week there was a twenty packet of fags for me on Saturday mornings.

I'd had two years extra schooling under Bobby Little from the age of fourteen, whereas all the other lads of my age had started here when they were sixteen, so I had a great advantage. There are numerous ways of using a file and most of them didn't know how to use one effectively. It was certainly also an advantage having Pat as a partner.

When I started at Clarkies none of the other apprentices bothered me at all. Usually a new boy had to undergo a certain amount of ragging and had tricks played on them, but it never happened to me. Maybe I was too big, or maybe Pat was so popular no one wanted to upset him. I did find out why eventually, but it took almost four years.

One day Pat told me that his brother was starting work in our section in three week's time, so, as expected, we

---

[14] The term four by four meant that the cylinders were four inches in diameter and they had a four inch stroke. Editor

had a tale every day as we ate our lunch together.

I might add at this stage that we all had our lunch, sandwiches and flasks, sitting on the bench together. Lunch time was talking time, although that was the polite term for it.

For the next three weeks Pat told us of his brother who was coming back from overseas. There was no shortage of listeners.

Pat's brother had jumped ship in Australia, went from sheep farming to gold mining, but decided this was too hard for too little, and besides Australia was much too hot. He then decided to go to Canada. When he arrived there the only job he could get was working in the forests as a lumber jack. However he had to get out of there because someone had picked a fight with his other brother during a drunken row and the brother had nearly killed the bloke. They both got the sack. He thought he might go home and see the family and wrote to Pat. Pat told him there were jobs going so he had decided to come home for a while.

Everyone was waiting for the day that Pat's brother would start work. After another two weeks of Pat's stories we all knew Pat's brother really well. Tall, sunburnt, fifteen and a half stone, we could just see him coming through the section.

I was bending over adjusting a bearing when I felt a tap on my shoulder. I looked up to see this chap standing there. I stood up and Pat said, 'Ern, I'd like you to meet my brother.'

Pat was smaller than I was, his brother was shorter still! But after the build-up over the last three weeks he was still given a great welcome. That was Pat.

After working with Pat for three months I was given a stand with a winch of my own, and within the time I'd worked with Pat, I was confident that I could manage. I would have to. I was the only improver to have a winch of my own, and there were older lads than me in the shop. If I did need help the next stand was only a yard away.

It took me a little longer to complete the first job to testing. I had to make sure, particularly on my first one, I couldn't let Pat down. However I managed to complete it in three weeks, and off test without any trouble, so I was on my own from then on.

As soon as I was eighteen I was approached by the foreman who wanted me to do a spell on the night shift. I wasn't averse to this idea at all. It was more money, and it would be a new experience, I'd never worked all night before. So come Monday I started work at 8.30pm until 7.30am. As it was my free time I had arranged with my mother that all my overtime pay was mine, it meant a lot more money.

Night work was only during the summer months as this was the time when the delivery of the winches became urgent. The shipbuilders worked inside the hulls during the winter months and all the deck work was carried out during the better weather, for obvious reasons. The purpose of the night shift was to get the specific machines when and where they were most needed.

During the winter months the opposite was the case. Winches weren't wanted on site, so from November to February the vast majority of the men were on the dole. They were paid off early November and the winch department was staffed by apprentices and a dozen royals[15] who were the favoured of the foreman and supervisor. Therefore it was a festive atmosphere when all the fitters were re-engaged in early March.

This was common practice during the hard times of the thirties. If a small firm, or even a large one, needed a little brickwork done they only had to get in touch with the Labour Exchange and a bricklayer was sent down to work for a day or couple of days. Then back to the Labour Exchange. Any man with a regular job considered himself very lucky and did everything in his power to hang on to it.

Spells of night work didn't last long. It was only ever to catch up with back orders which usually took about three weeks, and only about six of us worked nights. I don't know why I'd been chosen. I suppose it was cheaper to employ me rather than a man, as I was the only improver with a winch to myself doing the work of a man and only taking home a boy's pay.

We had an hour off for supper. This we took in two half-hour periods as a whole hour tended to make one fall asleep. Even trying to work and stay awake for six hours after half-an-hour's sleep was no joke. However they say that the body gets used to anything, although I'm not so sure but working nights did get easier after the first week. During the day there was always a wait to use the machines or the grindstone so working nights one could get on with work without any interruptions.

Talking of grindstones, one incident might be of interest; at least it was to me. The bolts in the crosshead guides had to be of exact length and it was customary to

---

[15] Blue eyed boys. Editor

measure the bolts, then grind them to length on this particular grinder which stood on a cast iron pedestal, about two foot six high.

The grinding stone was eighteen inch diameter with a steel guard over the top. The wheel, which ran at one thousand revs per minute, was supposed to run in a trough of water but due to lack of maintenance the trough had dried up and grit from the wheel had filled the trough and solidified until it resembled concrete. This only left a very small space under the wheel. The bolts, eight in all, lay on the tray in a handy position, ready to be picked up as and when required.

As I was grinding the vibration caused one of these eight bolts to begin to roll under the wheel. I daren't grab it in case my hand caught the wheel and I dropped to the floor beneath the protective tray just as the bolt rolled, or tried to roll, under the grindstone. I felt rather than heard the explosion and then the machine began to race. I knew then that the danger was over, so standing up I reached out and switched the machine off.

When I saw the result I was glad that nature had given me quick reflexes, after all I'd only seen the bolt moving out of the corner of my eye. The stone had disappeared, as had half the cast iron table and the guard over the wheel. Next morning in the daylight, all was explained.

Half the stone, which must have weighed half a hundredweight, went through the roof thirty foot high and the hole was there to prove it. A quarter of the stone hit the table and finished up twenty feet away, fortunately I was under the other half of the table. The other piece of stone was never found.

The apprentices weren't too pleased, they had to

shorten the bolts by cutting them with a hacksaw, then filing them to fit, but in a few days we had a new grinder. This time running in water, which was cooler and so there was less chance of burning your fingers.

Two days later a note was left in the night shift line up telling me to stay behind after work to see the supervisor. I dutifully sat in his office the next morning, waiting. He explained that it was about the accident report which he had to fill in, so it was just a case of recalling it as it happened.

Working at night was strange in other ways. Sleeping during the day was a new experience, then leaving work at 7:30am instead of coming to work, cycling home, having breakfast then deciding what to do. This was all new and I had to learn to make arrangements a day or two in advance.

Arriving home at 7:50am in the morning was too late, or too early, to make arrangements for that day, so I divided my week up into days. On Monday I did this and on Tuesday I did that, and so on every week; if a change was made it had to be arranged well beforehand. The long weekend was also a novelty. I enjoyed finishing work on Saturday morning at 7:30am, and not starting again until Monday night at 8:30pm.

Most of the gang had jobs, even if some of them were part time; Alan however was still unemployed. He had served his time at Clarkies, but stomach trouble dogged him wherever he worked. He had worked at numerous jobs, but after a few weeks or months he ended up in hospital. The only jobs that suited him were outside jobs. He did find the perfect job ten miles away in North Shields, in a bicycle shop. He enjoyed that job, and worked there for a couple of years, but it went bankrupt and closed. Jobs were few and far between in those days.

Usually Monday and Tuesday mornings were spent with Alan in the Cosy Billiard Hall in Low Fell, the attendant always had a table ready for us for 10:00am. We played until noon, then Alan went home and I went to bed after I'd had dinner. Afternoons were spent in bed. Wednesday was a change. I slept in the morning and had the afternoons out; sometimes at the pictures, sometimes with one of the gang, whoever had Wednesdays off, or sometimes with a girl friend. The billiard hall though was the main pastime, at least three times a week. Cycling was still there for the weekends and we ranged far and wide on Sundays.

Soon after coming off nightshift, I had another move, this time to the shaft department. Here the rotating parts of the winch were put together.

There were six men in this section, counting me as one of the men, and a labourer. He kept an eye on every one of us, and foresaw every thing we needed as our job progressed, so it was waiting there behind us when it was needed. When one of us finished a shaft it was lifted out of the vice by a crane and taken to the winch section. The labourer would have another on the floor behind, ready to be lifted into the vice.

Completing an engine shaft took a whole day and was an exercise in key fitting and what I call general common sense fitting. It was harder physically and not as varied as fitting the winches together, but there were occasions where one had to put one's thinking cap on, for example when fitting the clutches. Five minutes spent thinking before starting could save a good half hour's hard work.

These assemblies were finally filed to within .004 of an inch and were intended to stay together for all time. Every shaft assembled carried the mark of the fitter who built it and the builder could use any mark he liked as long as he used the same mark every time. My mark was 'I.V.I', and if it turned out to be faulty it came back to me. It was pride in one's ability that none ever came back. This mark was carried all over the world by ships which carried Clarkies' winches.

The two longest serving fitters in this section were Bob Morland and Bill Sherrif, but the latter was always known as Sam. Why? No one ever knew, not even Sam. We had a foreman but he never interfered with our jobs as long as everything went out of his section as it should do. He was content to do his book work. He couldn't tell these lads how to do their jobs, they knew what to do and how to do it.

It was hard work at first, but as certain muscles built up from the daily use of a two-pound hammer and a seven-pound sledge hammer, things became easier and before long I was lasting the day without too much distress.

Unlike Birtley Iron Works where I couldn't find the toilet, here it was just around the corner. It was built on the outside wall with wooden steps up to the door, as if the builders had thought of it at the last moment and stuck it there. Just inside the door was a little cubby hole; inside a little man sat, and as we passed a small window a voice was heard, 'Number?'

The entrant gave his name and number and received two pieces of toilet paper for his trouble with a warning, 'Three minutes.'

145

If anyone took longer than the three minutes, the occupant of the cubby hole came along and made his point by kicking the door. If the person in the toilet still didn't make a move, his name and number was reported to the office with varying results.

I never heard of anyone being suspended for this offence, but it was always advisable to tell the foreman if one had even a hint of stomach trouble. He would sign a note for the little man in the cubby hole which allowed one to visit the toilets whenever one wished, but only for that particular day.

No washing facilities were provided, so the usual way of cleaning hands was to wash them in a bucket of kerosene. In a small section like ours the labourer came along with a bucket of hot water fifteen minutes before knocking off time. With kerosene first and the hot water afterwards we set off home with reasonably clean hands.

Our labourer was a real treasure, supplying hot water when needed, making our tea at lunch time and for our overtime break. Anything he could scrounge he did, including bottles of milk at a penny for a third of a pint and sandwiches from the canteen. He looked after us really well.

There was a strange clocking on system at Clarkies, there were no clocks. Instead two big twenty by ten foot gates were swung open to let the workers in. However, at 7:28am the steam buzzer sounded and these gates began to close slowly, until on the stroke of 7:30am they came together. Anyone outside stayed outside.

The only way to get inside now was to wait until your foreman arrived at 8:00am to accost him and make your excuses. Anyone with a bad record had to wait until after lunch and missed half a shift, if you were in the foreman's good books. If the foreman had got out of the wrong side of the bed that morning he wouldn't allow you in and you missed a whole day's pay.

Inside the door, on the right, was a rack with rows of hooks. On the hooks hung wooden tiles, about five inch by three inch, with numbers etched along the top, and the worker picked off the tile with his number on as he passed. Mine was 125, so I'd lift it off and take it with me. After a day's work I'd rub the face with white chalk and with a pencil write 'eight and a half hours, winches'. These tiles were then thrown into a large basket by the door as we left the factory to go home.

Clarkies manufactured not only winches but windlasses, capstans - both steam and electric, davits, boilers and all manner of ships' auxiliaries. There was also the foundry, both brass and iron.

Thousands of men and boys had to break the monotony of some of the jobs carried out there and as one would expect there were a number of pranksters in a factory of this size.

A popular target for these pranks was the night watchman whose job it was to patrol the works at night with his Alsatian dog. He was not a popular person as one of his nasty habits was to come up behind someone busy working by himself and have the dog bark. Understand that the only lights were the ones around the winch, the rest of the place was in total darkness. Not only was it a nasty fright but it was positively dangerous, as a sudden jump or start would be enough to hit your head on the many sharp corners that were all around.

He raised the alarm one night, ringing the police to

report that he'd found a man hanging in the boiler shop. The man was hanging from a high beam having apparently jumped from the crane with a rope around his neck. The police arrived, coming down in force. By this time all the night workers had heard the news of the event and were all standing by, looking on. The constables cut the rope, and when they reached the ground they were not pleased. Someone had made up a good dummy, with a face mask, a good pair of dungarees, boots and all.

Whoever had made it certainly made a good job of it, and eighteen feet in the air, it looked real enough. The authorities never found out who was responsible, and the watchman kept out of the way of everybody for a long, long time.

Making something and especially something that actually works is a great feeling and we had a great deal of pride in our handiwork. It's said that pride is one of the deadly sins, but when one has built something from a heap of inanimate castings and seen it actually work, just by turning a steam valve on and off, one couldn't but feel a sense of pride. I don't think that could be classed as a deadly sin.

Eating our lunch at noon didn't take an hour. Some of the men passed the time by playing darts; on a fine day some took a walk down to the river which ran about a quarter of a mile away behind the works, some passed the time away sitting on the workbench talking on various topics, while others snoozed.

While sitting reading my newspaper one lunch time I was approached by another apprentice, John Henderson. He told me he was interested in boxing and had a set of gloves at home, how about a little sparring practice behind the works? In the works it was a sacking offence, but there was plenty of waste ground outside around the works.

It was boring sitting on the bench every day so I agreed, it was a little bit of exercise anyway. Neither of us was much good however, but I did find out about something that had puzzled me for a number of years. John was expecting me to teach him, to give him a few hints in the art of self defence and he wouldn't take no for an answer.

'Look John,' I said, 'I know nothing of boxing. The only boxing I've done is with the Boy Scouts years ago.'

But he wouldn't have this and insisted that I give him some coaching in the noble art. 'Come on, everybody knows that you're the junior champion of the Cornellion Club in Newcastle.'

When I'd stopped laughing I told him that this was news to me and asked him where he had got this from. He told me that Pat Murphy had let it slip just after I started. He had told them to be careful how they handled his new mate, otherwise we'd run into trouble. I laughed, and told him that I thought they would all have known it was one of Pat's stories, after all Pat had worked there long enough.

However I would always be grateful to Pat for giving me such an easy passage at Clark Chapman's. He so enjoyed any success with his story-telling, he must really have enjoyed this one. So I asked John not to mention it to anyone. He replied that no one would believe him if he did, and he certainly wouldn't chance it.

So we continued our sparring. It was good exercise

and no doubt if we were seen, anyone would think that John was having a lesson. Suffice to say we became good friends. I have an idea that we almost met in Hong Kong a year or two later, but that's another story.

Alan and I were still enjoying our trips on the tandem and a great part of my leisure hours was still spent at number four, St Alban's Terrace. Although on quite a number of occasions Alan and the rest of the gang had visited forty three, Beaconsfield Road, and had some pleasant evenings in the company of my sisters.

How many girls had I dated? Very few, the only one to make a lasting impression was a young lady from Gosforth. Bert Moderate lived in the same street as Alan, and next door to Bert lived the Barnes' girls, Ivy and Rita who had a cousin called Edith. I think it was in 1936 that I first met Edith Heald.

A tattoo was being held at Ravensworth Castle, a few miles from home in the Team Valley, now a large industrial estate. Two thousand or more soldiers must have taken part with three countries represented, England, Scotland and Ireland. The Scots soldiers came by rail, and the whole of Gateshead and Newcastle turned out to see them march from the Central Station to Ravensworth Castle. They marched across the Tyne Bridge with their kilts swinging and bagpipes skirling, refusing to break step as they crossed so that the great bridge swayed as they proceeded. The latter is hearsay, I wasn't on the bridge at the time, but it was well recorded.

The show lasted from 9:00pm to 3:30am. It was a beautiful summer night, and Bert, Albert and I escorted Ivy, Rita and Edith. There were only country roads for access, so we had to walk the three miles each way. We three, the male escorts, had already been vetted by Rita's mother, Mrs Barnes, and we had to get the girls back safely. We had a wonderful night. The big finale was an enactment of the attack at Rourks Drift, which took place during the Boer War. The enactment took place at 2:00am. The scene was floodlit with thousands sitting on the grass in the natural amphitheatre, watching a wonderful portrayal of the great battle. And then the long walk home, with arms around waists.

The next time I met Edith Heald was when she gave a party shortly afterwards, this time Rita wasn't there. It was held at Gosforth and we arrived there in time for tea which had been arranged by Edith herself, oddly enough her parents weren't there. Edith had invited some of her local friends, the drawing room had been cleared for dancing, and we had a good time.

Unfortunately we lost track of the time, and we missed the last tram. Ivy could not walk the eight miles home so she stayed overnight with Edith. I wasn't looking forward to the walk home myself, and I had a further three quarters of a mile to walk. Her parents would probably be worried and as there were no phones in either house, Bert was to remember to call in when he arrived home. We all arrived home safely, if very tired, but Mrs Barnes wasn't happy with the explanation.

When I next called at Alan's house I was informed that Ivy's mother wished to see me, and she wanted to see me as soon as possible. I had to call and convince her that everything was above board. That is all the lads came home together, and the only reason that Ivy stayed with Edith was that we didn't think it right that she should have to walk eight miles at midnight, also that all we did was dance and play charades. I think the entire Street knew about that party.

One evening I started out on my bike to see Edith at Gosforth, all dressed up, wearing a new overcoat and new trousers. I was taking care when this black cat jumped from a high wall and landed on my front wheel and I landed on my back. My hip had a piece of skin the size of the palm of my hand missing, with a hole in my trousers to match. The back was torn out of my new coat and a piece out of my ankle. I was in a bad way, however the bike was undamaged and that was the main thing.

I rode home and took myself to bed. I was sore all over and had a lot of bruises, but I had managed to keep my head off the road. Dad came up to my bed later and sympathised. The new coat and trousers were no great problem, they could be replaced. The important thing was that I wasn't damaged, although I felt that I had been.

However, the letter I sent to Edith explaining was never answered, so that romance never really got started. Someone up there was looking over me; they wanted me for someone else.

One evening when I called on Alan he was about to visit his Aunt in Walkergate; to keep him company I went with him on the tandem. This was when I met Phyllis for the first time, Phyllis was Alan's cousin. I also met his Aunt and was made welcome.

At that point I was only interested in cycling, Edith Heald had been an exception. I was shy, even though or maybe because I had five sisters. To me girls were friends as other lads were friends, but I think that Phyllis had different ideas.

On occasions Phyllis invited me down to her place

and we'd have a walk to the park, this was while I was on nightshift. Then she became a regular visitor to St Alban's Terrace, staying the weekend.

If the weather was very bad or Alan was indisposed, I often attended church on Sunday mornings, sometimes by myself or with one or two of the lads. I was confirmed at Christchurch in 1935 with four of the gang. Phyllis decided to attend church with us, but to the lads church was only for the occasional Sunday. Sundays were for cycling and I'm afraid that Phyllis came a poor second.

Christmas in 1937 fell on a Saturday, if my memory serves me right, and Alan had been persuaded to gather a few lads for a party at Phyllis' place on Boxing Day. Alan managed to get Bert, Albert and myself to attend. On the day we duly presented ourselves at his aunt's house dressed in our Sunday best, all polished, in time for tea and introductions. We had decided to have a good time that evening, all four of us. Why not? It was Christmas. We were there before the girls turned up and were sitting on the settee smoking our heads off, when there was a knock on the door. Then the girls walked in and we were introduced.

I knew that Phyllis was after me, but when I was introduced to Edith Lamb I knew Phyllis had shot herself in the foot by inviting Edith to that party. During the evening I couldn't take my eyes off this young lady, even though she was sitting at my side. Edith was slim, about one hundred and four pounds in weight, and beautiful. It was love at first sight, and I knew that she was for me. I can't remember the rest of the evening.

I hung on to this young lady and made sure she was by my side when we walked her home. I also made sure that

I was the first in the queue to ask her out in the near future. To my surprise Edith agreed to go out with me on New Year's Eve, the following Friday.

Our first date was a visit to the Heaton Picture Palace to see Irene Dunn in *One Night of Love*. Was that an omen? We didn't have a lot of money between us, in fact we had very little, but Thursday nights became our picture nights. A bag of pears or a quarter of chocolate éclairs and two back seats in the stalls were our idea of heaven. Some of the picture halls had double seats along the back row and these were much preferred.

After tea on Thursday nights I rode across the bridge through Newcastle and so to Montrose, the name of the house in which Edith lived with her parents, her brother George, and her sisters Joan and Audrey. On the fine nights we walked and talked, well wrapped up against the cold. On the wet nights we stayed in and played cards, unless we had the coppers to go to the cinema, then of course we chose the cinema.

In those days we had a good choice of cinemas, it was quite easy to visit a different picture hall every night and twice on Saturdays, there were no bingo halls. The cinema was the ordinary people's sedative for all their worries and troubles, a few hours in a fairy-tale world. It was cheap, sixpence each at the box office, four pence for chocolate, and ten cigarettes for sixpence.

To keep things in perspective depending on overtime, my pocket money was only five to ten bob, twenty five to fifty new pence, and that was to cover all my expenses for a week.

So the months passed, courting, cycling and working. Taking Edith out on Thursday evenings, sometimes

Saturdays as well, cycling on Sundays, while Wednesday evenings were spent with Tommy Jobe and company. January and February came and went. Then as March blew itself out the weather became kinder, and thoughts of the open road invaded the mind.

Alan was suggesting that we went touring at Easter and for the summer holidays. The question in my mind of the bike on one hand and Edith on the other started to pull me two ways. I loved them both. It was becoming harder and harder but I knew that I had to make my mind up. I had to choose one way or the other, and it became more difficult as time passed.

If I gave up cycling and later regretted the decision, would I tend to blame Edith? If I left Edith would I regret the decision later? I told Edith how I felt but she didn't understand, she had never had a bike, couldn't even ride one. Edith thought it was such an easy thing to decide. She was probably right. Years afterwards I thought it was easy but not at the time.

So we agreed to part. Although she couldn't give any assurances as to the future, I hoped that a few months apart would tell me one way or the other, and if the bike didn't completely satisfy me, then maybe Edith would consent to resume our relationship. I had to be sure for both of our futures, courtship and marriage was for life.

While at work the day before Good Friday I was unfortunate enough to get a piece of grit in my eye. I felt it first on the Friday morning so it nearly put paid to the Easter tour which Alan and I had planned in Scotland. We decided to take a chance and as we passed through Newcastle we called in at the eye hospital, where I had the eye examined and the piece of grit removed. I explained the circumstances and was told to keep the eye covered for a couple of days. We pedalled off to Edinburgh on the first leg of one hundred and six miles with Alan on the front and me behind with my head in bandages.

We always liked to keep to the secondary roads if possible, so we rode by way of Wooler, Coldstream, Greenlaw and Musselburgh, arriving at Mrs Handcorn's lodging house, our destination in Edinburgh, at 4:30pm. We had no problems on the way, although it was hard lines on Alan who had to ride on the front all the way. As in a car, the driver sees less than the passenger, so I had a lovely time coming over the Lammermuir Hills sitting up enjoying the scenery.

Knocking on the door we eventually made ourselves heard and the good lady Mrs Handcorn came to the door. Alan had stayed here before and he was welcomed like a long-lost son. We were right away despatched to the wet fish shop along the street for 'some nice pieces of fresh cod' for our tea, and after tea we sat in front of a roaring fire talking of, I think, everything.

We told her of our plans for the next three days and that we'd be going around and coming back to her on Sunday night, if that was suitable. So everything was arranged and she would leave our beds ready for us Sunday night.

That night we walked around the city leaving the castle to be visited when we returned in a couple of days. This was my first visit to Scotland and the furthest I'd ever been from home. We'd been up until 2:00am the night before in conversation with our host, so when she woke us up at 7:30am we were yawning and rubbing our eyes. We washed and then found that we both had razors but no blades, and when we turned up for breakfast with stubble on our faces she exclaimed, 'Ha' ye no razors at 'aal?'

She told us to get on with our bacon and eggs and she'd get us a blade. She did. She asked another of her guests for a razor blade and sterilized it even though it was a new one, enabling us to shave. We left our lodgings at 9:00am, all our gear aboard and enough sandwiches to last a couple of days. Mrs Handcorn had put up a pile of bread and ham, 'Just in case you get hungry,' she said.

We threaded our way through the Scottish capital, along the famous Princes Street towards Queen's Ferry. The ferry then crossed the Firth of Forth about where the new bridge now crosses the water. This was a pleasant crossing during which we compared our route with those of the other cyclist passengers, some going to the east, some to the west and some to the north.

Disembarking, we rode north towards Kinross where we turned left towards Crief on a country road. A short way into the country we found a grassy slope with the beautiful warm sun shining down on it, just right for a snooze. Leaning the tandem against the fence we hopped over and lay down on the short grass. The ground fell away into the valley from where we lay. The light clouds had disappeared and the warm sun shone down. With our hands behind our heads we lay there and admired the Scottish countryside for the next half hour.

This is the beauty of cycling, just taking one's time, being lazy when one feels the need. But one must get on, and soon we were passing the famous golf course of

Gleneagles with its magnificent clubhouse surrounded by pine trees. Then on to Crief for dinner which consisted of the sandwiches that Mrs Handcorn had supplied, although we'd eaten a couple previously as we lay on the grassy bank. Next was dessert consisting of cups of sweet tea at the cafe in the High Street. After a rest here we set course for Callendar, later to become famous as the setting for *Doctor Finlay's Casebook*.

From Crief we rode through wonderful scenery to Comrie, then on to St Fillans at the eastern end of Loch Earn. Whenever we arrived somewhere new the first thing we looked for was the usual tea place, but we were out of luck here. As usual we tossed a coin in the air to decide who was to knock on a front door and ask for water, and as usual I lost so I had to do the asking. Very occasionally we've been lucky and received tea. While this wasn't our lucky day, we received water for which we were very grateful.

After thanking our benefactor we crossed a little bridge over the River Earn. We decided to follow this road rather than the motor road on the other side of the loch. It looked much more interesting than the usual main road, and so it proved.

The high road, running along the south of the loch was no more than a path for most of its length, and as we looked down on the motor road across the Loch with the mountains behind, we were sure that we had made the right choice. Our road, we found, was only paved for part of its length. At times we walked pushing the tandem, sometimes carrying it, the path only a couple of feet wide, trees on both sides with the water of the loch scintillating in the afternoon sun.

Since those days the charm of the south road and the loch has greatly deteriorated. The road or path has been widened and paved to take motor traffic, a lot of trees have been felled and caravan sites built along the road. In places the loch is now covered with a fine film of oil, due no doubt to the motor boats. In the thirties only sailing boats were allowed on the loch.

As we travelled along this pathway we found small headstones by the wayside, these told of grim times past. 'Here lies the bodies of three MacDonalds, killed while attempting to harry', was the text on one such stone.

Many years later, while we were touring by car, Edith and I looked for these stones. Not finding them we made enquiries and learned that when the new road was built the headstones were removed to the local museum.

How much more romantic they were when Alan and I first found them by the wayside in 1938. I was pleased that Alan and I had seen this road when it was only a pathway. Since then Edith and I have made this trip twice, but on neither occasion was the beauty and mysticism there. I would have loved Edith to have walked this path as Alan and I had.

At the western end of the loch was Lochearnhead, and here we turned south towards Callander. Travelling through Strathyre forest along the shores of Loch Lubnaig and through the Pass of Leny, we arrived at our destination. Our first thought was finding a bed for the night and after a short walk we found a house with a Cyclist Touring Club (CTC) sign over the door. It was only a small stone cottage, but we knocked on the door and spoke to the old lady who answered and booked our room for the night, together with shelter for our willing mount.

The sign of the CTC was the guarantee that one would be offered a clean room and bed, and not least a good breakfast. They were run by motherly old ladies who stood no nonsense. They weren't averse to giving anyone a playful clip around the ear if the guests didn't behave themselves.

The cost for bed and a good breakfast was the same wherever one rode. The cost for the night was four and sixpence and often the good lady gave us supper. Mind you, Mrs Handcorn was an exception; her place was the only one where we had a day's sandwiches included.

After seeing our room and that the bike was sheltered we had a wash, which we both needed, then we walked around the town looking for a teashop. We had a couple of sandwiches left, bless you Mrs Handcorn, and we ordered a pot of tea with our supper. It was a lovely warm night and we sauntered through the town, removing the tension from our legs and preparing for a good night's sleep.

In 1938 Callander was a sleepy market town, now it's a big tourist centre and holiday resort. Even as far back as 1853 when John Ruskin the writer and the artist Millais paid a visit it was noted for it's beautiful surroundings. This whole area is steeped in Scottish history and folklore.

Next morning was a rude awakening. Inside the cottage it was lovely and warm, we'd had a restful night and were raring to get moving again, but a glance out of the window made us fear for the worst. Three inches of slush and snow, it looked horrible.

We sat down to bacon and eggs, sausage, fried

tomatoes and bread and butter, then finished off with toast and half a dozen cups of sweet tea each. Then we planned our route for the day and after paying our host we prepared to leave. So saying goodbye we picked up our saddle bag and panniers and stepped outside, then straight back in again. We'd seen the slush through the window but hadn't realised how cold it would be. The freezing wind went right through to the bones, and getting back indoors we reopened the bags and took out our heavy jerseys and gloves.

Outside again we got the tandem from under cover and proceeded to strap on the saddle bag and panniers. As soon as we took our gloves off to manipulate the straps the cold struck, but after three attempts and a couple of skinned knuckles we managed to get the job done. We were fortunate that we had decided to wear our plus fours and not shorts for this tour, if we hadn't I think our knees would have frozen solid. It was only cold for the first mile or two and we warmed up quickly on our way to Doune and Stirling, aiming for Falkirk and then Edinburgh for the night.

By lunch time we were feeling hungry and looking for somewhere to eat, this wasn't unusual. What we wanted was something filling and something wet, and it had to be cheap. These were the essentials and we found such a place in the shape of a small wooden hut by the side of the road. Inside we found a big open fire with a table in front, just the place to thaw out.

This was the signal for the owner to come out from the back room and enquire as to our requirements. He first informed us that the stove in the kitchen was giving trouble, not a good start, but he could supply us with smoked ham and bread and butter with plenty of tea. We told him not to apologise and that was the very meal we needed.

In a short time he was back with our lunch, all he'd promised plus a big jar of pickles. It was lovely to see the giant teapot with a full loaf of sliced bread, and a pound of smoked ham with pickles. We had a feast and soon we were sitting back with full tums and satisfied smiles on our faces. When we rose and thanked our host for such a feast he apologised for not being able to give us a hot meal on such a cold day, and only charged us one and sixpence each.

So filled to the brim we started off again, hoping to get to Edinburgh before 3:00pm. We wished to see the castle and didn't know how late it was open for visitors, but surmised that it wouldn't shut before 4:30 or 5:00pm.

There were still places in the city that we wished to visit, but these could be visited after the main attraction was closed. Travelling through Stirling we would have liked to look over the castle there, but decided that if the choice lay between Stirling and Edinburgh castles we would prefer to visit the latter. So we pushed on towards our next destination, Falkirk, through the industrial area of Scotland.

One must understand that the roads of 1938 were in no way comparable to the roads of today. The A9 was similar to the A1, a two-lane highway, just like the B roads of today. There was very little traffic so the conditions were totally different to those facing the cyclists of today. These days cyclists take their lives in their hands every time they mount their bikes, whereas in 1938 lack of motor traffic made cycling as safe as a stroll to the shops.

Eventually we reached the big city and straightaway made for our digs, parked the tandem and checked with our landlady, who was glad to see us safely back.

We toured the castle and had our photos taken beside Mon's Meg. Mon's Meg is a big gun on the castle ramparts to defend the castle, it was forged about 1455 and in it's hey day could throw a five hundred weight stone one and a half miles. After walking around the castle we walked the streets looking for the graves of the body snatchers, Burke and Hare, without success.

On our return Mrs Handcorn had our supper ready and as we ate she regaled us with stories from her past. We were still nattering past midnight. She told us of her earlier life, her marriage and how she lost her husband during the war. She then worked as a cook and eventually became head cook at a posh hotel in Ardlui, where she met numerous big names in the film industry and politics. One person she remembered very well was Herr Von Ribbentrop, the German ambassador. She described him as a very correct, charming man. After she retired from the commercial kitchen she started her B&B business.

Mrs Handcorn had a host of stories about the perils of this concern over the years. She also said that she'd met lots of lovely people and made countless friends.

I dropped off to sleep that night, thinking of Edith, wondering if she thought of me, as I thought of her. I thought how much she would like the mountains of Scotland and wondered if we would ever see them together in the future.

While we ate breakfast with Mrs Handcorn we discussed our day's journey home, and decided to take a different route and travel via Peebles and Melrose. This way we could visit Melrose Abbey then push on to Carter Bar on the border, Otterburn and Belsay through to Newcastle. This time we hoped to miss the stone wall at the Rothbury-Belsay road fork.

Easter Monday turned out to be much warmer than the Saturday or Sunday, and it was dull but dry when we said our goodbyes to our cheerful hostess, promising to return one day. She would only accept fifteen shillings for the two nights we'd stayed with her, breakfast, supper the previous night, the tea when we arrived on Friday and the huge amount of cheese and ham sandwiches and banana sandwiches, one parcel of which was packed in our saddle bag. This food supply was to last us all the way home. Mrs Handcorn said she liked the lads who cycled through, they were always welcome.

Alan and I set out at the usual time, but had some difficulty finding our way out of the city. The roads were smaller and poorly marked, much less built up than the way we had entered Edinburgh the previous Friday. We had an uneventful journey back home, taking a few photographs and visiting Melrose Abbey.

We took an hour out at Melrose as Alan was interested in the history, which was supposed to be the burial place of the heart of Robert the Bruce. It was to have been buried in the Holy Land, but Sir James Douglas who was carrying it there was killed in Spain fighting the Moors. According to legend he hurled the casket containing the heart at the enemy shouting, 'Go first, brave heart'.

Bruce's heart was later returned to Scotland and buried here at the Abbey. I can't vouch for the authenticity of the history; however Sir Walter Scott had connections with

Melrose, his home being two miles to the west at Abbotsford.

We next stopped at Carter Bar to admire the view and to change the driver, and of course the inevitable smoke. We didn't intend to stop at the next place but Alan said, 'Stop! Oh yes, I remember this was the wall we hit in the dark.' This was the first time we'd passed this place since it happened, and although we looked we couldn't see any marks. The next stop on entering Belsay was also unexpected.

We had changed drivers again and I said 'Stop!' There were two young ladies on the bridge who seemed familiar. Alan stopped and I dismounted as one of the young ladies was Edith Heald. I explained what went wrong with our last date, about why I didn't turn up, and we wished each other luck in the future. I was more concerned with another Edith and Alan was eager to get home, so we waved goodbye and set off on the last lap.

We'd had a grand tour of four days, travelling three hundred and eighty miles, an average of ninety five miles per day, with a variety of weather, sun, snow, wind and rain, warm sunny days and freezing cold ones. Four days of wonderful scenery and empty roads. For me the only thing that spoiled it was that Edith wasn't there.

It was nice to be home again and to lie in a nice hot bath, then to jump into my own familiar bed, but the thought was there, at the back of my mind, work the next morning. Even so I had friends at work, and such a break gave us a talking point whilst working.

The next morning it was back to those big black gates and into the dirty work place again, but we had to have money and unfortunately it had to be replaced when spent. In those days it was no work, no pay. We weren't paid for holidays so we had no choice but to work, and at that time of the year overtime was plentiful. An extra six hours work during the week and another four hours by working Saturday afternoon gave the opportunity to save a little. Sunday working was not so common. Instead at Clarke Chapman's they had another idea.

Clarkies had a three shift pattern. A man worked his ordinary shift, 7:30am to 5:00pm Monday to Wednesdays, went home and returned to work at 8:30pm, working with an hour's break until 7:30am Thursday. Friday he returned to work 9:00am until 5:00pm, reporting for work next at 7:30am on Saturday for four hours, with Saturday afternoon off. Needless to say Saturday afternoon was spent in bed. Another group worked the same way over Friday night.

These hours were supposed to be voluntary but no one ever refused. The foreman had the power, the unions none, and any man refusing could say goodbye to any future overtime. It was the only way that a married man could keep his head above water, wages were low and jobs at a premium. There was also the fear of the winter lay-off. Get on the wrong side of the foreman and there was the fear that one would not be recalled when work picked up in the spring. So all the workforce welcomed the extra work and money, but it would have been nice to have the choice now and again.

About this time I began to suffer attacks of indigestion similar to the trouble that Alan had over the years, but it was neither as bad as Alan's, nor as persistent. Milk of Magnesia tablets seemed to keep it under control, and as it disappeared over the weekends I put it down to the dirty atmosphere inside the works. Also our section was very near the doors of the foundry.

Fumes from there continually drifted through the factory, again it was no good complaining, no one took any notice. The men couldn't do anything, if they complained they'd be told to do the same as I was at Birtley. The men had no bargaining power, there were too many unemployed, and we had to put up with these conditions until men were needed in great numbers as is the case during wartime.

Cycling continued to be the main occupation outside work. Wednesdays at Tommy Jobes were still attractive, and Alan continued with his cycling articles without success. The billiard matches came to an abrupt end when Tommy sold the table to pay an unexpected bill. If we had known of this bill, all of us would have clubbed together and helped him out of his difficulties. However we still had the darts and tiddley-winks as well as the table tennis.

My bike was now only used to get me to and from work, unless of course Alan was indisposed for any reason, but the machines had to be kept clean and serviceable for use at all times. From new my own bike had been stripped down to basics, cleaned, oiled and reassembled every two or three weeks.

Mr Mathews was a very unusual chap. Only once have I seen him sit down with his family. He appeared to live a most insular existence at home. Whenever I was there he occupied the front room, furnished with one easy chair, a sideboard, a table with his record player, and a cabinet in which he kept his mainly classical records. I saw him very seldom, he sat in his room smoking and playing his records, the ash from his cigarettes falling down the front of his beautiful suit. He preferred to burn wood in the grate, and Alan made it his job to keep the wood box filled.

During the evening while Alan, his mother and I were talking in the big living room, he'd occasionally enter by the back door carrying a couple of carrier bags. These were sometimes filled to the brim with two-ounce bars of chocolate, at other times with packets of five or ten cigarettes, and a bottle of whisky in each coat pocket. As he came through the living room on his way to the front room, he'd stop and wish us good evening. Then, offering the carrier bag, he would invite us to help ourselves. This offer was never refused as you could well imagine, we were always hard up. Alan told me that he drank a lot of whisky, yet it didn't seem to affect him in any way.

One thing I knew about Mr Mathews was that he held the position of Secretary of Clarke Chapman's. Company Secretary that is, which was to become very convenient for me later on when I needed a reference at short notice.

16. Sincerely Edith

CHAPTER SEVEN
Cycling and Romance
June 1938 - March 1939

My eldest brother Tom was now married and living at Staines with his wife May. Some months after our Easter tour of Scotland I received a letter inviting me to spend my annual holiday with them. I thought well of this, but money-wise it was difficult until I thought perhaps Alan may like the challenge of cycling down there.

After talking it over with Alan I wrote to my brother and asked if he minded if we both came down. They could meet Alan and we would be company for each other as Tom, having different holidays, would be at school. So the invitation was extended to Alan. As neither of us had ever visited London, and held no hope of being able to afford the trip without financial help, we thought that this was a golden opportunity. Not only to visit London but also to have the experience of cycling there and back.

We only had four weeks to arrange our trip, agree the route and to get some miles in our legs before we started. Our proposed journey would be all of three hundred miles there and the same back, and we proposed to ride the journey down in one leg. We intended starting out at 3:00am on the Saturday, hoping to get to Staines around lunch time Sunday. We would take two days to ride back.

We were going to be busy as we would have to overhaul the tandem as well. New tyres, chains checked, new brake blocks in the third brake, spokes checked and adjusted and then the extra training. We decided to ride one hundred and twenty miles on Sundays, sixty miles after work on two weekdays per week, and another fifty mile on Saturdays, making two hundred and ninety miles a week for three weeks. For the last week before the journey we would rest.

After the first week of training, we substituted the two midweek trips of sixty miles to one trip of a hundred miles. The hundred mile trips were to Wooler, fifty miles there, a bag of chips, then fifty miles back home, and a nice lie in a hot bath. This training programme wasn't intended to speed us up, but only for stamina as neither of us wanted to race. We preferred to keep up a steady pace, having a short rest now and again at a pleasant location or place of interest. Any good excuse for a fifteen minute break.

We did have one blip in the programme. On one of our trips to Wooler we had trouble with the fourteen toothed sprocket on the back wheel. This particular toothed wheel was very important, being the one most used. A replacement had to be ordered, so we sent off the postal order and asked them to send it to Tom's address at Staines. We hoped that the old sprocket would last the journey down. Satisfied that the bike was as reliable as we could make it and all other contingencies taken care of, we set off as arranged.

We went to bed very early Friday night, Alan sleeping at number forty three, Beaconsfield Road, with both of us looking forward to the journey ahead. Our route was to take us over some minor roads which would increase the mileage to over three hundred miles, as we didn't want to travel on the main roads all the way.

We didn't need the alarm clock; we were both awake at 3:00am and spent some time putting up a load of sandwiches. We had learned this from Mrs Handcorn, and it was essential to save money. Alan had a grand total of six pounds in his pocket and I managed three pounds. Not a lot, but if one remembers that a man's wage in the factory only amounted to three pounds a week, it was a reasonable sum. After all, a man had to pay the rent and feed his family on those three pounds, as well as clothing them.

So, saying cheerio to Mam and Dad who were still in bed, we set off on time. Down the road to Doncaster, both tired out, wondering what on earth we were doing at this unearthly hour of the morning. But that is the way it goes, we always found that the worse one felt when starting out, the better things went later in the day. And so it proved once again. By 9:00am we were feeling on top form and the tyres sounded great, 'thrumming' on the tarmac.

During our cycling careers, Alan and I had never ridden together south of Richmond, North Yorkshire, so south of Richmond was new ground. New ground was always special as getting away from the cobbled streets was always a tiresome business, and riding over roads that were new to us was something to be appreciated.

We passed Catterick and Boroughbridge, Leeds and Doncaster and, as the roads were free of traffic, we kept to the A1 to Bawtry. Then off on the A1 to Nottingham, where my brother Arthur had studied for his first class honours degree just a few years earlier.

Wending our way through, we eventually came into

open countryside again, taking the A606 to Melton Mowbray - home of the pork pies - and then to Oakham, Uppingham, and Market Harborough. Kettering was our next stop at 11:30pm, we both smelt the sweet smell of fish and chips, and it was irresistible. We followed our noses and were soon in the queue, eating them on a seat by the wayside. There were no teashops open so we had to forgo our favourite beverage, but the fish and chips refreshed us and we set off for Bedford.

Riding along, the darkness slowly changed to a half-light with a lighter layer on the eastern horizon, when, out of the corner of my eye I saw a lion walking along the top of the hedge. I thought to myself, this is no place for lions to be running loose. I thought that I'd better tell Alan, he may not have seen it. On being told he remarked that in the circumstances we'd better get a move on.

A couple of miles further on we came across a quiet spot out of the way, and Alan suggested a little shut-eye wouldn't do us any harm; by now I'd realised that I'd been seeing things and I wasn't averse to the idea. So with our heavy woollies and capes on we had half an hour's sleep in a potato field, under the hedge.

In fact we slept for an hour and woke up cold and hungry, our thoughts only on food and how to obtain it. Packing up our capes and gear we ran up and down the road to get our circulation going, then mounting up, we set off to Redford in search of food.

When we arrived at Redford at 6:00am on the Sunday morning the streets were deserted. However, we rode down the main street and found signs of life, a good lady scrubbing her front step, and above the door was a bed & breakfast sign.

We stopped and told her we were cold and hungry, could she help? She asked us how far we'd travelled and when we told her that we'd cycled from Newcastle, she threw her hands up in the air and exclaimed, 'Oh you poor lads, come in and sit you down.'

The good lady took us inside, up the stairs and opening one of the doors said, 'There you are, you can strip off and have a good wash and shave; I'll have a good breakfast ready for you in half an hour or so.'

When our hostess called we were ready for that breakfast, and what a meal! When we were finished neither of us could eat another bite, all our tired feelings had gone and we both felt as good as new. After thanking our hostess and checking the tandem, we said goodbye and promised her that we would call on the way home and stay the night. The lady only charged us four shillings and six pence for both of us, although for what we had we would willingly have paid four shillings and six pence each.

From here we had misgivings about the route we'd chosen, but we carried on to Hitchin. With hindsight we should have taken the Leicester road when we left Nottingham, then to Banbury and Oxford, Henley to Staines. This way we would have avoided the London area which we found was much too congested for our liking, at least compared to the cycling we were used to.

Now we were heading for Welwyn, Hatfield, St Albans, Rickmansworth and Uxbridge. Here we got lost having no street maps and we realised that we should have spent a little more time on research before setting out. The roads weren't as well marked in 1938 as they are now, although the traffic moved much more slowly.

However, we found our way to within ten miles of Staines, at which point we had to ask for directions.

We stopped and dismounted, lit a fag, and looked around for someone likely to know the way. We plumped for an ice-cream man on his tricycle, one of the clan we thought, so we stopped him, bought two ices, and asked him for directions to our destination. We couldn't have made a better choice. He must have enjoyed his beer, as he dictated as we wrote;

'Down this road until you come to the Red Lion, turn left and carry on past the gasworks until you come to the Fox on your left. Bear right at the next fork and keep going till you get to the Ship on your right. Turn right here and carry on for two miles where you'll see the Station Hotel on the corner'. He carried on for five or six more pubs and then asked which part of Staines we wanted. We told him the small estate opposite the Jolly Butcher, so we were directed there in no time at all.

We asked him how he knew the district so well. We understood when he told us that he'd been selling ice-cream around this district since he was sixteen. He also told us that he liked the open air, so during the winter months he worked in the HMV factory in Hayes, but when the sun shone he couldn't stand being locked up.

We thanked our good friend, and mounted up. Alan took the front with me behind reading the directions, and marvelling how anyone could navigate for ten miles by public houses only. But one thing was certain, he knew his pubs as we had no difficulty at all reaching our base.

We had a great welcome from Tom and May. May offered us a hot bath to take the stiffness out of our legs, and there was plenty of hot water. After a good soak,

May announced that a meal was waiting. May must have read our minds, a hot bath waiting and a meal besides, and we were starving. We apologised for being late, but as Tom said, five hours late after a three-hundred-mile cycle journey was pretty good.

The house was a three-up and two-down semi, backing onto a huge field with a big garden, and a nice lawn with deck chairs and table. At the far end of the field was Tom's school. In the field, just over the fence, was a concrete channel, thirty inches wide and about four feet deep, the water in the channel was flowing from left to right. It connected two reservoirs, so Tom said, but what made it special were the big trout swimming slowly against the current.

We wondered how many fish suppers were enjoyed by the inhabitants of that estate. Most of the trout were near to the eighteen-inch mark and reminded me of Thrum Mill, near Rothbury, Northumberland, where Alan and I used to lie on our stomachs watching the trout coming upstream in the River Coquet.

We were up next morning at 8:30am. May must have heard us moving about upstairs as she was already cooking breakfast. Tom had left for school and as the field was muddy in parts, he cycled. Knowing Tom I thought of a way to repay him, we'd overhaul his bike whilst we were there.

Neither of us had visited London before or seen Windsor Castle, and Alan wanted to visit Hayes to see if there were any jobs going at HMV. Being a radio ham he was quite a whiz kid in electronics. Frampton Court and Bushey Park were both quite near so were also places to be visited.

At breakfast we had a good chat with Tom and May's father. Steamboat, as he was known, was a seagoing engineer in his prime, now he was retired. He had lost his wife a year or so back so he lived with his daughter and Tom and did the odd jobs around the garden. He said he was just sitting back now, a little bit of gardening, stopping now and again for a sit down and a few draws on his pipe.

Over breakfast we learned of the swimming pool a few hundred yards down the road and, as we always carried our trunks with us during the summer, we had to take advantage of the situation. So Monday morning was spent in the swimming pool, which pointed out to us both how fit we must have been. A three-hundred-mile bike ride, eight hours sleep, then into the swimming pool.

We followed this with a walk around the district to get our bearings, and the afternoon was spent lounging in the deckchairs in the garden, recovering under a warm sun.

Now it was leisure time. This was tea and biscuits on the lawn, with Steamboat giving us all the gen and advice, where to go, what to see, and how to get there. He was a mine of information, and had the bus times and brochures of all the local beauty spots.

Tuesday we rode to Bushey Park, making friends with the local deer. They were tame enough for us to stroke their muzzles and to accept biscuits from our hands. There were notices up not to feed them but the little deer enjoyed the biscuits which May had given us. During the week we visited Windsor and Egham, and even got to Hayes to see if there was any work going, but apparently summer was one of their least busy periods.

We had a little parcel delivered one morning

containing the new sprocket for the tandem, so we had a working day. The tandem only needed the new sprocket which didn't take long, and then for a couple of hours we concentrated on overhauling Tom's bike. It needed it!

It was stripped down to the last nut and bolt, every thing cleaned and rebuilt, with new parts where needed. When we were finished it looked like a new bike, in fact it almost was, but we were only too pleased to do something to repay their kindness and hospitality.

After tea on Wednesday we sat in the garden and discussed our trip to London. As neither of us had been before, May suggested we travel by bus on Thursday morning with Steamboat as our guide. She said that he was looking forward to showing us around and we would certainly see more if we had a conducted tour, rather than just wandering around by ourselves. Next morning we were up bright and early, and caught the bus at the end of the street.

Old Steamboat made sure that we understood he was in charge. He'd had his instructions to show us all the main places of interest, Buck House, the Tower and so on, and to cover all expenses. We had the most wonderful conducted tour. We saw the changing of the guard, had a grand lunch, and then more tourist spots.

Over lunch he told us that after 4:30pm we were on our own, as he thought we'd like to wander around ourselves for a while, or do a show. He wrote out the bus routes and the number we required, where to get them and where to get off. He also gave us a door key so that we didn't have to come back early if we didn't wish.

We had seen the London New Cross speedway team ride at Newcastle when they had visited Brough Park. As we were both fans when at home we thought it would be a good idea to see a race meeting on a London track, and we decided to pay a visit to New Cross stadium. That night the New Cross team were riding against Wimbledon, the result didn't matter, but after seeing the New Cross stadium we were disappointed as it wasn't a patch on Brough Park.

It was now 11:00pm and we had to find our way across London to catch the coach at Victoria. We found our way there following our former guide's instructions, we made sure it was the right bus, and then climbed aboard. I was ready for bed, the last few days had been tiring and soon my head was nodding, but we daren't drop off.

With a heavy head and half asleep, my mind was straying, thinking how nice it would be to share all these places with Edith, and dreaming back to the Easter holiday. I'd already sent a birthday card on the sixth of June, before we came to Staines. I had to send another card and hope that Edith and I could get together again and explore all these places together. I'd made my decision.

Back at Staines we crawled from the bus, crossed the road and let ourselves in. We crawled into bed at 1:00am and I believe we were both asleep by ten minutes past.

We'd had a wonderful time with Tom, May and Steamboat, but we didn't think that we could manage another three-hundred-mile trip in one leg. Not after walking around London as we had the day before.

I had to go to work on Monday so we decided to take our time returning north. Coming down in one leg was an experience, but not one that could be repeated too often.

So we came to the conclusion that this was a holiday. If we left early on Friday morning and travelled one hundred and twenty five miles, followed by one hundred and twenty five miles on Saturday, that left fifty miles for the last leg on Sunday, and that would be it.

We'd made our intentions known to all, and May had kindly put up some grub to help us on our way. Getting up early on Friday morning we said thank you to our three hosts, explaining how much we had appreciated their kindness towards us. We had bought a small present each for Tom and Steamboat, and a nice bouquet of flowers for May. These were presented as we left for Bedford, there to keep our promise to the lady at the B&B. I posted cards to Mam and Dad as well as to Edith, and reminded Alan that he had a mother too.

We made our way towards Bedford, not exactly by the route by which we came as we took May's advice and avoided the heavily built-up areas. We did get back to Rickmansworth, but then we turned to Hemel Hempstead and Dunstable, and so to Bedford. We arrived late afternoon, rather tired, but we'd been taking things easy for almost a week and the traffic was awkward.

It would have been easier to have gone north through Oxford, there would certainly have been less traffic and, although I didn't know it at the time, Edith was on holiday that particular week at Oxford.

We called in at our chosen B&B and fortunately the good lady wasn't fully booked up. The house was on the main road, just north of the bridge over the River Ouse; at least I think it was the Ouse. On the south side of the bridge there were steps down to a riverside walk and gardens, it looked the perfect place for an evening stroll.

181

Supper wasn't served at the digs so we did what all cyclists do when hungry, we stood in a queue at the nearest fish and chip shop. Then we walked back down the steps to have our supper on a seat among the flower beds. What would we do without the fish and chip shops?

After a comfortable night's sleep and a big satisfying breakfast we set off early on the long middle leg of our journey. The previous day's ride had got our legs moving again and we felt fit.

We were soon back on the country roads away from the streets of houses, shops and factories. The tyres were singing again, changing their tune on the different road surfaces, the sun shone, legs turning in unison. It made me feel great to be alive. Although we hadn't ridden far the day before we were making up for lost time and the bike seemed eager to travel.

We made our way to Higham Ferrers, but instead of Kettering we carried on east to Thrapston, Oundel and Stamford on the A1. We had found by our experience on the way down that traffic on the A1 was very light, so we continued on to Newark, Bawtry, and towards Doncaster.

We rode a few more miles, and as we didn't wish to search Donny for B&B, we stopped at a small village to look for something to our liking, to stretch our legs, and as an excuse for a smoke.

It was a colliery village, no different from the Lintz and dozens of pit villages in the area. Old Faithful was left leaning against the railings on a small terrace at the side of the road. A little further down the street, with his head over the railings, was a big brown horse. We walked down and had a word, stroked his muzzle and apologised for not having any sugar lumps. We usually carried a few sugar lumps in our pockets for emergencies, unfortunately this horse was unlucky, we could only apologise.

Over the fields the grassland stretched for miles. I thought, what a great view the houses in the terrace had from their front windows. We turned around and leaned against the gate studying the houses opposite.

They were stone built for the mining communities of that time like thousands of others, but one had a CTC sign on the wall beside the door. This gave us something to think about, we had ridden one hundred and forty miles, why not spend the night here? This would leave us eighty five miles to ride tomorrow, just in time to get home for tea. So we walked across the road, made enquiries, booked in, and then went for a walk over the fields, waiting for the fish and chip shop to open.

We got back quite early, and we had the usual question, 'How far have you ridden today?'

I believe that people thought that anyone riding over fifteen miles a day was superhuman. As soon as we mentioned one hundred and forty miles, the old dears made you sit down, brought a cup of tea, which was never refused, put a cushion behind your back and asked if you were comfortable.

We loved being spoiled, but here we had to eat another supper, the good lady refused to believe that we'd just finished a paper of fish and chips. As is still often the case with landladies today, our landlady was ready to spend half the night chattering, so we got to bed at 1:30am.

We enjoyed our stay there, supper, bed and breakfast for the sum of four shillings and sixpence each. We still had a little money left and thought what a smashing holiday for two, for less than nine pounds.

We set off for home at the usual time, and after an easy ride arrived home as anticipated. Alan dropped me off at Low Fell, 'See you tomorrow Ern.'

He didn't wish to stay, he needed a bath, as I did, and we only had one bath at home. So Alan carried on home, and we agreed I'd collect my gear the following evening. Talking about tomorrow reminded me tomorrow meant work.

I'd bought a present for my mother, but after sixty five years I think that I could be forgiven for not remembering what it was. I only bought one for Mam, Dad had told me on numerous occasions, 'Don't get anything for me, but always remember your mother.' After a hot bath and saying hello to all the family, I felt a lot better.

Next morning I was back at work, and as usual after a holiday the main topic was, 'What sort of holiday did you have?' All down the benches whilst eating lunch, the same question.

Holidays rarely took place in Italy or Spain, and in the nineteen-thirties no one at Clarkies could afford it. The ordinary worker would consider himself lucky if he could afford a week in a boarding house for himself and family. More often the parents took their offspring on picnics down the woods and visits to the pictures or theatre.

When I told my mates that Alan and I had cycled to London and back I was told that I needed my head seeing to, but I know that there was a lot of envy there too.

I was coming up to my twenty first birthday and I was thinking about Edith and saving. As was the custom then, at the age of twenty-one apprentices only received three quarters of a man's rate of pay, and were termed 'improvers'. To receive full pay the improver had to leave the firm and find a new job.

I was giving serious thought about this, as there was no way that I could save money on my present wage. If I was to ask Edith to marry me, I'd need money. I didn't even know if Edith would have me back, but I thought she wouldn't have sent me cards and photographs if that weren't so.

Talking to men who had had the same problem of saving for the future or to get married, I was told all sorts of things, but the serious ones I listened to. I learned that some had left home and found a job working as a travelling fitter on outside jobs, where expenses had been paid by the employer. Others had found jobs on capital projects and lived in hostels on site. Some went to sea as engineers and received their board and accommodation; working as they did at Clarkies on ship's auxiliaries they had the job at their finger tips.

The pay was in most circumstances higher than I earned in the factory, and then again if I was confined to a ship, there was no need to spend. Old casual clothes were the norm on board and only one good suit would be needed for going ashore. According to the majority of those who had been afloat it was the best way to save quickly. The drawback of course was one didn't see the girlfriend as often as one would wish.

There was a card from Edith waiting for me when I arrived home and I knew that we could get together again. I replied with a letter telling her how I felt. Could we meet again and talk things over with the idea of getting back together? Over the last few months I'd thought things over in my mind and come to the conclusion that my future was with Edith and that cycling would take second place.

We met in Newcastle and walked through Jesmond Dene. Talking everything over we decided that we belonged together and began making plans that only concerned we two.

During the rest of the summer we visited the local beauty spots, occupied our favourite seats in the local cinema, and went on picnics on Sunday afternoons.

Our favourite spot was on the banks of the Tyne at Wylam. We took the tram to Newburn, up on the top deck, swaying from side to side along the Scotswood Road and hanging on to each other to prevent falling on the floor. This was a trip one had to experience to believe. It was a six mile ride for tuppence h'penny[16] return over a cobbled road that should have been resurfaced a decade ago. We got off the tram at Newburn then took a short walk to Wylam village where just before reaching the village, on the right, stood the small cottage where George Stephenson once lived.

This piece of the north-east is now taken up by sports fields and a golf course, but we knew it as a piece of land by the side of the river with scrub and small bushes, which was ideal for picnics. We usually had the place to ourselves, a flask of tea with ham sandwiches and dates and nuts.

My eldest sister Maggie was an expert in picnics with lots of ideas in this respect, so she kindly made up our teas. But picnics of this sort were only feasible during hot

---

[16] Two and a half old pence. Editor

summer days. Other times we walked miles together, and often there was no need to talk, just being together was everything.

While walking Edith and I discussed everything concerning our future; what we would like to happen, marriage, how and when, getting a house, how many children. We talked everything over.

One particular night I called at Montrose and was told that Edith was in hospital. I blurted out, 'Which hospital?' Before Edith's father could explain, I was on my bike and on my way. I must have been in shock as I forgot about the visiting times until I read the notice when I got there, 7:00pm to 8:00pm. I walked to the reception desk, but as soon as they found out that I wasn't a relative they wouldn't tell me anything, so I had to wait an hour until the bell rang and everyone took off for the various wards.

I found Edith looking pale, her face small against the big pillow with both eyes bandaged, but when I spoke her face lit up, that was all the greeting that I wanted. She had been in for three days, and the operation had gone well. An hour's visit wasn't long, but Edith had only had the operation that day and was tired, so for the most part we just sat and held hands.

I sat on the chair by the bed, but the bed was low and the chair was high, so I knelt by the side of the bed. It was more comfortable for me and our faces were closer together. I proposed that day, kneeling beside her bed, but we were not officially engaged until March 16th, 1940.

Edith wasn't in hospital long and a couple of days later she was much more cheerful, however she still wouldn't tell me why she needed the operation.

When Edith was released from hospital she only had one eye bandaged which she wore for a long time, but it didn't prevent us from going on long walks, or even going to the cinema.

I remember one day we walked to North Shields at the mouth of the Tyne, intending to get the train back home, but we ran into trouble when there was a power cut. We were sitting in the train unable to get off for three hours. We didn't get home until after 11:00pm. Edith, drawing sickness benefit, was supposed to be indoors by nine. Her mother went up the wall and Edith told me that things were rough until the breakdown was reported in the Monday morning paper. Oddly enough Mrs Lamb never mentioned the episode to me.

We were happy together, although we had very little money. All of our trips were low budget, perhaps a trip to town, occasionally with tea at the Dicken's tea rooms. This was a tea room decorated in the style of the Dickens era, with wood-panelled walls, and suits of armour around the place. It was warm and cosy on a cold day, with tea and scones, and we found the atmosphere quite romantic on a cold autumn afternoon.

I was still wondering how we were going to save enough money to enable us to get married. Neither Edith nor myself wanted to wait six years and working in the factory it was going to take that long, even if I went on to full money when I was twenty one. During the slump there were no shore jobs vacant or advertised, and at Clarkies the men were only working for nine months of the year, the rest of the time they were on the dole.

Edith wasn't earning enough to save; besides her

mother took all her wages and only gave her a little for her pocket. No one could save under those conditions. There seemed to be a need for junior engineers at the time and the case for going to sea became stronger in my mind, and so we decided.

Nowadays young people of eighteen can often earn enough together to set up home, but we were very old-fashioned in the thirties, and in any case no one could earn enough to live on their own then.

At work, I was more than capable of holding my own. I was as big and strong as most of the older men, stronger than some, and could keep pace with them at the work bench. I was accepted as an equal, not only in the shaft department but in the electric and steam winch departments as well.

What I lacked was confidence. I was still worried about the usual things most twenty-year-olds worried about, and may still worry about today. When I leave this sheltered existence, will I be able to cope on my own? Apart from the new job at sea, I'd also need to get another job to keep both of us after we were married. Looking back I need not have worried, but no one can read the future.

My older mates at work were my confidants as we ate our lunch sitting on the bench. Dad wasn't easy to approach, although I'd sought his advice on many occasions. I supposed that the men in the factory, correctly as it worked out, had had similar experiences to myself at one time or another. And just as they had done, I would have to rely on what I had learned over the past seven years.

Then something occurred. At the time it scared me

rigid, but later on I realised that my good fairy was still looking after me.

A new ship, the *AMRA* built at Swan Hunters on the Tyne, had come back from its trials with a faulty warp end on the forward winch. One of our fitters had been down there a week trying to get the faulty drum off the shaft and replace it with a good one. He'd failed, so someone else had to get down there and get the job done before the ship sailed to India on the tide, 4:00am Sunday.

During Friday afternoon I saw the foreman having a word with Sam Sherrif, one of the two senior fitters. I noticed Sam shaking his head and I wondered what they were talking about. The foreman then went to the other senior, Joe Morland, and they had a few words together. This was very interesting. I saw Joe shake his head, then they both looked at me; my heart leapt up into my throat. What had I done now?

Shortly afterwards the foreman came over to me and told me that he had a job for me over the weekend. Sam and Joe had dropped me right in it. I had to go to Swan Hunter's and get this warp end replaced by another before 4:00am on Sunday morning. I was still an apprentice and this other guy, with over thirty years' experience had failed after a week. I didn't even have a weekend. Apparently someone had more faith in my ability than I had in myself.

The foreman said to me, and this is true, no fairy story, he said to me, 'All you have to do is take the gear down there, take the damaged warp end off and replace it with the new one.' It didn't sound very difficult the way he said it, but my heart was right down in my boots.

I was told that the lorry would be ready at 7:45am the next morning, and to my disappointment, it was. I did get one concession; I could take another apprentice with me, although I had to ask for him. So John Henderson was picked to give me a hand, two lads on a man's errand.

Saturday morning I turned up for work, I had hardly slept at all. John was there, he and Joe were going to see Jackie Milburn play that afternoon at St James Park. Joe called me over and gave me two shillings. He told me they weren't for me; they were to buy two twenty packets of Players to give to the slinger when I got down there. One was for the slinger and one for the crane driver, and to tell the slinger that you might need a lift in a hurry to get the job done in time. Going down in the lorry I felt sick, I turned to John and told him we were in it up to our necks.

'This is not my job,' he said, 'I'm only here to give you a hand.' Those words made me feel much better, as you can imagine.

We reached the dock gates, and the gateman came over. I told him we had business on the *AMRA* and he told me where she lay. When we reached the dockside I went in search of the slinger, gave him the fags, and got the assurance that when he was needed I could give him a whistle and he'd be right there.

I went on up the gangplank and looked at the warp end, as I expected, the end of the shaft had been mauled. There was no way that we were going to get that warp end off, not with the tools at our disposal. I looked away at the ship, how clean it looked. I wonder if this was the job to ends all jobs, sailing with this ship, looking after the winches, getting paid for sailing around the world.

This was the first time that I'd been on the deck of an ocean going vessel. It was wonderful, and I felt happy, until I remembered why we were there. My heart sank and I turned back to the winch.

Then I started laughing, suddenly everything was right with the world. John wanted to know why I was laughing, and I told him that the foreman was going to give him a rise.

We'd only been looking at the warp end. I pointed out to John that the winch was central with an extension on each side, and on the end of the extensions were the warp ends. We didn't have to take the drum off, we could take the extension off and take it back to Clarkies complete with warp end, and let Sam and Joe do the job.

We got busy taking the bearing off the shaft and undoing the bolts holding the extension. We whistled up the slinger, and down he came right away to lift the warp end and extension shaft onto our lorry. We tied it down so it wouldn't roll and set off, back to the shop.

When we arrived back at base I saw the foreman, told him the shaft was coming down on the crane, and could he get Sam and Joe interested. Using the hydraulic equipment the drum was replaced, a new key fitted and hammered home in no time at all, and at 11:30am we were ready and on our way back to Swan Hunter's yard.

When we were finished we thanked the slinger and crane driver, loaded our tools onto the lorry, then told the driver the job was done and he was free to return to base. We were all finished by 1:00pm, so now we were going to look over the ship.

To be truthful, apart from the little ferry across the Tyne, this was the first ship that I'd been aboard, much less explored, so we enjoyed the walk around. While walking around I felt really at home. I felt that I belonged here, and I was comparing the surroundings with our filthy factory in which I was working at the moment.

The *AMRA* was built for the British India Line, her maiden voyage starting at 4:00am on the Sunday morning. It was more of a passenger ship than the *City of Kimberley*, which was to be my first ship, and although it was only a little bigger than the *City* - four hundred and sixty feet against four hundred and thirty seven feet - the *AMRA* had beauty salons and hairdressers. The *AMRA* was also driven by twin turbines instead of the triple expansion, low pressure turbine and electric drive of the *City of Kimberley*. This new ship was also faster, sixteen and a half knots against twelve and a half knots.

We visited the engine room and galley, and as we opened doors in our curiosity we found the hairdressers. The barber offered us a haircut but time was pressing so we had to refuse. Also we didn't have enough to cover the tip, so we wended our way home.

We called in at Edith's to let her know I'd be a little late, and explained why. Edith made us a cup of tea while her mother looked at us in our dirty overalls, wrinkling her nose. I don't think she fancied Edith marrying someone who worked in a factory.

Monday morning came as usual, and back at work I gave Joe his two bob back that he'd given me to buy the fags, and the foreman gave me a sheet on which to claim my expenses. Apart from the two bob for the fags I'd had no expenses, but the foreman must have been pleased as he insisted that we charged a good lunch, tram fares and for the cigarettes. So we were paid our expenses, even the bribe of the fags, and we were paid to 5:00pm, even though we were finished at 1:30pm.

I don't know how they knew, but the apprentices were all talking about our weekend job. Everybody was happy, Joe and Sam because they saw the football match, the foreman because he was able to report that the job was cleared up, and me because my first real job on my own had been so successful. Apart from the fact that everyone was happy, my reputation had gone up and the foreman addressed me by my first name. Maybe I didn't have as much to worry about as I thought.

My twenty-first birthday came along. That Wednesday evening as usual I was on my bike and down to Tommy Jobe's place to meet the others, but to my surprise it turned out to be a special evening.

After the various championships they presented me with a special gift, a handsome de luxe leather toilet case containing a brush and comb and shaving equipment. They'd kept it a very close secret. What a wonderful evening, it was really something to treasure.

But at the age of twenty one I had other things to consider, I had to think seriously of what was in front of me. There were adverts in the papers for junior engineers at sea with better money than in the factories as well as being more permanent, so the tide took me in that direction.

I needed references before I applied for any post so I called in the office and enquired as to the correct procedure. I was told that no references were given unless the apprentice had served his whole five years with the company. I explained the circumstances, and said that my prospective employer wanted a reference.

The clerk behind the counter wasn't being helpful, in fact he was quite nasty, and so I told him I would be back. Mr Mathews, Alan's dad, was the man to see.

When I saw Alan that night I asked if his dad was available. Fortunately he was, listening to music in their front room as usual. Alan waited for the break in the music and then went in and asked him if I could have a word. I went in and we talked about the situation. When he heard everything he exclaimed, 'What a load of rubbish. If you write out a draft of all you've done whilst you've worked there, leave it with me and I'll see to it first thing in the morning.'

Two days later the clerk came down to see me on the factory floor, and asked me to call in at the office when it was convenient. There I received a very good reference detailing all my work whilst I'd worked for the company, and a handsome apology from the clerk. He asked if I knew Mr Mathews personally. When I told him his was my second home, the clerk's face dropped, he was Mr Mathew's personal secretary.

Next I needed a reference from Sanderson's to cover the period from when I was fourteen to seventeen years old. I rode down straight from work at Clarkies. It was just after 5:00pm and I was hoping that one or two of the bosses would still be there, otherwise it would mean taking time off.

However I was lucky that day, there was still a light on in the office as I walked in. The factory floor was in darkness, the workers had gone, but knocking on the office door had an effect. Mr Race came to the door, recognised me and asked me in, pulling up a chair for me as I entered. This was the man who sacked me and then had to reinstate me. I was a good bit bigger and older now, and maybe that made a little difference.

We had a good talk of old times and the company then and now. I told him of the past three or four years, and said now I was off to sea and needing references. 'Nothing easier,' he said, and putting paper in the type writer he started typing.

He read the reference back to me, asked if I was happy with it, and then signed it with a flourish. So we shook hands, and I said that if I could I would come back and say goodbye to all the others, given that the staff had left for the night. He'd only stayed himself to finish off some work otherwise he'd have been off too.

When I looked at the reference I noticed he had signed the manager's name. I knew that I wouldn't be back. Just being there that time, seeing the old place, remembering Bobby Little and the rest of the men brought a lump to my throat. I thought then, would the thought of this place affect me in the same way in fifty years time? Sixty-five years on, I can now say it does.

Edith and I had talked this over, time and time again. On the down side, we wouldn't see each other for a long time, six months, maybe twelve. On the up side, we could get married in perhaps two years instead of four or five, and the usual temptation of courting couples would be non-existent while I was away. Edith was nineteen years old, I was twenty one. Edith's mother wanted her at home as it was Edith who did the housework and brought money in from her job. Edith's mother was against her getting married, full stop. But in two years time Edith would be twenty one, then we would be married.

Elsie, Alan's sister, lived just across the road, one

hundred yards away from where Alan lived, and her husband was a wireless operator at sea with Elder Dempster. She took the paper published by Lloyds which listed all the shipping information.

We made a list of the companies, the ships, routes and so forth. Tankers were out, there were too many restrictions. Besides they had very little time in port, being able to load a cargo of oil in twelve hours and then off to another oil terminal to unload in the same length of time, allowing almost no time ashore for the crew.

Then there were the passenger liners. No, that was too much dressing up for my liking, as engineers weren't allowed on deck unless wearing uniform. Elsie wrote down what I would like, a ship that visited as many places as possible, out east or all over the world, good money, and good grub. Out of the mass of information, Elsie came up with Ellerman and Bucknall and a cargo liner.

Other companies such as the Port Line ran regular trips to New Zealand and Australia, carrying frozen cargo, but the only countries that I would see were probably the two named.

I wrote to eight shipping companies and had ten replies. I never found out how, but I actually received two replies from companies that I hadn't contacted.

After the letters arrived Alan, Elsie and I sat down together, and all the replies were read over and discussed, adding up the pros and cons. With Elsie's knowledge of the shipping lines we settled on Ellerman and Bucknall, offering the post of Fifth Engineer.

According to Elsie, they were the best bet, with a line of first-class ships. They paid over the average, the food was good, they sailed all over the globe and they were liable to call at any port, in any country. In her opinion I couldn't do better than accept their offer. I wrote straight back; although I didn't have the job yet, the post was offered on the assumption that my references were satisfactory.

However, the next week I received a letter confirming my appointment, and instructions to stand by. The letter also returned my references and informed me that I would receive further instructions as to when to offer my notice to Clarke Chapman's.

I must thank both Elsie and Alan for all the help that I received from them, they made it so easy for me, and I don't think that I could have done such a good job by myself. I also have to thank Mr Mathews for his help.

This was the start of a new phase of my life. The familiar butterflies began to intrude at times but after a couple of weeks the letter I'd been waiting for arrived, my ship, the *City of Kimberley,* was lying in Huskisson Dock, Liverpool. Enclosed within the envelope was a travel warrant for the train journey to Lime Street Station, Liverpool. I had just two weeks to make all my arrangements.

The next two weeks were hectic. I gave in my notice to the office and a week later was saying goodbye to a lot of good friends, some I never saw again. The day I left, my thoughts were very confused. I was sad to leave this place, I'd enjoyed working here for the last four years and hated leaving it and my friends. On the other hand, I was leaving on a great adventure which was to change my whole life. I wasn't frightened of the challenge, but I was very nervous.

At 4:00pm, when the time came to actually say my farewells, I looked around the section, then down the length of the factory to the winch bay, and felt a hand on my shoulder. It was the hand of Joe Morland, beside him stood Sam Sheriff. Joe said, 'Ern, nervous of the future?'

'I am Joe,' I replied.

'Not to worry,' he said. 'Look down there in the winch bay. You know that there's not a man down there that's better than you. You know your winches as good as anyone there, and a lot better than some. And I'll tell you another thing, this ship you're going on, no one on that ship will know as much about winches as you do. So stop worrying lad. Just give us a thought now and again, look after yourself and good luck.'

I went along to the winch bay, to say goodbye to my old foreman and Pat. No, I couldn't go without seeing Pat. He'd done me some real good turns; after all it was he who had made me a boxing champion.

As Pat was coming towards me he attracted the foreman's attention, he spoke to Mr Kirton, 'My old mate's leaving and going to sea, he'll need a couple of valve spanners, can you help?'

Now valve spanners are specially bent to get into very awkward places. When setting the valves they are essential, and mine went back into stores when I moved into the shaft department.

The foreman turned to the nearest fitter and asked him for his valve spanners, then handed them to me. He then shook my hand and wished me good luck. Pat turned to me and said, 'See that Ern, you get nought if you div'ent ask, and when you get to that ship of yours just remember you're a champion. Div'ent let anybody get on top, give them hell first.'

We said our goodbyes. I felt bad at leaving them all and thought to myself, 'Will I be so happy in my new job?'

The two spanners, by the way, were handed over to the new fifth engineer when I was promoted to fourth. Maybe they're still with the *City* as she lies in her ocean bed.

I didn't have the money to own a large wardrobe, so all I took was one good set of clothes, one not so good, two pairs of shoes, my cycling jacket - which I thought might come in handy - and my leather cycling gloves. The two latter items came in very handy later, very useful indeed.

I had been informed that clothes were so much cheaper out east that I didn't buy any extra, but I bought two large expanding suitcases. In fact it was rather strange, on my return I still had to buy an extra one.

When I called and said goodbye to Alan and his family, he gave me a model of a galleon mounted on an ashtray. He said he had made the model himself expressly for this occasion. It stood about three inches high and took pride of place alongside Edith's photograph. Edith's photograph was always there on top of my chest of drawers, the same photo that at this moment stands on my sideboard.

I also had a quiet word with Mam. I pointed out that Edith and I were saving to get married, and hoped that we had her blessing. Mother told me that I owed her nothing, but I asked her if I paid the rent of the house while I was away would she accept it. So we were happy with that arrangement.

But the hardest thing was saying goodbye to Edith. For the last two weeks we'd been out together more often than at any time since we met, but we had the comfort of knowing that we were doing something for our future together. We had a lot to look forward to, the rest of our lives together.

I said goodbye to Dad, and asked him if he'd look after Edith whilst I was away. He said that he'd look after Edith as if she were his own daughter and said that he hoped she would visit them every Sunday while I was away.

All goodbyes said, the only thing was to catch the tram, then the train at the Central Station. As I sat in my corner seat I realised that this was the first railway journey by myself, and if one discounted the South Shield's ferry and the *AMRA*, when I boarded the *SS City of Kimberley*[17] it would be the first time I'd been aboard a ship.

The train pulled out of the station. I was looking from the window wondering how long it would be before I was to see this station again. My first leave I expected in either six months or twelve months time, and I had to learn a new job all over again. And then I thought, it's not a new job, I'll be doing the same job that I was doing at Clarkies, only in the fresh air instead of that dirty factory. I began to feel much more cheerful.

---

[17] The *SS City of Kimberley*, 6169 tons, was built in 1925 by Wm Gray Ltd , at the Wear Shipyard, Sunderland, for the Ellerman and Bucknall Lines, which lost 58 ships in World War Two. On the 5th September 1964 the *City* sunk off Hong Kong during a storm, breaking loose while being towed to the breakers' yard at Shanghai. Information found with my father's manuscript. Editor

My mind went over the past, when I first left school to start work at Sanderson Bros., then the short stop at the slave pit in Birtley Iron Works and then Clarke Chapman's, the basis of this new adventure. And I wondered how an apprentice can go to bed an apprentice, and wake up on his twenty-first birthday as a skilled man.

Sixty five years later I realise how inexperienced I really was, or should I say how little I knew of the world, or indeed how lucky I was then. I was big and healthy; I'd had a good grounding in the three R's and a good, no, very good, training as a fitter and turner. I had everything going for me.

When I was seven, I wanted to be a cowboy, so much so that it physically hurt. Many years later the same longing returned, only this time it was for ships. I think the headmaster at Kelvin Grove School, Mr Sedgewick, may have had something to do with my interest. Following the journey of his two sons from port to port, around the world, and discovering what cargo went to which port.

Then building winches among a gang of ex-seamen must have had some effect. But even earlier, I was sailing ships of my own making on the pit ponds of the Lintz and Tanfield Lea. I'll never know where I got my love of the sea and ships, from my father, perhaps?

He was in the Royal Navy during the First World War, and he told me stories of his time at sea when I was a baby. When we were at South Shields he also took me to the end of the pier to see the ships that sat close to hand when they entered the River Tyne. Maybe it was my dear old Dad all the time. Thanks Dad.

17. *SS City of Kimberley.* This is an old post card and the only detail I can find is © E & A Feilden, Liverpool

18. The Officers from left to right, 2nd Engineer, Chief, 4th and 3rd, 1939

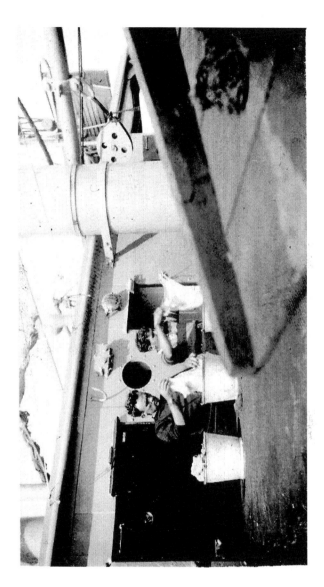

19. Washing at sea

CHAPTER EIGHT
Preparing for Sea - 1939

It seemed as if the train was in no hurry to get to its destination, although maybe it wasn't the train but my excitement. But we did arrive eventually at Lime Street Station and, dragging my two cases, I stepped onto the platform. Carrying my case to the barrier, I thought to myself that I could do without these things. There wasn't much in them, but it would be hard dragging them around if I had to do any looking, so I went into the left luggage office and left one there.

I had no idea where Huskisson Dock was, but the station porter came in handy, and he told me the way to the docks. We had porters to carry the luggage in those days, if you were fortunate enough to grab one. I caught a tram to the pier head, then the overhead railway to the appropriate dock. I never thought of a taxi, never having been in one.

The railway ran right along the dock road overhead and stopped at the gates, but I hadn't realised how big these docks were. The place was crowded with ships, and as I didn't know what my ship looked like I spent some time looking. Then I did what I should have done in the first place, I walked to the gates and asked the man on the gate. I learned that the ship had moved to another dock for coaling, Langton Dock, so I turned round to go back on the overhead railway. It wasn't far and I was learning all the time. This time I asked the man on the Langton

Dock gate for directions straightaway and was directed to the right berth.

Standing on the dockside with my case I looked up. The ship looked enormous. I walked up the gangplank and onto the deck. The chap at the top knew I was a crewmember by my case and he enquired who I was. I told him that I was the new Fifth Engineer. He told me where to find my cabin and where to get the key, he also told me where to find the Second Engineer.

I collected my key from the Mess Room Boy, a lascar seaman from Bombay whose name I never found out, we all called him Boy or Raj. He answered to either, but to us he was a godsend. He was the man who woke us up in the morning with a cup of tea and biscuits, and again at 3:00pm. He served us at mealtimes in the mess-room, cleaned our cabins, and looked after us generally.

Dumping my case in the middle of the floor, I stood and looked around, my very own cabin on my first ship. I was struck by how small it seemed at first. Probably because it was small, just nine foot square. It was a room in miniature and it looked really quite luxurious.

Opposite the door was the bunk, two and a half feet wide and six and a half feet long. At the head of the bunk was a wardrobe, two and a half feet square. To the left along the bulkhead or wall was a two and a half foot wide settee or day bed with padded back and head end. It was upholstered in bright red fabric, embroidered with Prince of Wales feathers in gold, and was a wonderful bed for an afternoon kip.

On the wall at the head of the settee was a small bookcase and on the opposite bulkhead to the settee, near the bottom of the bunk, was a small steam radiator.

Standing next to this was a chest of drawers, three feet wide and two feet deep, with an electric fan above it, both of which were fixed to the bulkhead.

Alongside the chest was a wash stand in polished wood, with a lift-up lid which concealed the wash basin. Under the wash basin was a small cupboard which held a bucket, and when one pulled the sink plug it emptied into the bucket. There was also another small cupboard under the bucket, inside which was a metal jug which held a gallon of water. The jug was for hot water, which was delivered by the Mess Room Boy before we came off watch and when we woke, ready for shaving.

Beneath the bunk, which was three feet high, were two large drawers and four smaller ones. In the chest there were six small drawers and a pullout leaf, baize covered for writing purposes. The drawers were all lockable, not solely to outwit thieves, but also to prevent the drawers from sliding open during heavy weather.

The room was completed by one deck head light, one table lamp clamped to a small shelf at the side of the bunk, and two portholes, or scuttles, one near the head of the bunk and one near the foot.

There was also a hole in the roof, or deck head, to which was connected the ventilator. This could be turned from the outside to allow air to be blown into the cabin, or it could be turned in the opposite direction allowing the stale air to be drawn out.

Lifting the seat of the settee revealed storage space for four large suitcases; there was also a large board in here which could be clipped to the side of the bunk to prevent one rolling out during heavy weather. I never had occasion to use it, simply because I didn't know its purpose. I found that when the heavy weather came I could stay in my bunk quite naturally by using elbows and knees. At least, I never had any difficulty even when we had some extra heavy weather twelve months later.

There was no planned colour scheme in the cabin. The woodwork was stained dark oak, the bulkheads were all panelled in wood, and only the deck head was painted white. The red carpet complemented the red settee and the gold coloured fleur-de-lys finished the decor. Altogether a very comfortable box, measuring nine feet by nine feet by six feet high, and I found out later that the bunk was extremely soft and comfortable.

I left my case in the centre of the cabin and turned to leave. Across the passageway was another door without a name on, being nosey I opened it and found another entrance to the engine room. This was for access during bad weather, so we didn't have to go outside to get to work. Along the passage were four cabins. Coming from aft they were for the use of the Carpenter, the Fifth Engineer, the Fourth Engineer, and then a double cabin for two Quartermasters.

Through the door to the engine room was a long gangway, 'the iron bridge', just like a steel ladder but with the rungs closer together and handrail on each side. One could walk from one passageway across the engine room to the passageway door on the other side which gave access to the other engineers' quarters. Through that door, from aft, were first right the mess-room, first left, the bathroom, second left was the Third Engineer's cabin, third left was the Second's, and the fourth and fifth doors led to the Chief's cabin and office.

Standing on the iron bridge, between the two doors,

provided a wonderful bird's eye view of the engine room. It felt very unsafe, but it was surprising how quickly one became accustomed to using this quick way to work.

With, if not my name, my occupation in print on the door of my very own cabin, Fifth Engineer, I felt that I had risen up in the world!

After I'd taken off my overcoat and parked my suitcase, I made my way down to the engine room to find the Second Engineer. I found him by the desk near the bridge phone, chaos all around. I realised later that in port this was quite normal, although at the time I didn't know that it was organised chaos. In fact there is very little floor space in an engine room, and with everybody taking things to pieces and laying them around there was less room than ever.

I arrived as the Mess Room Boy was handing tea out to the three engineers, just in time for the Second to ask him to get another cup for the new Fifth. While we drank our tea we made our introductions, and the Second asked me if I'd settled in. I told him that I had another case at the station. He suggested that I collect it right away and that tea was at 4:30pm. 'See you then. Don't stay down here in those clothes, you'll ruin them.' With that he finished his tea and was off.

I had time to collect my case from the station and just got back in time for tea, which was more like a dinner with a menu and water glasses on the table. This was a real change of life-style, like going to a restaurant for meals.

After tea the Third and Fourth excused themselves and the Second and myself were left on our own. I think he was quite happy when I told him that I came from the

211

north-east. He came from Middlesborough, so now there were two English, two Scots, the Chief and the Fourth, and one Welshman, the Third Engineer.

I was asked where I worked and what I'd done. When I told him that I'd served my time at Clarke Chapman's, it made his day. I told him, if necessary, I could build a winch up from the base plate and set the valves, in fact anything he wanted doing on a winch, I could do. He said it would be a relief to leave them in my hands. I then had a rundown on my duties.

We started work at 7:00am. That is, we assembled on the starting platform when I would be informed as to the job for that day. Breakfast was served from 8:00am until 9:00am. Then work was until 12:30pm when we stopped for lunch or dinner, then back to work until 4:30pm. In a home port it was dinner at 12:30pm, while at sea it was lunch at 12:30pm. However I was to find out that lunch and dinner were very much alike, they were both three-course meals.

I also learned that the Third, Fourth and Fifth took turns in rotation to stay on board during the evenings, as the boiler or boilers had to have an engineer in attendance at all times. There was a donkey man down there to keep steam up for the generator and so forth, but one of us had to be in charge.

Sounds daft, doesn't it? Here was I, a novice, in charge of the engine room at night and I'd never seen an engine room before, at least only one. I was told that one of the others would keep me company for the first week or two, but that didn't stop me from worrying. There had to be a first time on my own, I needed to find out quickly what was likely to happen, and why.

After tea I changed and wandered down to the engine room to have a look around on my own trying to get the feel, or rather trying to make sense, of the maze of pipes and machinery. One must understand that this was my first introduction to a ship's engine, I had no idea that they were so big. I began to doubt if I would ever be at home here, although at that moment it looked beautiful.

I walked up and down ladders, I walked back and forth on the catwalks around the main engine and traced pipes from here to there, although I didn't know or understand what they did. Standing by the telegraph I looked up towards the skylights. It looked less forbidding than looking down from the top. The catwalks with just a single handrail looked decidedly dangerous.

The first level was about seven foot six inches from the floor plates, the second level was about the same distance again and level with the top of the engine. There were no plates on levels one and two, just grating, so from the top of the engine one could look between one's feet and see the bottom floor plates fifteen feet below.

One side of the second level was plated, however, and this area was taken up by the low pressure turbine and the generator. This is where one gained access to the boiler tops where a couple of dozen steam valves were housed. These directed the steam to various parts of the maze. The oil and water separator was also there.

Behind the turbine was the auxiliary oil pump for the turbine; this supplied oil to the turbine bearings as it was slowing down, or starting up. When the turbine was running normally it had its own lubrication pump.

Whilst walking around I realised how easy it would be to slip and fall between the grating and the single handrail. I also learned that wearing rubber-soled shoes in the engine room was extremely hazardous as the gratings and the handrail were coated with oil to prevent rust in the hot and humid atmosphere. I would have to seek advice on this matter at the next mealtime.

After an hour or so I returned to my cabin and unpacked my suitcases, which was when I realised how little I had brought with me. Most of my drawers were still empty, however the two cases went into the hole under the settee seat and everything had its place. I tried the electric fan; this was the first time I'd ever used one, and it worked as did all the lights. Someone had been in and polished, I could smell it, and the cabin was spotless. Just as if someone was hinting, this is the way that they wanted it kept. I tried the mattress and decided that as well as being well fed, I was going to be comfortable.

So a couple of letters home, one to let Mam know that I had arrived safely and was settling in, and one to Edith to remind her that I loved her and was thinking of her back home. That night I slept like a top, to be awakened between 6:30am and 6:45am by the Mess Room Boy, who came in with a cup of tea and a couple of biscuits, shaking me gently with a quiet word, 'Tea, *Sahib.*'

Out of bed at the double, I pulled on my blue boiler suit over my old trousers, and by the time I had my overalls on the Boy was back with my hot water for a wash and shave. A quick wash and down the ladders to my first day's work.

On our ship, although I suppose the same practice is carried out on all ships with five engineers, the Third was the electrician who also worked on the main engines with the Second, the Fourth looked after all the pumps, the

Fifth looked after the valves and boiler mountings, and at sea he also looked after the winches.

But this is just a guide, as when needed, everyone looked after everything and if anything went wrong, everybody was involved. Everyone on the ship was on call twenty-four hours a day, seven days a week, and three hundred and sixty five days a year.

My first job was to help the Second to renew the cast steel baffles just inside the furnaces. These baffles protect the doors from the fierce heat and deflect the air that is blown into the furnace, so that the fires burn more efficiently. The old bolts were distorted and hardened by the fierce heat acting on them over the last twelve months. They had to be cut through and replaced with new ones, and then the new baffles fitted.

I was inside the firebox holding a long chisel whilst the Second wielded the sledgehammer. The boilers were still hot, and crawling into the firebox was very difficult. I had to be wrapped up with sacking to prevent myself from being burnt, especially the knees and elbows, and I wore thick asbestos gloves.

It took us three days to replace the eight baffles in the two boilers, and there were four more to be cut out and replaced in the other boiler when it was available. We had three boilers, but when in port only one was used to generate steam for the generator and winches.

I sweated so much that I must have lost pounds during those three days. Such was the work in the thirties. Nowadays with modern tools we could have done the job in three hours, and there would have been no need to climb inside the firebox.

We stopped work at 8:00am for breakfast, my first

breakfast on board. The mess-room was small. The table was thirty inches wide, with three stools on each side, and the table and stools were fastened to the deck. The stools had no backs, but they were fitted alongside the bulkhead and this acted as a back rest. The stools also swivelled to make it easier to get in and out, so those sitting at the far end of the table had to get in first and out last. It worked very well really as there were only four[18] of us; needless to say the Second sat nearest the door.

The serving table was on the left as one entered; the main table on the right. The serving table had racks above it, for the plates and crockery and so forth, and a washbasin at one end.

The food was brought from the galley and served onto the plates from the serving table, and seconds were available when there was any left. From the menu on the table I chose grapefruit, then three rashers of bacon, two eggs and a plate of freshly fried chips, finishing off with toast and jam. The bread by the way was freshly baked every day.

With a three course lunch and a three course dinner every day, and enormous breakfasts, I was never hungry; the only danger was putting on too much weight.

All that day the engine room crew was cleaning the inside of the boiler, chipping scale from the boiler plates, and after a while I was in there with them, suffering.

The noise was horrific, a dozen men chipping away with pointed hammers. Although I was supposed to be keeping an eye on them, ensuring that they were doing

---

[18] The size of the ship indicates there must have been another mess-room, so this suggests that this one was solely for the use of the four engineers. Editor

the job properly, I'd never even seen the inside of a boiler before, but I had to learn. I learnt that it was much more comfortable outside the boilers.

Replacing these blocks was another job that had to be carried out whenever the boiler was opened up. It was an unpleasant job crawling around the boiler and over the boiler tubes while a dozen men chipped away at the scale. We needed cotton wool in our ears and a mask over our mouths to keep the dust out. By the time we got out of the boiler, coming out into the fresh air seemed like heaven.

Another of my jobs was to service the valves on the boiler tops. Steam pipes can stay hot for a long time and care must be taken when breaking them open or taking the top off, as hot water could be released. A warning in Urdu had to be shouted down before the valve was opened up, so the first phrase I learned was, '*Kabadah nichi, goram pani.*' This means, 'look out below, hot water.'

That was how it sounded, how it was spelt I don't know, but it always worked. The engine room crew scattered right away, not bothering to look up.

As I stated previously, looking after the boiler mountings was the duty of the Fifth Engineer. However, as I had to learn the whys and wherefores of things first, initially all my instructions were issued by the Second who showed and instructed me. The stop valves were leaking on the boiler tops so we had a look at one. Opening it up, he showed me the marks where over a period of time the steam had cut small channels across the faces. It was through these slight marks that the high-pressure steam was getting through, and the marks would

217

be etched deeper as the steam escaped past them.

The usual way to deal with them was to grind them in with carborundum paste, as one would do in the case of a car engine, but unfortunately the marks were too deep. While some modern ships have well-equipped service departments, we had to do everything by hand. When he saw the condition of this valve, he said it would take too long to grind the leaking places out, and we would put a spare in. I asked him why not file them out, which would mean filing all the way around the valve a little at a time until the marks disappeared. He said he wouldn't try, but asked if I could do it.

It was ready to be ground in that same day, and when the Second saw it he wanted to know where I'd learned to file like that. I told him that I'd had three good teachers. I ground it in the next day and we had no further trouble with it, the only trouble was that I was then concentrating on valves for quite a while. But this was boosting up my confidence and I stopped worrying so much. I was finding things a lot easier than I had thought they would be, and said a quiet, 'Thank you' to Bobby, Joe and Sam.

When the two boilers were ready, that is, all cleaned out, the zinc blocks renewed, gauge glasses cleaned and checked, and the valves all checked and OK'd, then the boilers were filled to the bottom of the gauge glasses. As the water was heated it would rise up the gauges.

Once the boilers were fired up to pressure, the valves on the top would be opened very gradually until we had two boilers in operation. Then the fires were put out in the remaining boiler, and after the valves were shut and it was isolated, it was left to cool. When it had cooled down it was drained, then it would be ready for the same treatment the following day or the next day. It took a long time for a boiler to cool enough to be worked on.

The following day the Second and I started work on the baffles in the third boiler, which was worse than the other two. The boiler was hotter and I needed all the sacks that I could collect around me. I had so much padding around me I had great difficulty wriggling into the firebox, but we got the job done. The boiler itself was still too hot for anyone to work inside so we had to wait a little longer, even though we opened the inspection door to help it a little.

Eventually, all the boilers were ready for use, all the pumps had been overhauled, the main engine had been checked and all repairs carried out. There was a certain degree of tidiness appearing, and there seemed to be more room to walk around.

The handrails and the bright steelwork gleamed, the engine room plates were clear of all obstructions, polished and oiled, and the painted areas had all been washed and where necessary repainted. The engine room had been transformed, it was beautiful.

It is amazing how much one can learn in a couple of weeks. I was able to take my turn in staying aboard by myself, and looked after the engine room without needing to kneel down and say a little prayer that nothing untoward would happen. Yes, I was quite comfortable walking down below every half an hour, checking the water level in the boiler and having a look at the working machinery, knowing what to do and when to do it. Mind, I was living in ignorance. Months later there were times when unexpected things happened, but by that time I had a little more experience and could cope.

After the half hourly trips down the ladders I was back to writing letters or reading. I had a small radio the previous Fifth Engineer had left behind. The reception wasn't as it should be, which was probably why he left it, and the stations didn't line up with the dial, but I got used to it after a while. I could keep up with the news and the music from the big bands from 10:30pm to midnight.

I had no desire to roam around Liverpool on my own, I was quite comfortable in my little box writing or reading, or getting to know the new world downstairs. I can only remember walking into town on four occasions before we sailed. Once to see the great Nel Tarleton, the champion boxer of his day, making his comeback, twice to the pictures with the cadets, and once to do my shopping.

I'd been concentrating on my shopping list, asking all and sundry what I would need, as I had never before shopped for the everyday needs of a household. Thinking about these things it was astounding how much I had to buy for the future, although if one ran short of a razor blade it could be borrowed.

I bought a patrol suit to wear on board, not while I was working, just to save my good clothes. We wore the patrol suit when looking around the engine room on our nights aboard and for general wear aboard ship. While ashore we wore civvies or our uniform, if we had one. We never visited the engine room wearing our best suit.

I also bought a new suit for ashore, made to measure by a visiting tailor for £2.50, but as I'd previously been warned by the Second I saved a pound by refusing to pay the £3.50 that he wanted. It was navy blue and the jacket had pockets in the usual places, but it had no lapels and buttoned right up to the neck.

Inside the boiler, at each end, were bolted blocks of zinc about six inches by six inches by two inch thick; these were to compensate for the electrolytic action caused by boiling the same water again and again. As the water became acid it attacked the inside of the boiler; and the zinc was there to prevent this as the acid attacked the zinc instead and gradually ate it away.

The *Cassop*, or Engine Room Storekeeper, would wash my overalls so I'd need a dozen and a half bars of hard soap to keep him supplied. The custom was to give him a pound note and promise him another after the voyage. Similar arrangements were made with the Mess Room Boy.

I approached the two concerned but promised them a pound now and two pounds at the end of the trip. Both the *Cassop* and the Mess Room Boy went away very happy, '*Pan Sahib*, I keep your boiler suits very clean indeed, first class A1.' I wasn't disappointed in either case. The fact that I'd promised them two pounds at the end of the trip made a big difference, the money was well spent.

The Mess Room Boy, as well as his other duties, kept my cabin scrupulously clean and polished. During the good weather in the tropics he took all my clothes out of the little wardrobe, brushed them down, and hung them out on deck to blow in the breeze. Airing and brushing clothes in the tropics is to keep them free of insects that are worse than moths. Besides this he always kept seconds for me of my favourites, beef olives and banana soufflé.

While in foreign ports any clothes left lying on the

bunk or floor were picked up, everything taken from the pockets, and then hung up in the wardrobe. Any money from the pockets I always found intact in the top drawer of the table.

He was always ready with good advice and if it started to rain whilst we were down in the engine room, our boy always went around shutting the scuttles, to prevent our bunks from getting wet. He also made sure that these were shut and door locked while the cabin was unoccupied in foreign ports.

I had been in Liverpool about three weeks when, while in town, I saw an advert for cheap day trips to various destinations looking down at me from a poster. Reading down, I saw that Newcastle was on the list of destinations, 10:00am start and return any time before midnight. That night I wrote to both Edith and home and before Sunday received a reply that Edith would be at Low Fell that day, so on Sunday morning I was on that train to Newcastle.

Oh, it was so slow. Possibly I was impatient, but the train seemed to stop every mile or so. They must have been repairing the line all the way to Newcastle. I eventually arrived at 2:30pm, to be greeted by the family and my dear Edith. At first everyone was trying to talk at the same time, but the table was set for lunch and we talked as we ate. After lunch Edith and I were excused, we walked hand-in-hand around Wreckenton and over the golf course, one of our favourite walks, then home for tea with the family.

After tea I managed to get Dad on his own to have a quiet word with him, and asked him again to help Edith in any way he could. He told me that he'd had a word with Mam and they had talked it over, and would tell Edith to come over to Low Fell whenever she wished and not to wait for an invitation. If she came over every Sunday, they could get together and acquaint each other of my news and wellbeing.

I also had a little time alone with my mother. Mam had looked after me for a long time but I was leaving the nest, everyone had to do it sometime, and now it was my turn. I loved the family, and still do. I was moving out into the great wide world, as they say in the storybooks, but this was real and a war was forecast. I know that my mother took it hard, there were tears in her eyes, and I promised to write.

I told her how much I loved her and thanked her for the way she had looked after me and how much I appreciated my wonderful childhood. I asked her if there was anything else that I could do, but all she wanted was for me to come back again, safe and sound. Time passed all too quickly, and soon it was time to go.

Saying goodbye was just as hard as it had been the last time. We'd worked out the time of departure to get into Lime Street Station for 2:00am, so all I had to do was to get the tram down to Central Station.

The journey back was a nightmare, much worse than the trip in the other direction. I arrived in Liverpool five hours later than expected. I had to be down in the engine room at 7:00am, and I only had five minutes to get there. Dashing from the station I took a taxi to the dock gates, then ran through the dock arriving in the engine room twenty minutes late. I took a good dressing down from the Second, no excuses accepted, but it was worth it, sleepless night and all.

With evidence of sailing time getting nearer, there'd be no chance of another quick trip home, so letters had to be written. I enjoy writing, so this was no hardship and after breakfast I wrote a couple of quick letters to tell the family and Edith that I'd arrived safely, and not to worry.

Later that week down in the engine room we felt movement; we were being towed, or pushed. We were going to the coaling berth, which we'd been expecting.

I'd heard and read about coaling the ship, how it was done, and that it wasn't pleasant. Coal dust gets everywhere so the ship became covered in dust, and now I was going to experience it. Fortunately the Mess Room Boy knew all about it.

He'd been around the cabins closing the scuttles and making sure that the ventilators were stuffed with paper to prevent the entry of too much dust. Even so, he had to clean out five cabins after coaling was finished and it was three or four days before he got those cabins as he wanted them.

My shopping list was almost complete, including things that I'd never purchased before, such as soap, both hard and powdered, toothpaste and a spare toothbrush, a few medicines and plasters to make a small first aid kit, a pair of scissors to cut my nails, writing paper with envelopes, ink and a spare pen, a good pocket knife and a torch. A sewing kit was also needed, so needles and thread were included in the bill.

I also took the advice of the Fourth and bought a pair of boots with soft uppers, like gloves, elastic cuffs round the top and good leather soles. The boots were solely intended for the engine room. The leather soles were safer than rubber on the oiled plates and catwalks, although one still had to tread carefully, but best of all the elastic tops prevented hot ashes from getting in when the firemen were cleaning the fires. Fortunately while in port we were paid weekly, so that I was able to buy the stuff that I needed.

Apart from the daily work it was a lazy life. My cabin was cleaned by the Mess Room Boy, although I liked to keep it tidy myself, if I didn't he would do it. My meals were cooked and served on time, every day, no washing up. The only thing we did for ourselves was our personal washing, our underwear and socks; our shore-going shirts were also important, and of course that cup of tea last thing at night before we went to bed.

Our underwear was boiled by putting it in a bucket of cold water near the engine room feed pumps, an open-ended steam pipe was then put into the bucket, and the steam turned on. Within a few minutes they were being boiled. Ten minutes boiling, then rub and rinse, and hey presto, sparkling whites to hang on the line in the turbine flat, or in the tropics, on a line on deck for a few minutes.

By now I knew most of the crew, the white crew that is, there were eighteen all told. There were two crews, the engine room crew and the deck crew, I should say about eighty altogether. At first they all looked the same, but then as one worked among them, one or two stood out, then more as time passed. Of course the people we met every day were soon recognised, the *Cassop*, who washed our overalls, was recognised on sight right from day one, as was the Mess Room Boy. As time passed I recognised other deck crew members more easily, but it was a long time before I was well acquainted with the entire engine room crew.

My first meeting with the ship's carpenter occurred when we were in Gladstone Dock, and it wasn't a happy one. From conversation in the mess he liked his booze, and at such times when he'd had a few it didn't take much to upset him.

I was lying in my bunk, having just finished listening to the 10.00pm news, when the door flew open and the Carpenter burst in demanding that I turn my wireless down as he couldn't get to sleep.

The bulkheads were steel but none were soundproof, and one could hear anything that moved in the corridor outside the door, so I knew that he certainly wasn't in the habit of going to bed at 10:30pm. I also remembered Pat Murphy's advice when at Clarke Chapman's, 'Kick him first before he kicks you,' or something to that effect.

So I told him that as I had heard the news he could turn the wireless off and take a seat, which he did. I think he thought that he was going to get the offer of a drink and a sort of apology. After he was seated I said,

'Listen Chippy, I don't like anyone bursting into my cabin as you've just done. Next time you'll knock on the door, just like everyone else, and wait outside until you're asked in. If you come in again like you did just now, you'll go out quicker than you came in with a boot up your backside, OK?'

He pulled himself out of my chair, mumbled something that sounded like, 'Sorry,' and then went out shutting the door behind him quietly. We became quite friendly, and I was later introduced to his pet mongoose as we sat on the hatch cover one night before turning in.

The Second and Chief seemed to get on well together, although the Chief was a man by himself except when on ship's business, whereas the Third and Fourth were near the same age and seemed to stick together having known each other over two or three trips. I suppose the Second had some responsibility for the Fifth; the Third and Fourth had their jobs to do, so the Second was lumbered with the poor Fifth who knew nothing at all.

Then the day arrived, and we were told to attend the saloon to sign on. So one by one we went to the table and signed our names along the dotted line, we were told how long we'd be away and asked if we wanted anything stopped out of our wages. Those married could have stoppages taken out for anything, but the single chaps could only have one person to leave money to, their mothers. Mam had said she didn't want anything from me, but the least I could do was to pay the rent whilst I was away. So I signed the articles for the rent to be deducted from my monthly salary and sent off to Mam.

The results of loading coal had been attended to and now the engine room crew were engaged in the final spit and polish, the handrails shone, as did the brass work and glass in the many gauges. All three boilers were linked up and in operation and the main engine was warming up. Steam was escaping from drain cocks and glands and it was everywhere. When the engine reached working temperature, the leaks would seal up, the drain cocks would be closed and the clouds of steam, or water vapour, would disappear.

We'd already been moved to Gladstone Dock, where the cargo had been loaded, and the Blue Peter was flying at the masthead, so we knew that we were sailing within twenty-four hours. The engine was warming through and that also was an indication of our sailing soon as it took twenty-four hours to warm sufficiently.

The following morning after breakfast we were all in the engine room when the Stand By was rung down on the telegraph. I had been well-versed on my position; as Fifth Engineer I had to answer every ring on the telegraph by swinging the handle and speaking the message loud enough for all to hear. We took up our positions, the Second by the main steam valve, the Third by the reversing handle, and the Fourth at the desk, with telephone and log book. Every ring of the telegraph, every bump that we felt or anything unusual was written down, with the time, in the logbook. For me it was very exciting. I'd never seen the engines turning over and I was waiting for the first movement of the engine, but I would miss being on deck as we left the Mersey.

Standing on the pier at South Shields watching the ships entering the Tyne I had tried to imagine what it must feel like being in the engine rooms. Now I knew, I was actually there, just waiting for this giant engine to start.

Dead Slow Astern the bell rang. I rang the message back whilst shouting out the command. Stop. Dead Slow Ahead. Stop. And so it went on for fifteen to twenty minutes then, Half Ahead.

As there were no signals for a while, I thought that we must be sailing down the river and out of the dock. We continued down the Mersey with the Pilot on the bridge for a while until the telegraph rang Stop to let the Pilot off. I could imagine him climbing down the rope ladder into the pilot boat.

Then the message rang Half Ahead, then later the Full Ahead. I couldn't take my eyes off the engine. Shortly the telegraph rang again, a double ring of Full Ahead, I answered the double ring and the other engineers got busy. I just stood and kept my eyes open.

The main condenser was already in service; the water heater was switched in and the feed pumps synchronised, the auxiliary oil pump was started up, then the low pressure turbine. Immediately the speed increased and the main engine ran much smoother. All this activity was new to me.

Being down below we saw nothing of the departure from Liverpool, not of the town nor the river itself. This is one of the disadvantages of working in the engine room, but we had one advantage - in the cold weather we were always warm.

Twelve months later, during the war, I did all this myself in total darkness.

20. At work

21. More work

22. Taking a break

23. Manhattan Skyline, 1939

24. The Apprentices in a rowing boat, Sydney Harbour

CHAPTER NINE
Liverpool to Auckland
April 1939 – May 1939

When I came on deck it was almost noon. The Third Engineer had just taken over the watch from the Fourth, and the Second had given me a job for the rest of today and tomorrow, which he wanted finished by tomorrow night.

As Fifth I was on day work, so I didn't keep a watch as the Second, Third and Fourth did, I wouldn't know how. I only went on watch with the Second on Sunday mornings, at 4:00am, without breakfast.

When I reached the deck, the ship was rolling just a little, I felt a little light-headed. Was this the first sign of seasickness? I hoped not. I looked over the water, turning right around and could faintly see the last of England, or was it Ireland? Seeing all this water around, the ship seemed small in comparison; I thought to myself I'll get used to it, I hope.

Standing there on the open deck, I realised that I was on my way around the world. After the waiting on the swing bridge just to see a ship pass through, all those childish dreams had come true. It was really wonderful. I just hoped that I was not going to be sick, and then lunch was ready. After lunch it was work.

At that moment we had a leak in the auxiliary condenser and it had to be repaired. The auxiliary condenser is smaller than the main condenser, and is usually only used in port when only one boiler is in use. The leak was probably very small but due to the pressure of the circulating water, which is seawater, salt was getting into the boilers. The Second tested the boiler water for salt every day.

The Second had explained the job that I had to complete, and he was off to his bunk, having to take over the watch from the Third at eight bells, 4:00pm. I made my way down the ladders.

So there was I, in a very cramped position, curled up on a little platform, six feet above the smelly bilges. With the smell of hot oil in my nose and my head swimming due to the motion of the ship, I thought to myself that there was a price for everything.

Most of the work must have been completed by the former Fifth, as the new condenser tubes had already been fitted, and all that was required was to replace the packing around the tubes and carefully screw in the new ferrules. This was an exacting job as the cast iron body was old and granulated and the ferrules had a very fine thread. There were no short cuts. Every packing and ferrule had to be one hundred per cent, if the job was finished with the covers back on and the leak was still in evidence, we'd have had to start again right from the beginning.

I concentrated on this new job, making sure that all the ferrules were fitted correctly and that there was sufficient packing to do the job that it was supposed to do. I was tucked away against the ship's side, and although the railing around the small platform was only two feet high, in bad weather it was indispensable. Falling off into the bilges could be fatal; there were far too many sharp projections on the way down.

The ship was now moving up and down and sideways. We had moved out of the shelter of the land and were in open water. Restricted as I was, the heat and smell of the oily water began to tell on my stomach, my head was aching, and I felt awful. The quicker I got this job done the better, I thought.

At one bell, 3:45pm, the Second came down to take over from the Third, ready for 4:00pm. The watches were 12:00 to 4:00, 4:00 to 8:00 and 8:00 to 12:00, all these times being eight bells, one bell for every half hour. There was also one bell quarter of an hour before the watch, telling the oncoming watch keeper it was time to take over.

It took fifteen minutes to go round the engine and engine room, checking to see that everything was to the oncoming watch keeper's satisfaction. If he was dissatisfied on any point, he could refuse to take over the watch until such time as he was satisfied. After he'd taken over the watch anything that went wrong was his responsibility.

After the Second had taken over the watch, he came to see how I was getting along. He looked quite happy with my progress and maybe noticed how pale I looked, for he told me to knock off for today and get ready for dinner. When I reached the deck I looked around and saw nothing but water, Ireland or England had disappeared completely. I looked again, straining my eyes, but all traces of land had gone.

It would be twelve months before I would see England again. I turned with a lump in my throat and walked to my cabin, washed, then walked round to the mess. I wasn't hungry but I thought that I'd better get something down. I ate and felt better for it. At least I wasn't sick, my dinner stayed with me and that was a good sign. Fortunately I never was sick, even though I felt heady for a couple of days each time after leaving port.

After a couple of days the job on the condenser was completed. I knew that I'd taken longer than expected, but argued that it was better to take an extra day than risk having to do it all over again. The Second agreed and I was delegated another job, this time on deck preparing the winches ready to unload the cargo in New York.

While we were having breakfast, the Second outlined what I had to do that day on the winches. He said that I'd be disgusted with their condition, but they worked, and they never caused any delay when unloading. Winches straight from the factory gave trouble due to the bearings deliberately being too tight to leave some space for expansion. After breakfast I wandered down to the workshop and selected the tools that I would need, including my two valve spanners. I made sure the steam valve that controlled the deck steam line was shut tight, and then started work.

As I examined the first one I came to, I realised that there was a lot of work here. All the bearings were so slack I could afford to take out half the slack, it was unbelievable. But when I felt the cylinders they were still too hot for comfort, and steam was still leaking into the deck steam line. The next thing was to look on the boiler tops. I found the valve, traced the pipes and shut the valve I thought was responsible, and carried on working.

I was working away when the Second Engineer came running out of the accommodation block and straight across the flying bridge, and disappeared down towards the steering engine. Hello, I thought, what's up? Back he came, then up to the bridge, down again and then came over to me.

'Have you shut any valves on the boiler tops?' he asked. I told him what I'd done and why.

'Have a look behind you,' he said. I did, and saw a strange sight, one that I've always remembered. The ship's wake was a big round circle, and we were going round in circles.

The Second said, 'Go down and just crack open the valve, give me ten minutes, then open it fully'. Down I went and did as I was told, and then walked back to the winch. The Second came back to me after 15 minutes, laughing his head off. I'd shut off the steam to the steering engine which unfortunately was on the same line as the winches.

He said, 'Not to worry'. He'd had a good chance to rip off the Second Mate, blaming him for not keeping the hydraulic line primed.

After dinner I went down onto the boiler tops and memorised all the valves, I still had some left to learn. I don't think that the Second Engineer and the Second Mate liked each other, or maybe they just liked scoring points. Anyhow I heard nothing more on the subject, except when the incident was recalled much later.

Nine days after leaving Liverpool we reached America, New York itself. We were all down in the engine room, the engine turning over slowly, coming up the Hudson River, when the Second told me to nip up and see where we were. I wouldn't know where we were, I'd never been here before. But I dashed up those ladders with my heart beating like a steam hammer, to see my first sight of any foreign country. I was only on deck for a few minutes, but long enough to see the Statue of Liberty as we passed and the silhouette of Manhattan up ahead. We were still moving slowly up the river when I returned below and informed the Second that we had just passed the great statue. I realised later that with his experience of New York, the Second would have known exactly whereabouts we were at that time.

I think, with this being my first trip abroad, he knew how excited I was and enjoyed showing me the parts that I shouldn't miss. When passing famous locations over the first six months, he never failed to send me up topside to experience the sights from deck level.

When the telegraph rang, Finished with Engines, I knew we were there for over a week because the Second gave orders to shut down two boilers. Then the pumps were changed over to harbour working and the auxiliary condenser put into operation; we'd see now whether or not my job on it had been successful.

When I came up to breathe the air of America and view the Hudson River that second was sheer nostalgia. *Tugboat Annie* immediately came to mind, the scene was exactly as in the film. The skippers of the tugs were shouting across the water to each other and I was expecting to see Wallace Beery at any time. It was a most wonderful sight, a wonderful experience that I can remember and relate to even now.

I was also remembering all the stories of Indians that I'd read about since I was seven years old, living in their tepees on the banks of the Hudson River. I was back to my childhood again, living in another world. I never thought that I would be so affected, and if it was all like this, I didn't want to grow up.

When we were in a home port we were paid weekly, but after signing on we were paid at the end of the voyage. Before we had reached New York, the Third Mate had been to all the crew and taken a list of how much money we all required for our stay. The captain had then radioed the agent and informed him of how much was required, so the money was waiting when we docked. I'd been chatting to the others while in the mess, and had been informed that this was the first place for cheap deals.

The pound then was worth four dollars. I needed a small present for Edith, small enough to post in an ordinary envelope, and some cigarettes. I asked the Second for advice on the cigarettes. He told me how much they cost, which turned out to be one quarter of the cost at home, so I asked him to get two thousand for me, at a cost of twenty five shillings. After paying a shilling for twenty at home it was great to get them so cheap.

Of course these would have to go into bond until we were out to sea again,, which was quite convenient really. They were kept under the care of the Chief Steward, and if we ran short of fags at sea we asked the Mess Boy to get a pack of two hundred from the Steward and leave them in our cabin. Whisky, duty free, was only seven shillings a bottle and was stronger than the whisky at home, although in those days I didn't drink spirits. Actually, before I went to sea I didn't drink alcohol in any form.

So I calculated how much money I would need to pay for this lot; it would come to a little more than the five dollars that I had asked for, and I was surprised how cheap things were. I was still a little short but the Second said he would cover it, and I could pay him back later.

During the day, while cargo was being unloaded, I patrolled the deck seeing the winches were OK, giving them a quick drop of oil here and there. My job was to see that the winches ran all day with no breakdowns, and so long as I was successful everyone was happy. We were docked in Brooklyn and the dockers were mainly of Italian extraction. I just strolled around with my oilcan within reach, chatting with the dockers who were very generous with their fags. They were very happy as we had no breakdowns.

In numerous ports throughout the world cargo was unloaded by the dock cranes. In that case our winches wouldn't be needed, and I would be working in the engine room. Nowadays, with giant container ships, I don't suppose there are winches aboard for the purpose of loading and unloading, but in the nineteen twenties and thirties these giants didn't exist. All cargo ships had derricks and winches of various sizes, the drivers of which were very skilful.

There was one winch for lifting the cargo from the hold in big nets, and another winch to swing the load from ship to shore. The dockers emptied the nets, and then back they swung for another load. The Second Deck Officer stood by the open hatch and checked everything that went in, or when unloading, everything that went out. Crossing out items or writing on his clip board as he watched. The Third Mate would be at another open hatch, and if more winches were working the cadets working together would be helping.

Talking with the dockers during the day I learned quite a lot about Brooklyn. I was warned that it wasn't the worst place in the world, nor the most dangerous, neither was it the best place or the safest. I was warned not to rush to the assistance of any female, young or old, who seemed to be distressed or in trouble, as I was likely to be mugged myself, especially at night. I also learned how to get around on the underground.

In fact I was surprised how much I learnt about New York during the first day's work. I needed a camera but was advised to wait until we got to Singapore or Hong Kong, which were duty free ports and therefore that much cheaper.

I'd been in contact with the two cadets and arranged to go ashore with them after dinner. We three innocents abroad, it was their first voyage too, were off to discover America, and as we walked down the gangplank onto American soil it was my first step anywhere foreign.

No passes, no passports no hindrances of any kind, and while every other visitor was required to have a visa, we were free to walk anywhere. This was just as well, because when I joined the ship in Liverpool it never occurred to me that I may have needed a passport.

We weren't complaining, we found the right platform in the underground station and put our five cents in the slot to go through the barrier. Any single journey on the underground cost five cents in those days. The train came along with the destination on the head, Broadway, which was the stop we wanted. We alighted at Times Square and came up to street level, almost next door to Forty Second Street. How many times had we heard of Forty Second Street?

I couldn't get over the fact that I wasn't dreaming. I could hardly believe that I was actually in New York. We walked around, and looked up at the great skyscrapers. It was all too big. We found a shop, or should I call it a store, and found a present for Edith, appropriately a fountain pen. It was about three inches long in mother of pearl, with a small silk tassel[19] on the end and in gold letters, New York, was engraved along the side.

The letter to be posted consisted of six sheets of paper and when folded over there was room in the fold for the pen, some tissue stopped it rattling when shaken. I posted the letter, the first one from many parts of the world.

We walked up and down Broadway until our feet were sore, taking in the new sights and trying to find streets that we could remember from films we'd seen. We also sampled the soda bar at the drug store, however it was getting late and we thought it was time we were getting back to the ship. We were tired, but we were looking forward to lots of other new places.

We were at New York for only a week, but during that time we became well acquainted with the underground system and the post offices and shops we would need around Brooklyn. Next time we visited we'd feel at home.

Then the boilers were steamed up, the engine warmed through, and we were off to New Zealand via the Panama Canal. As we sailed south, I could actually feel the temperature rising day by day. Working on deck was sheer delight, the land in the far distance, islands drawing closer then slowly disappearing astern into the fine mist, and the gentle pulse of the engine. Totally unlike the

---

[19] Many years later, when the nib had broken, the pen found its way into my toy box. The little green tassel was still attached. Editor

244

vibrations of a motor vessel such as the Tyne ferry. This was a slow, friendly beat, as if the ship had a heart, and with the gentle movement of the hull through the water, the creak of the masts and rigging, altogether a most peaceful existence.

After dinner I was off duty, but there were no picture halls to attend and TV hadn't been invented, at least not for the masses. But I had my wee wireless, even though the programs faded out and new ones in foreign tongues took their place. Letter writing, playing cards, reading and sleeping were the main occupations, unless one paid a visit to the Quartermasters' cabin.

Quartermasters steer the ship, and in port stand at the top of the gangway to vet anyone who wishes to come aboard.

There were four Quartermasters, two young ones and two old. The two old ones lived on the ship; that is, they had no home ashore and even spent their leave on board. One of these old salts spent his off duty hours making lace, huge balls of it. The kind of lace one finds around tablecloths. When he got back to England he had contacts to whom it was sold.

These old shellbacks started their careers during the time of the sailing ships and if one was to pay them a visit and catch the two old ones together, one had a good chance of being entertained for the rest of the night with hair-raising stories of the old clipper days. The two apprentices and I often took a couple of bottles to visit, hoping to get them talking, although we weren't always successful.

But letter writing was the most popular off duty occupation. Two pages each night soon built up to a

Liverpool to Auckland

sizeable letter over a week, and of course letters weren't only to Edith and Mam and Dad, my sisters and Alan had to have their share, they all had a place in my thoughts.

I loved writing to all at home because while I wrote I was there. Even the writing pad and pen were friends, and it was easy to write as there were always different things to write about. I never had to sit back and wonder what to say next.

We posted the letters whenever we went ashore, but any one of the ship's company would post them if they were going ashore. At some ports we only stayed overnight. On those occasions when the ship's agent came aboard, as he did at every port, the Third Deck Officer came around collected the letters for posting, and handed them to the agent who posted them on our behalf. This was quite popular as without local stamps, or money to buy any, the company paid for the lot.

As there was so little to do in our spare time, visiting each other for a chat was very popular, one never knew who was going to pop in at any given time. If one was busy and didn't favour company, one just said pleasantly that they were busy, the visitor would beetle off, and no offence was ever taken.

The Third and Fourth were studying for their exams, so it was customary to speak to them and make arrangements to call when convenient. You couldn't just walk off the ship so no one could be any other than friendly. Everybody had to work together, any disagreements like the one that I had with the Carpenter were resolved in no time. Just say what you felt and that was it.

As I lay in my bunk at night waiting to drop off to

246

sleep, I would lie there, really relaxed and comfortable and the day's experiences would go through my mind. Every day there was something new that needed thinking about. The only down side was the absence of Edith, family and friends, and of course the bath.

The bath, salt water only, was heated by turning a steam valve releasing steam into the water. This heated it up nicely, and although you can't get lather with ordinary soap in salt water, we managed. We rinsed off with fresh water, and besides, we couldn't expect everything to be perfect. The cargo ships weren't designed for luxury in 1925 when the *City* was built. None carried enough fresh water to cater for fresh water baths, and the evaporator was too costly to run to provide enough water for baths for all on board.

We had no freezer or fridge in those days, only an icebox, so the long trip from the canal to New Zealand was marred by there being a lot of tinned food on the menu. But we still ate well and the Indian cooks worked miracles.

We arrived off Colon just after dinner. In fact we'd had an early dinner that night to cater for the fact and Stand By, the signal to go down below, was rung just as we finished eating. After ten minutes the 'movements' began, Half Ahead, Slow Ahead and so forth, and soon we were stopped and the anchor was dropped.

Watches were still kept, however, and a message came down the telephone to the effect we'd be going through the canal at 8:00am the following day. I was informed that I wouldn't be needed until 7:00am, my usual time for starting work. We were anchored in the bay for the night and no one could get ashore

I had a bath and changed, and wrote a few pages telling Edith that we had reached Colon, the port at the Atlantic end of the canal. Before I had left home I'd obtained a map of the world, marked with all the shipping routes, so that Edith could chart my progress around the world as she received my letters.

Edith had also received a list of the shipping agents with addresses and an itinerary of the ship's route, with the approximate date of arrival, so she could send letters to the respective agent. If the ship had already sailed when they arrived, the letters were forwarded to the next point of call until they caught up.

When I came on deck again it was dark, night falls very quickly in the tropics, almost as soon as the sun sets. This night there was a warm, soft breeze blowing from the shore, what a beautiful night. I could smell the land, the trees and the grass. It smelt very strong, due I suppose to smelling nothing but salt water for so long.

I was sitting on the forward hatch, admiring the twinkling lights ashore tumbling along the shoreline, when I heard footsteps. Turning my head I saw the Carpenter approaching, he sat down beside me with two glasses and a bottle of whisky in his hands. He never said anything, just offered the glasses which I took and held while he poured a generous amount into each glass.

'Good health,' he said. I returned the compliment and thanked him for the drink. 'You looked lonely sitting there by yourself,' he said, 'so I brought my mate along to introduce to you.' Right on cue a little nose peeped out of his inside jacket pocket, and then the rest of the animal came out. The Carpenter introduced his pet mongoose, which is very like a ferret. I put my hand out towards him, or her, but the ferret was none too pleased and disappeared back into the pocket.

I took this introduction to his ferret as an apology for the Carpenter's actions back in Liverpool, but it was never referred to. It was just forgotten, as was every little upset that happened on the ship. As we sat talking, the two cadets came along and joined us, adding to the conversation which continued until around 11:00pm. Knowing that we had an early start in the morning and needing our sleep, we left the scene, the lights still twinkling ashore.

I was awakened next morning at 6:45am with the usual cup of tea and biscuit, and was informed that breakfast would be early, at 7:30am. As soon as I was dressed in boiler suit and shoes, I went below and was told to have breakfast and then hang about until the Stand By signal. I was up those ladders in a flash. If it was going to be a quick breakfast, I thought I'd better have an early start, I was hungry.

The Stand By rang at 8:45am, and with the Pilot on board and in control we all made our way down the ladders and took up our places, ready to move. Slow Ahead and we had started. At first there were few signals, we were out in the bay and had to reach Colon to enter the canal, but before we reached Colon the Second spoke to me.

'You haven't been through here before, have you Fiver? Up you go, everyone should see this at least once. Come down every hour and tell us where we are.' I didn't have to be told twice, I was saying my thanks on the way up the ladders. I called into my cabin and changed from my boiler suit into my patrol suit. The boiler suit was worn over one's underwear as it was too hot down there otherwise. It was a lot cooler up on deck.

We stopped at Colon and I was amazed, it seemed that half the population boarded the ship. Within half an hour the deck was covered with blankets and sheets, every available square foot was taken over by a market, fruit and vegetables, small toys, handmade native hats, shawls and shoes, you name it, it was being sold right there on the ship.

I saw the Mess Boy in the crowd and as he came past he told me that he'd shut the scuttles in the cabins, and told me to do the same whenever we were in port, or if strangers were aboard. A common practice was for thieves to be armed with a hooked stick to lift things from the cabins through the portholes. I moved off the deck up a short ladder onto the boat deck, from here I had an uninterrupted view of everything going on.

I didn't bother buying anything, I had no money, but through this experience I learned to keep a small amount back from every port. All these people selling stuff were moneychangers as well, and we could spend any currency in the ports we visited.

The first lock lay just ahead, and as the ship inched slowly towards it lines were thrown aboard and tied fast. These lines were hitched up to small electric locos running alongside the lock, and as the ship's engine stopped they pulled the ship into the lock. Then, as in all locks, the gates closed, water flooded in and the ship rose to the next level.

This sequence was reversed and the little engines towed the ship out of the lock, making sure it didn't touch the sides. The towing ropes were then cast off and the ship made its way to the next lock, Dead Slow Ahead, or Half Ahead if the way was clear.

There are three locks to negotiate going through the Panama Canal[20]. From Colon the first lock is Gatun Lock, then Gatun Lake, next is the Gaillard Cut followed by the Pedro Miquel Lock. Last is the Miraflores Lock, and then on to the port at the Pacific end of the canal, Balboa.

We sailed slowly through between high walls and dense forests. I was even tempted to miss lunch. However, we had a late lunch half way through while at anchor in the lake waiting for ships travelling in the opposite direction to come through.

After lunch we were on our way again, eventually reaching Balboa at the Pacific end of the canal. Here, all the traders left the ship and we prepared to leave for Auckland, New Zealand. I should imagine that all the traders boarded another ship going from Balboa to Colon. I thought at the time that they wouldn't do much business on our ship, maybe they were hoping for a cruise liner.

When we left Balboa the next morning I was in my usual place on the starting platform, answering the telegraph. When everything was running normally the Fourth took over the watch and the rest of us carried on with our usual jobs. When I reached the deck the coastline was on the horizon, almost out of sight. It was as if the canal had never been, except for the strong memory that would remain with me.

---

[20] The canal is forty three point eight four miles long, three hundred feet wide and fifty seven feet deep. The average time taken to go through was eight hours. It was opened on 1st of August 1914. Reference note provided by my father. Editor

About three days later we crossed the line, the equator. Most ships, especially the passenger liners, have a ceremony on this occasion but I'm glad we didn't have one on the *City*. I had no desire to be shaved and dipped by Father Neptune, and possibly wasting time on such frivolities wasn't to the Captain's liking. Three weeks now to New Zealand, three weeks of hot sunshine, so now was the time for haircuts. This operation was usually carried out on the first Sunday after leaving the canal on the hatch of number three hold. Why on this particular day? No one knew, it had always been so and today was the day.

About 10:00am, four bells in the morning watch, a chair was placed in the middle of the hatch, just aft of the engine room accommodation. For anyone wanting a haircut this was the time and place, with the Second supplying the tools for the job. We were all practising barbers and eager to try, if anyone would allow us. The Second's haircut was easy, all over with the shears, but not shaved.

Others were more choosey than the Second and wanted a short back and sides, and the hairdresser tried to please all his customers. I was the new boy and no one knew if I could cut hair, so when asked I said 'Yes I can cut hair. Who can't?' So I got to practise. Fortunately we had no mirrors, besides it had three weeks to grow again and you can grow a lot of hair in three weeks.

When we reached Auckland the apprentices and I visited the barbers to have a trim. The youngest cadet[21]

---

[21] The terms apprentices and cadets appear throughout the book. This paragraph suggests that they apply to the same role and are therefore interchangeable. Editor

was first, no comment. I was next and as soon as I sat down the barber burst out laughing, 'Who in God's name cut your hair last?'

I made sure my sea mate didn't cut it again, and he had a piece of my mind when we got back to the ship. But our hairdressing skills improved over the next eighteen months.

CHAPTER TEN
Auckland to Penang
May – August 1939

During the week I worked eight hours per day, five days per week, four hours on Saturday mornings and four hours on Sunday mornings spent on watch with the Second Engineer.

Whilst I was the Fifth Engineer Sundays were my worst days, although I realise they were the most important as far as my learning was concerned. It meant getting up at 3:45am, then being in the engine room from 4:00am until 8:00am.

Getting up at this time of day with nothing to eat and only water to drink until 8:00am really got to my stomach at first. I felt weak and dizzy in the heat, one hundred and ten degrees Fahrenheit, but after the first hour or so, the discomfort lessened somewhat. I felt sorry for the Second Engineer; he did this every day as long as the ship was at sea.

But interesting it was, very. It was school but with a teacher/student relationship of one to one it was an opportunity to ask questions and get answers at length. I learned about the various pumps, which did what and why, how to check the running temperature of the engine bearings and what to do if there was anything wrong. I learned the uses of the fans and how to clean a fire properly. We traced the whole steam cycle from the boiler back to the boiler.

I learned why and how to clean or blow the boiler tubes, how to check the level of water in the boilers, which was not easy in rough weather but vitally important in any weather. Changing fuel oil filters was a simple job if done correctly, but if it wasn't done in strict sequence it could kill. Boiling oil under pressure is very dangerous stuff, especially as the filters were shoulder high.

There was, of course, the safety of the ship to consider, fire in the engine room was the last thing anyone wanted.

Testing the big end bearings was, at first, a dangerous experience which gave me a lot of trouble, as well as a lot of bruises.

Every bearing was felt by hand to ensure that it was not overheating, the big end bearings being most important. The idea was to stand to one side and as the crank web came towards you, you quickly put your hand in and rubbed your fingers on the inside of the web getting a thick film of oil on your fingers. As the oil came from the big end bearing, the condition of the oil denoted the condition of the bearing. Rubbing the oil between the fingers you could feel if it was free from grit, and if the oil was slippery and clean then the bearing was OK.

The small end bearings were tested standing on the first platform, half way up the engine. They passed quite near, about eight inches from your chest, and just a couple of touches with the back of the hand were all that was needed.

However there are two sides to everything so you had to be ambidextrous. As the bearings were turning over at seventy eight revs per minute, I had bruises on both

256

hands from mistiming the hand movements until I learned the art or rhythm. Any hesitation to get the hand in position and you were too late, resulting in a painful thump. Practice makes perfect and once I learned I never had another bruise.

Another important job was to ensure that the water level in the boiler remained constant. Two glass tubes, surrounded by armoured glass, were mounted at water level on each boiler in such a way that when the level was correct the water showed in the centre of the tubes. This level was controlled by a valve on each boiler which, when opened or shut, controlled the flow of water into that boiler from the feed pumps.

The watch keeper had to keep an eye on these six water levels and compensate by opening and closing these valves by half a turn or so. He had to make sure that the water in the glass tubes never got so high, or so low, that they disappeared. It's possible to take the lid off a kettle and look inside but not on a boiler, and the consequences could be serious. Too much water and solid water could get to the cylinder and wreck the engine, or too little and the boiler could be damaged and in extreme cases could blow up.

The last thing was to read the log book. Anything out of the ordinary that had happened was recorded here, including when we were burning oil which tank was in use for the fuel oil. The log book was our bible and lay on the desk next to the starting platform. All the controls were around here, telegraph and clock, the telephone to the bridge, and the voice pipe to the Chief's cabin. Just above the head were two dials, the steam pressure and vacuum gauge, and to one side, the mercury level gauge which showed how much air the fan was pushing into the fires. All these readings needed to be entered into the log book.

When everything had been checked and you were satisfied that everything was as it should be, then and only then, did you tell the engineer on watch that you'd take over. After that you had full responsibility for anything that happened.

The native crew were a friendly bunch, but the Second impressed on me the necessity of keeping them ignorant of the fact that this was my first trip, otherwise they'd try to take advantage. He advised me to give orders clearly and see that they were obeyed right away. Also to learn enough of their language quickly, just to get by, because people react quicker if you can speak in their own tongue. Any hesitation in carrying out orders could mean someone could get badly hurt, and even a slight knowledge of Urdu helped greatly.

Yes, the Second was a fount of knowledge, but best of all I really enjoyed being down there in the engine room. It was hot, humid, and not particularly noisy, more like a loud grumble. A comfortable noise, if it could be so described.

But my mentor also asked questions, as at school, and soon I was looking forward to Sundays, even though I never got used to the early start. I enjoyed this life so much that I'm sure this would have been my career if Edith hadn't been waiting for me at home.

Sunday morning was also the day that the Captain made his round of inspection. At six bells of the morning watch, 10:00am, he walked the ship making his inspection of the mess-rooms, cabins and galley. If he was happy with what he saw, he said so. If he wasn't happy he had a word or two with the Second Mate by his side, and those things that he was dissatisfied with were referred to the *Serang*, who then dealt with the matter.

The *Serang* was the crew boss, the Bosun. Actually it was his crew; he gathered the crew together and appointed the leaders. Of these the *Tindals* were the foremen, the *Cassop* was the engine room storekeeper, and the greaser was the *Tail Wallah*. *Tail* I'd been led to believe meant, oil. The poor chap who cleaned the heads or toilets was the *Topas*, he was a member of the lowest caste and didn't have many friends on ship, if any.

By our standards they were all poorly paid, but after being at sea for two or three trips they could go home to their villages and live in comfort for a year or two. Of course the *Cassop* and Mess Boys earned a little more in tips.

As Fifth Engineer I was very fortunate, I worked during the day and was then free to do as I wished from dinner until 7:00am next morning, although there were exceptions to this rule.

At sea the watch keepers were in charge twenty four hours a day, but in port, with only the generator and pumps working and no watch keepers, then the Fifth had to work nights.

On these occasions I was in charge from 6:00pm to 6:00am, and worked from 8:00pm to 6:00am with an hour off for supper. The Second left notes in the logbook of jobs he wanted me to do, and I had to get them done as far as I could without making too much noise. It was surprising how noises, like using a hammer travelled through the bulkheads and the deck.

After work I always bathed and changed into clean clothes, it made my off-duty hours so much more pleasant. In the tropics we wore a clean boiler suit every day which was usually soaked by the end of the shift, so it was a delight to take it off. I usually took mine off outside the cabin, it was that dirty. After dinner, washed and dressed, I felt as if I was on a world cruise and at those times I was.

A favourite pastime of mine was sitting or lying on the forward hatch watching the light clouds drifting past. The masts swaying from side to side, creaking as the ship slowly rolled. In the water the flying fish would break water as they fled from their predators, and porpoises raced the ship, criss-crossing the bows as if daring the ship to catch them.

Leaning on the rail after dark I enjoyed a quiet smoke in the soft breeze, with maybe a small bottle of Worthington E, gazing over the ocean and watching the moon's reflection in the black water with the stars twinkling overhead. On rare occasions when the lights of a distant ship appeared, I wondered where it was going to or coming from. One night I saw the *Rangatiki* cruise liner with all her decks lit up, near enough to hear the band playing the latest dance tune.

Another night I called out to one of the Quartermasters, who was over on the port rail, as a few miles off to starboard a square rigged vessel in full sail passed by. He'd been to sea for years and never seen one under sail. In six months I was to see two, although one of them was at anchor in Auckland harbour waiting for a favourable wind.

There is little twilight in the tropics as darkness comes

very quickly as the sun sets, but darkness at sea can, in some ways, be more beautiful than the daylight.

Just imagine a bright moon overhead, the tips of the small waves shining as they break, twelve inches of bright, bluey-green phosphorescence all around the ship, and the lights in the ship's wake curling astern. It's like a picture from fairyland, with the sound of water rushing along the ship's side, and the gentle grumble of the engines to complete the effect. Anyone experiencing such wonderment could never forget.

Nearer Auckland a group of us was sitting on the forward hatch and watching a wondrous display of the southern lights, the Aurora Australis. They were like huge draped curtains of all colours, high in the sky on the horizon. They were a wonderful sight, but after half an hour we had to leave them, it was past our bedtime and we had work in the morning.

One thing I had no trouble doing and that was sleeping, it was so easy in my bunk or on my day bed. The rhythm of the engines and the gentle movement of the ship was a natural sleeping draught. I closed my eyes and never even dreamed.

The three weeks from Balboa to Auckland meant that we suffered a deteriorating menu. We only had the icebox and water too was scarce, so we couldn't have the usual fresh water rinse-off after our bath. We could make a certain amount of water from the boilers, but it was cheaper to buy fresh water than it was to make it with the evaporator.

At times the Pacific was a wonderful place. We had a blue sea, a blue sky and continuous sunshine from dawn till dusk for almost three weeks, but at times we were wishing for rain. It was this first crossing of this ocean that taught me a big lesson.

Never again would I stay in the sun for twenty minutes without a shirt. I did it only once. The following day I was in agony, my back was one big blister, standing out a full half inch. No way could I lie except on my stomach. Putting on and taking off my boiler suit was agony, and the heat in the engine room almost drove me round the bend. But the blister did burst eventually. I took care that it didn't burst prematurely, and I was glad it didn't burst whilst I was in my bunk. It was fully healed when we reached New Zealand, but after that I always wore a shirt, and I bought a *topee* for my head.

Four weeks had passed since we left New York and I was looking forward to walking on dry land again. Apart from that, Auckland was some place new, a place that I had only read about. I wondered if the first impression would be as strong as my first impression of New York. I was disappointed, but I suppose that was natural. I'd seen so many pictures of New York and so few of Auckland. Again, I don't think that any other place would have a similar impact since New York was the first city of skyscrapers that I had seen in my life.

Auckland, at first glance, looked like a small English town until one noticed the roofs over the pavements, although the people called them sidewalks as the Americans did. I thought at the time, what a wonderful idea as it was possible to shop without getting wet in the rain. However the atmosphere was American rather than English.

Unfortunately we didn't have time to explore the town as we were only there for a few days, and even in port we worked an eight-hour day. I hoped that we would have more time there in six month's time, when we returned.

When in port at weekends, if Sunday was one's day aboard, one only had Saturday afternoon to get ashore. This was not a lot of time to have a look around, but if one had the Saturday and Sunday off then that had big possibilities, perhaps a good look round the town and even a meal out, which made a big break.

Oddly enough the ports in New Zealand appeared conveniently spaced out. If the ship sailed from Auckland on Monday we always seemed to get to the next port on Friday, and as we sailed around the New Zealand coast we always reached the next port in time to spend the weekend there. The next three weekends we spent at Wellington, Lyttelton[22] and then Dunedin.

At Wellington I walked around town, and bought a dartboard. Later on I discovered that I need not have bothered. I never thought of the fact that there is little timber in modern ships and that darts can not be expected to stick in steel plates. No, buying darts was a mistake. You only had to miss the board once and the dart needing the point attending to, and this happened so often that no one bothered to play.

The town itself was built around the bay with white, timber-built bungalows dotted about on the hills around the town. New Zealand is a volcanic country, but I remember Wellington for the wonderful views from the hills and the pleasant walks through the tree-covered surrounds. We climbed the hills surrounding the town for the exercise, which was much more interesting than walking around the deck on board ship.

---

[22] Lyttelton is the port of Christchurch. Editor

The next weekend we were in Lyttelton, a little port with a great reputation, it was usually the last port of call for explorers of the Antarctic. Climbing the hill behind the town and crossing the fields, we met the local farmer who turned out to be very friendly. The farmer even wished us 'Good day' as he passed. I thought this very unusual. My childhood experience of farmers was anything but friendly, especially if I was walking across his field without asking permission.

From the summit of the hill we looked over a wonderful view. To the south of the ridge on which we were standing, stretching away as far as the eye could see, were green fields gradually turning to white snow-capped mountains, which then faded into a bluey-white sky in the far distance. Down below to the west were vast plains running down to the sea, sheep dotting the green like white spots, with the beach a golden border. However it was too far to walk which was a great pity, as it would have been nice to walk along those sands. Oddly, the seaman sees so much of the sea and so little of the beaches, except from the deck of his ship.

After work the following day the two cadets knocked on my cabin door to say that they had discovered that Christchurch was only a short train ride away. Would I care to keep them company? We walked the short distance to the railway station and boarded the single carriage train to enjoy a twenty-minute trip to our destination. I say enjoy. It was a dark trip through the mountain tunnel, very much like travelling on the underground. But it was worth the trip, Christchurch was a beautiful city. It was reputedly the most English of New Zealand cities, and if this was so, it flattered England. It was bright, neat and scrupulously clean, not a sign of a discarded cigarette packet, or even a cigarette end.

The cathedral was an outstanding building, as clean as if it had just been completed. It pointed out to us the damage caused by the polluted atmosphere of our own country. We walked through the main streets, wishing we had cameras, especially when the sun went down and the street lit up, as the floodlights made the cathedral more beautiful than ever. Then we opted for a visit to the cinema. I don't remember the name of the film only that it was a comedy and starred Sid Fields. Eventually we took the same route home through the mountains and a short walk back to the ship and our bunks.

The next weekend we spent in Dunedin, which is the old name of Edinburgh. Unfortunately Sunday was my day aboard so that a short walk on Saturday afternoon had to satisfy my roving instincts.

After we left Dunedin we sailed south and round the southernmost point of New Zealand, across the shark-infested Tasman Sea. We arrived at Sydney about four days later, just in time to spend another weekend in port. There was no opera house then, but the bridge was there as a reminder of home on Tyneside.

When the Tyne Bridge was erected in 1928, (I think that's the correct date), I had no idea that I would ever see its big brother here in Australia.

It was usual in the thirties for tradesmen to come aboard to sell their wares as the ships tied up in port, and here was no different. I think the most popular was the lad selling newspapers. Relying on our wireless sets as we did everyone aboard wanted news, we received so little until we reached port. On occasions we could get the British papers, and the overseas *Mirror* was popular wherever we went. This was a weekly newspaper, the *Daily Mirror* bound in six issues. I often wonder if the overseas *Mirror* is still printed and if it is still available all over the globe.

In one of the local papers we found an advertisement, 'Small boats for hire', so the three of us investigated and decided to have a busman's holiday. For three pounds a day we hired a small rowing boat with an inboard engine and enough fuel to last the day. We did a lot of exploring that Sunday, sailing between the numerous islands, most of which were uninhabited. After lunch we were out again with renewed energy.

We had a rather a trying half hour during the afternoon as the local sailing club came out in force, and we found ourselves in the centre of their sailing space. We couldn't sail clear without endangering another, so we stopped and sat, and allowed them to find their own way. We just sat tight and took all the verbal abuse they could throw at us. We wouldn't see them again, so why worry? However we'd had a most enjoyable day and after dinner we took our craft back to its owners, thinking that the Sunday had been well spent.

After we'd left the boat we walked to the local pleasure park, Luna Park, and the two apprentices were on their own sampling the fair. Me, I don't like roundabouts, or rather they don't like me, I always feel ill afterwards. So I found a deck chair, lay back and listened to the brass band until it was time to return to our ship.

Work the next morning was in the engine room, curing a little problem here and another one there. The winches was never worked on while in port as they had to be available at a moment's notice, but I knew I would be taking them to pieces again when we sailed.

After a week in Sydney we left harbour and sailed north. This I remember well because sailing up the northeast coast of Australia was indeed the trip of a lifetime in itself. The journey was to take us to Thursday Island[23] at the most northerly tip of Australia, where the Pilot would be dropped and we would proceed without him.

With a clear blue sky above and the sea like a millpond, not a mark on the surface, not a ripple, the sea around looked for all the world like a sheet of glass. Working on deck improving the condition of the winches was an experience never to be forgotten.

The first few days steaming up the east coast we had a few showers. We could see the small dark clouds ahead in the blue sky, and could actually see the rain falling as we approached. It looked like a solid wall of rain. Then the ship's bows entered and as we sailed, so the rain wet the deck in a straight line and travelled slowly towards the stern.

Seeing the line approaching I could step back into the galley before it reached me and so not get wet, but the rain itself was very refreshing, and after the ten minute shower the latent heat of the deck sent clouds of steam swirling about. The deck was dry in less than ten seconds after we were through the rain and, looking astern, I could see the rain falling behind, getting further and further away.

---

[23] Thursday Island, in the Torres Strait, is situated approximately 39 kilometres off the northern point of Australia, Cape York. Editor

Two days steaming would bring us to Fraser Island.[24] It was here that we picked up the Pilot who would be advising the Captain until we reached Thursday Island. It was a hundred miles to the start of the Barrier Reef and from there to where we dropped the Pilot was a magical journey.

Although I had plenty of work to do there were times when I had to straighten my back and I admit that going up the coast my back was well straightened, the views were fantastic. At first the small islands were far apart, but eventually they became more numerous and so closer together. The sea was a beautiful aqua green and water snakes of all colours could be seen swimming just below the surface, the only ripples on the water caused by the bows of the ship as it cruised on.

During my free hours, after dinner and until my bedtime, I leaned on the rails regretting that I had no camera. I would have appreciated a deck chair as well, sitting on the hatch made uncomfortable viewing whereas a deck chair on the boat deck would be perfect. I made up my mind that I would have to get a camera and deckchair at Singapore.

The next day the islands were even more numerous. On one or two occasion we passed so close to the islands that we could see the facial expressions of people on the beaches who were happy to wave to us. It was a wonderful five or six days, and I was sorry when we dropped the Pilot at Thursday Island.

I spent a lot of time writing, trying to convey the beauty of the trip to those at home, but how does one

---

[24] Frazer Island lies close to southern Queensland and is the biggest sand island in the world. Editor

describe the beauty and colours with only pen and ink?

I have made that trip four times, but that particular trip was a one-off. The next time was north to south, and the third and fourth times were during war time. Under war conditions one sees very little, the ships stay out of sight of land as much as possible, to stay away from enemy eyes.

We sailed around the northern tip of Australia, through the Indonesian Islands towards Singapore and Malaysia, passing the Celebes (now Sulawesi), and then Borneo to starboard with Java and Sumatra to port. We were looking forward to Singapore. Singapore was the real East and this was to be the first eastern country we'd called at. Singapore lies at the southern tip of Malaysia, fractionally north of the equator. Hot and humid, even a ten-minute walk made one sweat freely.

Working in the engine room was an ordeal; at least it was for me. Until then I had only had my old blue boiler suits to wear, thick and heavy, whereas the others had linen duck trousers and cotton T-shirts. But the Second had told me that Singapore was the place to get kitted out.

That day we arrived in Singapore and received our letters, which were the foremost thing in our minds, and again Edith's scent filled the engine room.

I don't know what the various people who handled Edith's letters thought about the scent, but I don't think she cared too much as long as I didn't complain. Letters were the main concern of any seaman if they had family, and it was amazing how a letter affected a man's outlook.

The ship's agent brought them aboard as soon as we tied up at the quayside, or dropped anchor. We engineers were down below changing the engine room to harbour working, so the Second usually brought the letters down to the lower orders through the accommodation door, right at the top of the engine room. As he came through the door the usual cry, 'You've got one Fiver, I can smell it.'

If our hands were particularly dirty we'd put our letter or letters on the desk until we went up on top. Our boiler suits could be soaking wet and putting the letters in our pockets would ruin them. If our hands were clean we'd read one and keep any others until later. I think that Auckland was the first port that letters from Edith[25] found me.

Sometimes the letters followed the ship around the world for months, having a postmark for every port from which we'd sailed. I remember receiving thirteen letters when we reached home at London,, and most of the envelopes were covered both sides with postmarks.

And as soon as possible, the letters written since the last stop were sent on their way to our loved ones at home. Some of them were so thick we often had difficulty stuffing them into the envelopes.

The next day, after we'd docked, the usual tradesmen came aboard selling their wares and the Second was good enough to act as adviser. In fact, he did most of the buying to prevent me from being robbed. I bought twelve white boiler suits for £1.10 shillings, six pairs of white linen trousers at seven old pence a pair, a dozen sweatshirts and two-dozen pairs of cotton socks at one

---

[25] In one of those letters was the photo of my mother, see the end of Chapter 6, showing the latest hair style, which I believe was called the Marcel Wave. Editor

old penny per pair. The cotton socks were handy as they could be boiled with the T-shirts, which killed any fungi before they could get established. It must have worked, as I never had any foot troubles.

The trousers and sweatshirts were a godsend, and subsequent visits to Singapore were opportunities to top up on these things. However, the sweatshirts I found didn't last long. In the heated atmosphere of the engine room one sweated so much that to be comfortable we would take three down with us into the engine room to change into. But unless they were washed that day they seemed to disintegrate after a day or two, so whenever we changed, the T-shirts were dropped into a bucket of cold water until such time as they could be washed. The socks too, were prone to rot, so these were put into cold water as soon as we took them off. But at a penny per pair they were very good value.

At most ports there was a Mission for Seamen building. The Mission was a charity for Merchant Seamen the world over. All ships had some sort of library and all ships' crews could change the books here, on a one to one basis, at almost any port in the world. Every mission was staffed by a Padre, often with his wife, and I should think that the majority were ex merchant navy officers who had the necessary qualifications to help in any circumstance.

They held services on Sundays and visited the ships when they entered port to enquire if anyone needed help of any sort. Sometimes the smaller ports had only the mission chapel, but Singapore had a large building, more like a hotel. Here there was a concert hall, two billiard rooms with four tables in each, a restaurant and two bars.

One could also rent accommodation if one was waiting for a ship, or any other contingency. Quite often if a crewmember was taken to hospital after an accident, he would be accommodated here until such time as another ship of the same line could call and pick him up.

The first trip ashore was usually a walk around to see as much of the place as we could, always of course with prudence, and you will note that prudence is not spelt with a capital letter. There were places where walking alone was positively dangerous so we made a point of going ashore in twos or threes, or even fours, until we learned something about the place.

We visited the mission on two or three occasions to play billiards, and once to a concert. The billiard room was a grand place. I couldn't begin to compare it with the Cosy in Low Fell, which would be too ridiculous.

This one had four tables only, but it had wall-to-wall carpeting, and a bar with armchairs scattered about. All you had to do was sink into one of these chairs, and nod to a steward who would come over and take your order. He also brought the drinks over, asked you to sign for them, and if there was anything else you required. No money changed hands at this stage. Here we were regarded as officers and gentlemen, although this was a long time ago.

If you wanted to play billiards, you just mentioned it to one of the stewards. If the four tables were in use he would book one for you, and come over and inform you when it became available. The players didn't even have to score for themselves; a white-coated steward did it for you. It was luxury of the highest order.

After the evening was over and you wished to leave,

you tipped the steward who had scored for you, then walked across to the bar where the signed chits were settled. After tipping the drinks steward you could leave, or visit the restaurant if you felt hungry. Or the steward would call you a taxi, and until it arrived you could sit in the armchair and read the overseas *Mirror* while you waited.

This night out was quite cheap, even though it sounds expensive, but it was a charity. The drinks were cheap, English beer was available, the tips were small and the fees for the billiard tables only amounted to coppers. I wondered at the time why there were no ordinary seamen in there, but found out later that they had their own bars where the billiard tables were free, but they had to pay for their drinks up front.

The mission's hotels, and they could be classed as hotels, were all air conditioned. It was great to walk about and enjoy yourself, and not return to the ship with your shirt stuck to your back. The taxi back to the ship was only coppers and the way they hurried for another fare you were back on board before you started to sweat.

Engine room temperatures were often higher in port than out at sea. At sea the breeze caused by the ships speed acted as fans, and with four ventilators turned in two opposite directions they caused a vacuum, so in effect we had two ventilators pushing air down and two drawing it out. But in port, with no breeze, we were unlucky.

While the engineers were working down below, the deck crew were loading and unloading the cargo, at least they were helping. The dockers did the loading and unloading. We carried all types of cargo: latex, raw rubber, pineapple chunks (tinned), citronella oil and coir, indeed all manner of raw materials. The citronella oil was a deck cargo, contained in thirty-gallon drums, which typically had to be delivered a short way up the coast. If one drum was leaking, just a very small leak, a matchstick acting as a wick into a small bottle for a week could amount to enough oil to keep hungry mosquitoes at bay for quite a while.

It was at Singapore that I learned another fact of ship life; our ship could steam on coal or oil. Here we had to change over to oil by taking off the boiler doors and instead bolting on plates that held the jets through which the fuel oil was blown into the furnaces. Worse, I had to work nights until we changed over to burning coal again in the next port.

The theory was that we loaded coal at home, where it was comparatively cheap, and after we had used the coal the bunkers were swept out, making space for extra cargo. At the same time we began to burn oil, which was cheaper abroad than at home. We used the cheapest fuel, whether that was coal from England or Australia, or oil from West Africa or wherever.

The fuel oil was carried in tanks under the engine room, odd-shaped tanks, which could only be used for oil or water. The oil was pumped from these tanks into a settling tank, a large round tank standing on end in a corner of the engine room. The settling tank was just that, it held thirteen tons of oil but we only used the top ten. The three ton at the bottom was sludge consisting of all the settled impurities, and this was removed and disposed of when the tank was opened up and cleaned out periodically.

The oil was pumped from this settling tank to a much smaller one, which was fitted with steam pipes to heat the oil, and from here it was pumped through filters to the small jets in the furnace doors. As the oil was under so much pressure, and heated, it entered the firebox as a gas. Burning oil was a much more dangerous process than burning coal, and great care had to be taken to keep the oil at the correct temperature.

I suppose that on newer ships the temperature control would be automated, but the *City* had no such refinements, we didn't even have a revolution counter on the engine. The filters had to be changed at least on each watch, and this in itself was a dangerous operation.

There were two filters, side by side, one working and one ready for use when needed. A pressure gauge before and after the filters indicated when the one in use needed cleaning, and as these were full of boiling oil and under pressure, everyone took extreme care.

In the stokehold the fire bars in the firebox had been covered with asbestos, three quarters of an inch thick. This was then covered with a layer of clinker, which had been stored for such an occasion whilst we were burning coal. The normal doors when burning coal were akin to old-fashioned coal oven doors, and you just lifted the bar, threw the coal in, and then pushed the door shut.

The doors for oil burning didn't open. Instead of being hinged they were bolted on in the place of the original doors and were fitted with an observation hole, with a cover of blue glass. The jet was screwed into a jet holder that slid halfway through the door. This was held in place with a small hand wheel and screw which could be taken out to clean the jets. The oil or gas as it would be at that stage, burned with a fierce white light, hence the need for the blue glass covering the inspection hole.

Burning oil was much cleaner than coal. The stokehold plates were polished as they were in the engine room. It was also much easier to keep the steam pressure at two hundred and twelve pounds per square inch constant. No stokers were needed, only the *Tindal* was required in the stokehold. His job was to fit the correct jets to keep the pressure constant, and to clean the jets if they became blocked.

In port, while burning oil, I worked in twelve-hour shifts. It was nice to go ashore while everyone else was working, so sometimes it was quite convenient to work nights. On night duty I started duty at 6:00pm and had supper between midnight and 1:00am, this consisted of bacon and eggs, which I had to cook for myself in the galley.

The cook had his instructions to leave my supper out, but eggs and bacon can become very monotonous. The cook had no imagination at all, but I found raisins were a good supplement to my diet. They were in the second drawer down which was locked, but the top drawer wasn't locked and if one took the top drawer out one could quite easily reach the raisins in the second drawer.

I learned this dodge from Edith who told me how her mother rationed her husband's cigarettes by keeping them in the sideboard and locking the door. Edith's dad helped himself by taking the top drawer out to reach the fags in the cupboard beneath.

Lunch one day was interrupted by a cadet who put his head round the door and informed the Third and myself that the camera salesman was on board, but he was quite willing to wait until after lunch to do business.

After lunch we sat on the hatch and started haggling. He had four customers, two cadets, the Third and me. We all chose the same model, so it depended on the price. We told him he could sell four or none and that it depended on how much he wanted, he dropped his price and sold four Agfa's.

When comparing results later on we found that two cameras had very sharp lenses and two not so good. The two cadets were the lucky ones, but they suited our pockets at the time. The Third and I bought better cameras later in Hong Kong and sold the Agfas at a profit.

The cameras made a big difference to our excursions ashore. We also experimented in developing and printing, and even enlarging. The latter wasn't a success. Our homemade enlarger worked, but the results were very fuzzy and we had to content ourselves with the contact prints.

While working we were called on deck to be vaccinated and inoculated. The Second told us later that we were going to French Indo China. It is now Vietnam and the capital, Saigon, is now Ho Chi Minh City. How things change.

As far as I remember we had four, or was it five, pricks of those needles, and when our arms were most painful we had a couple of days off work. I never found out what they were for, nor did I know if they would have any effect. We were to be on our way in four days time and it would only take us two days to get there. Would they have any effect inside a week?

When we arrived off the river mouth we stopped and

waited for the Pilot to guide the ship into Saigon. As I would be working all night I had the day off, and so I was able to lean on the ship's rail and enjoy the trip upstream.

We had some cargo to unload and some to load. We were only staying overnight so there was no opportunity to go ashore, but I did enjoy the trip up river. It took the whole day, the river was so winding. So much so, that on occasions I saw the masts of another ship, half a mile away, sailing to port then shortly afterwards saw the same ship sailing in the opposite direction. There were paddy fields on both sides with water buffalo up to their knees in water with small boys on the backs, for all the world like wee jockeys.

We reached the docking area during late afternoon, and it was interesting to be on deck to see the docking for a change. As I watched the ship being pulled towards the dock my eye caught sight of a coloured jersey through the railings, at the back of the dock some teams were playing football. I climbed onto the boat deck to get a better view.

As I watched, the referee blew his whistle, the centre forward kicked off and virtually the whole team took the ball straight down the field and into the net, pushing the goalkeeper into the back of the net in the process. That was the end of the match. The spectators rushed on to the field, some players pulled off their jerseys, running as they did so. The last I saw of the man who had knocked over the goalkeeper he was climbing over a fence, blood streaming down his face. No, I don't think I'd like to play football there.

With steam on the winches, one could hear the hissing

as they warmed through and as dinner was due it was a hurried dinner, a quick change into my boiler suit and to work. I was there in case I was needed. If a winch had trouble it had to be repaired at once, but all that was needed that night was oil and grease.

By about 8:00pm, huge cargo lights had been hauled into position over the hold, they were so powerful they turned night into day. There would be no sleep for anyone this night as the noise of the winches clattering away would keep even the soundest sleeper awake. I would have a quiet sleep tomorrow.

But for me the noise of the winches was nothing compared with the attention of the mosquitoes. Mosquitoes the size of daddy-long-legs were loose among us and very soon I was back in my cabin. Even if the night was hot and humid, I was getting dressed up.

Two pairs of socks pulled over my trouser bottoms, a crewneck jersey, the wrists sealed with elastic bands, gloves, scarf and a balaclava. The last of my citronella oil was used around my neck. However they still got through. Never have I experienced such a night.

When morning came I was in my cabin, Flit gun going until not one mosquito survived. During the night I'd blocked up the ventilator and the portholes were shut tight, but they were still about. They must have liked me, I was bitten all over, whereas the dockers were working in vests and shorts, apparently without any problem. They must have had some sort of natural immunity.

A few months later I was engaged in closing down the boilers, which was a very hot job at any time. I was working actually on top of them when suddenly I was shaking like a leaf. I felt very weak. I sat down, sweat pouring out of me. I couldn't stand, and as I sat and shivered, the Second came through the door and saw me sitting there.

I was shaking too much to speak but he seemed to know what he was doing. He shouted to the Fourth to bring the Chief Steward, who acted as our doctor. After a short while he arrived with what tasted like a glass of water, this had a magical effect and inside of ten minutes I was working as if nothing had happened.

But there was a sequel to this. Two years later after I'd forgotten the incident and was married, I woke up on two or three occasions with the same symptoms I had experienced on the boiler tops. It frightened Edith half to death, but I remembered where I had contracted malaria.

I think that the only ones who enjoyed that night in Saigon, or Ho Chi Minh City, were the native crew. Ropes had been slung over the starboard side of the *City*, the side of the ship away from the dock, and a steady stream of girls were up and down those ropes all night in and out of the seamen's quarters in the stern.

Around six bells of the morning watch we left Saigon and made our way downstream. Since I'd been working all night, I had the day off. I stayed on deck for an hour or so then lay down on my day bed, had a couple of hours sleep, then came on deck again and continued observing the river banks and villages as we passed by. With my new camera I took a few photographs, but they didn't come out too well. We were in the middle of the channel and the river was so wide near the estuary that the interesting villages on the banks were far distant. The only decent snaps were of the local fishing canoes, taken as we passed.

Sailing northeast for about three days we came to the capital of the Philippines, Manila. It was dark when we arrived in Manila Bay, no moon and no stars. I couldn't see the water even though I was only a few feet away. Standing on the deck all I could see were the lights ashore.

Before we arrived, the engineers were in the engine room as usual whilst the deck officers manoeuvred the ship to her anchorage. When the anchor was down we could come up on deck, and the officer of the watch had the responsibility of nipping down every fifteen minutes to ensure that nothing was amiss.

The night was still, nothing stirred. It was warm and very pleasant leaning on the ship's rail, straining my eyes, trying to get a glimpse of anything in that black void. The Fourth was the first to hear the faint cry, a cry for help he supposed although it wasn't the word 'Help'.

We strained our ears, everyone holding their breath, and then it came again. We all heard it this time, probably as we were all listening for it. We heard the cry again, it seemed to be more urgent this time, there could be someone out there needing help. We found a coil of rope hanging by a lifebelt and the Third, being the strongest swimmer tied the end around himself, jumped over the side and swam towards where the sound was coming from. The call continued and the Third answered and swam towards the voice. After fifteen minutes or so we heard the Third call to haul him in. By this time a rope ladder had been thrown over the side and we were helping the rescued and rescuer on deck. They were helped into the galley, this being the nearest place with a light.

By now, there was quite a crowd around, towels had been brought as well as blankets, and both men were being given a hard rub down. Not that the sea was cold but both men were shivering with exhaustion. We laid them out in the galley; however the Third was soon on his feet.

The other chap was a short, heavily-built individual wearing nothing but a pair of underpants. At first glance he looked like a dead Chinese, but after a good rubbing with hand towels and half an hour lying in the galley, he turned out to be a live Japanese sailor.

He could understand a little English, but could speak less. We gathered that he had jumped ship and was very fearful of having to go back, we never found out why. We knew that the Japanese Merchant Navy was almost as disciplined as their Navy, unlike our own MN vessels. It was possible that he'd committed some crime, but whatever the reason, he was afraid to return to the ship that he'd escaped from. The Chief had to be told, and of course the Captain.

The rescued man was made comfortable in the galley, the warmest place on the ship. He was still shivering uncontrollably, but I don't think it was on account of the cold as it was warm. It may still have been shock, but I believe he was scared of going back aboard his own ship.

The Captain later decided to hand over the problem to the harbour authorities. He didn't want to be involved in any dispute, so the following morning the harbour police were informed and the man was taken ashore. That was the last we heard of him, but as a general rule on such occasions the man would spend time in the local jail then be escorted on board just before his ship sailed.

Later we thought of other reasons why he should jump ship, and later still we noticed how many Japanese were distributed throughout the east. The Philippines were a point in question and there is no doubt that when the war started there was a considerable fifth column in position.

Manila sixty five years ago was a really handsome city with large, imposing buildings, one of which was the cathedral, another was the post office. It was really two cities; whilst the new Manila was built adjacent to the old site, the old city was kept as a museum, part of which was used as a barracks.

Come daylight we moved alongside the quay. We were looking forward to trying out our new cameras, which would have been very handy the previous night if we had had flash equipment, and to visiting the post office to mail our letters. I was free to go ashore so long as I was back ready to take over at 6:00pm; the other engineers of course were working all day.

We were very impressed with Manila, the way the old and new buildings complimented each other. But if the new city was stylish, the old city was more so. The old city was very like the old cities of Spain, understandably so as the Philippines were originally Spanish. The post office was a most imposing building. We had no problem buying stamps, we could say 'Please' and 'Thank you' in a number of tongues, and in those days the people of these countries made us welcome, more so than in America.

Since those days things have changed considerably in certain ways. You didn't need travellers' cheques, all you needed was dollars or sterling, they could buy anything.

The shopkeeper and you worked out the rate of

exchange when you made a purchase. No one ever went into the banks to change money into the local currency. If we had money left over from our visit, there was no problem we could spend it in the next country. But you had to be wary as the rate of exchange varied from country to country, and you could be on the losing end.

American dollars and the English pound were accepted everywhere, but guilders, rand and coins from other countries were also gratefully accepted. However in some countries I had difficulty spending Australian coinage which was strange. In those days it was almost indistinguishable from our own but the native shop-keepers knew the difference.

In port the ship tied up alongside the quay, the crew lined up along the deck, and the Port Doctor walked along the line as an inspection. Then we were free to go ashore at any time. Even during the war we were allowed to take our cameras ashore with us. There was one restriction however, the old question, 'Have you anything to declare?'

There was the rule, any unopened bottle of spirits had to go into bond before we reached port, and the same applied to unopened cartons of two hundred cigarettes. That meant they had to go to the Chief Steward to be locked up until we left port.

Within a week we were on our way again and I was getting used to the Sunday morning watch with the Second Engineer. It was still hard getting up at 3:45am but I knew my way around now. At first everything had appeared so complicated, but week after week I understood more and more. Taken separately the components of the engine room were quite simple, taken together they were so dependant on each other as to be very complex, as any one machine could affect all the others. It was this complexity than I had to understand.

Often the Second concentrated on the storeroom entering stores that we were short of into a book, leaving me alone to continue the watch on my own.

My interest down among the engines never flagged, I think that I enjoyed this job because I loved steam engines and here was a large one that I could relate to. I could see it working, whereas you cannot see the working parts of a turbine. Here, as an engineer, I was one of five instead of being one in five hundred, as I had been in the factory. Yes, I liked this job and the side benefits, but I was always glad when it was breakfast time.

About five days sailing brought us to Batavia, now Jakarta, in the Dutch East Indies, now Indonesia. Here we took aboard some coal, though not in the usual way of loading coal from an overhead hopper and chute.

Here there were two planks from the deck to the quayside. All day long and at night, men and women carrying baskets of coal on their heads ran up one plank, tipped the basket of coal into the bunker, and then ran down the other plank to pick up another basket of coal. This process was repeated until the loading was complete. By loading coal here at Jakarta, I knew that I would soon be working days again.

The following morning we sailed for Surabaya, about four hundred and twenty miles down the coast. If we averaged thirteen knots this would take a day and a half. At the moment we were still burning oil, and we were expecting to arrive off Surabaya during Saturday afternoon.

During dinner we asked the Mess Boy if there was anything of interest here in Surabaya. He'd been here before and seemed a knowledgeable sort of chap. He could even get by in Chinese. He told us that there was a good swimming pool, where we could spend Sunday. One could swim, have a drink at the pool side, and have a meal at the same time. It would only cost one guilder for the day, and he said he could arrange it all for us, no problem. But then I thought of the problem. It was the Fourth's night aboard tonight and it would be mine tomorrow, Sunday.

Luckily he and the Third, boozing pals, wanted that Saturday night off and the Fourth would work for me on the Sunday if I worked the Saturday. And so it was arranged. We asked the boy to organize our trip for the following day, starting at 10:00am, so we could have lunch out and be back for dinner. Unfortunately things didn't work out as we had expected.

On the Sunday morning I prepared myself, washed and shaved, then went in search of the others. The apprentices were ready so we called at the Third's cabin, knocked, and got no reply. We thought he and the Fourth must have had a good night out. I knocked again and getting no reply, opened the door and went in.

He was still in bed but when I spoke he moaned, and when he turned over I was sure they'd had a good night out. He had a beautiful black eye with scrapes and bruises down the other side of his face. He didn't look too happy at all, so we had to revise our plans. We had lunch on board and then got all the news, bit by bit.

The three of them, the Third, Fourth and the youngest

of the Quartermasters, had visited a nightclub for a drink. They downed a couple of drinks then found out that there was no floor show and the place was quite dead, so they decided to move on to another club. At two in the morning, half-cut, they entered another club and saw three girls without escorts sitting at a table. There were no other tables vacant, so they crossed over and asked the girls' permission to sit.

They never heard the answer for, just as they were thinking of sitting themselves down, three Dutch sailors, big ones, grabbed their collars, dragged them outside and duffed the Third and Fourth up, leaving them unconscious in the gutter.

The Quartermaster was more fortunate. He escaped and ran into a nearby pub, which was so crowded it was easy to get lost in. He continued to drown his sorrows before he went back to find out how the other two had fared. When he went back he couldn't find them, so he went back into the pub and drowned some more of his sorrows.

The Third and Fourth were left lying in the gutter to be found there by a skipper of another ship. He brought them round, found out the name of their ship, and then brought them back by taxi.

The Quartermaster had so many sorrows that he passed out before he'd drowned them all. When he came round he was in a clearing in the jungle, and a girl was trying to pull him from a taxi. He had no idea of how he'd got there, no idea of what had happened or where he was. He didn't like the idea of being hijacked, but the driver of the taxi couldn't speak English or didn't want to.

However our Quartermaster wasn't to be outdone. He

got through to the driver by singing and dancing in the clearing, as if he was on stage, then grabbing the driver and waltzing in front of the taxi in the moonlight. The man got the message and took him back to the club, from where he eventually crawled back to the ship. We daren't ask him what happened to the girl.

After we had sympathised with all concerned we brought up the subject of the swimming pool. After lunch we managed to find a cab, the Mess Boy gave the cab driver his instructions, and then told us the arrangements.

We had no real idea where we were going, but five of us piled into the taxi and left everything to our driver. After we'd been on the road for thirty minutes or so, we found ourselves outside a wooden hut in the middle of the jungle. The road at this point was only a track, but the driver stopped and motioned us to get down and have a drink.

He led the way into this hut and when we entered we just stood and looked around, expecting Humphrey Bogart to be around somewhere. It was as if we had been transported to some film set.

Round tables were scattered about the room, four chairs to each table, a wooden bar at one end and sawdust scattered over the floor. As we sat down at one of the tables, moving an extra chair from one of the other tables, one of the waiters came across to take our order. A waiter I said, but he was more like a bouncer. Three others lounged against the bar talking among themselves, just keeping an eye on things. We wondered what sort of clientele they were used to on Saturday nights.

They were all dressed in the same sort of clothes, a pair of jeans and sweat-stained singlets, as you would imagine in some old film. Rays of sunlight found their way through the timber walls in places. I suppose the timber planks had shrunk due to the dry weather, although at certain times of the year the rainfall could be torrential.

Two chameleons clung to the walls, living flycatchers earning their keep, slowly walking occasionally to a new vantage point. However the beer was cold and greatly appreciated, and in these surroundings we had the feeling that we were extras in some Wild West film. That really was the feeling, something that I can't fully describe. It was a wonderful experience.

We finished our drinks and then climbed back into the taxi to continue our journey to the swimming pool. Swimming in fresh water was something that by now we were unaccustomed to, so we were looking forward to this pool without exception, and to having our photos taken there. Yes, we had our pictures taken. The only trouble was that the cameraman was one of the apprentices who had a cine camera, but no projector with him, so he was the only one that was going to see the result of his efforts. We must have really been off the beam.

But the swimming pool was an eye opener. The pool itself was fifteen foot deep, and bigger than any of us had seen before, with diving boards, both high boards and spring boards. Down one side of the pool was an area dotted with tables and chairs, you could have a drink or a four-course meal at any time of the day. Or if you wished, you could leave the pool, have a meal then return. The entrance fee to the pool lasted for that day.

The dining area could be separated from the pool by

sliding glass panels through which one had a panoramic view of a large bay, which under the sun was a brilliant blue, and the roof was glass with ventilators. Also at anchor in the bay were four British and Dutch giant flying boats, all four-engined,

We had a wonderful afternoon swimming and diving, then the taxi turned up on time to get us back to the ship for dinner.

From Surabaya we sailed north to Singapore we thought, but we guessed wrong. It was very difficult at times finding out where we were heading. The Second, close to the Chief, was our main informant, but sometimes even he didn't know. So all we could do was wait, although we always knew before we arrived.

Our next port of call was Penang, on the south-west coast of Malaysia. As I would be working during the night I had the day off, and I decided to have a walk ashore, just to see what the place was like. It was only a small place, every port was different, and I was inquisitive just as any lad of my age would be. There was little there as far as I could see but I may have missed the main town.

The streets were trodden earth and the buildings were mainly lapboard, but I did see a restaurant with a sign saying that no one was allowed in without a tie.

We only stayed there a couple of days. However, during those two days three of us, the two cadets and myself, managed to squeeze in a lunch at that hotel. The meal was cheap by our standards.

We had no money, or very little because we were only there for a day or two, and we had had no chance of drawing any. So we did our best with the odds and ends that we had in our pockets. During our travels we collected small change in various currencies, a pound here, a dollar there, guilders and pennies. They all mounted up, so we emptied our pockets onto the table.

It was quite an education paying for a meal in this fashion. The manager counted the odd currencies, told us how much we had in the local coinage, then we chose our meal to suit. The odd currencies, with a bit of haggling and laughter, paid for our shark fin soup and broiled fish cooked by Chinese cooks, and we enjoyed it.

We had no idea what kind of fish but it was a change from lunch on board, and after all we'd be able to tell our grandchildren. I hoped they would like to know of my experiences some day.

Soon we were off to sea again, the true home of the sailor. I didn't consider myself a true sailor, although if I hadn't had Edith waiting at home for me I may well have become one.

My heart was on Tyneside at that moment and my first thought as we set out across the Indian Ocean for Cape Town was to get down to writing letters again. Nearing port my first thought was of letters to read, especially those scented ones from Edith.

The warm days and nights were so very different from our home climate, and so far we had not encountered any bad weather. When I look back, up to that point, we hadn't met any really bad seas at all.

25. Funeral Cortege, Saigon, 1939

26. A Cadet and me (left). Saigon

27. Boston Skyline, 1940

28. World Fair, New York, 1939

29. *The Killoran*, Auckland, 1939

30. The Repulse Bay Hotel, Hong Kong, 1939

31. Back row from left to right, Cyril, Jack, Aussie Gunner, Wireless Operator, Cadet, me in front

32. From left to right, 3rd Engineer, Wireless Operator, Jack, the Carpenter

CHAPTER ELEVEN
Penang to Hong Kong
August – December 1939

The trip across the Indian Ocean was a dream, especially as I had purchased a deckchair and *topee* in Singapore. On Saturdays and Sundays I could relax in comfort on the boat deck, and on warm evenings I could laze in my deck chair instead of sitting on the hatch. We had wonderful weather as we crossed this ocean. The surface of the water was like glass most of the way, and with the ship steaming at a steady three hundred and fourteen sea miles every twenty four hours, the engine had an almost hypnotic effect.

But as we rounded the Cape a day from Cape Town, we felt the meeting of the seas, the South Atlantic and the Indian Oceans. This produced long swells, the ship pitching and burying her nose, then rolling as we altered course, then to some extent doing both at the same time with a cork-screwing motion. If I'd been liable to seasickness this would have been terrible. I'm glad to say it had no effect and I actually enjoyed it, wondering what a storm would be like. Twelve months later in the Pacific I was to find out.

Cape Town was only a stop to get supplies, food and oil, although of the latter only five hundred tons were taken in. Here oil was expensive, and as we were going up the coast to Nigeria where the oil was cheap, we'd fill the tanks there.

Taking in oil was a busy time for the deck crew, carpenter and engineers. The deck crew had to connect the five inch diameter supply pipes to the oil intakes on deck, but the carpenter had the hardest job. He had to keep dropping his steel measuring rod down the right sounding pipe to take a reading, judge the measurement, and shout to us down below when to change tanks. We had to be quick opening and closing the valves on the tank tops as once a tank was full we determined which tank the oil entered next.

Whilst we were loading the oil and the Chief Steward had been attending to the ship's stores, the ship's agent had been in conference with the Captain. As no one was going ashore we handed our letters to the agent. A few hours later we were sailing out of Cape Town harbour for Lagos, Nigeria, and leaving Table Mountain behind. Pictures of which even now brings back vivid memories of those times.

When we were near any English-speaking country my little wireless came in very handy for the local news. For the English news we relied on the Wireless Operator if he was in a good mood, but lately he seemed more difficult than usual, so we couldn't get any news.

Instead of cruising up the African coast we were now headed out to sea, out of sight of the land, and then we turned north. We had no sight of land until we reached Lagos about fourteen days later.

At Lagos we took aboard more fuel oil and filled the water tanks, boiler water and drinking water for our trip across the Atlantic. The Second and I spent four hours that afternoon stripping down and overhauling the drinking water filter on the boat deck. The heat was terrific and without shade the temperature must have been well over one hundred degrees. We were well covered against the sun, loose shirts and *topees*, but we were both exhausted when we'd finished. The Second always seemed to take the worst jobs himself. I just wished that sometimes he would pick someone else to help him.

I'd never experienced heat such as this, but we were all given salt tablets, quinine tablets, and so forth. I think at that time we were taking six tablets a day. We were only there a day and a half, but during that time we again filled both water tanks and the oil fuel tanks.

When we left Lagos the seas were running high, and as we sailed out of the shelter of the Ivory Coast the *City* began to dig her nose in, waves coming over the bows and running the length of the ship. What made it worse was the reason why we were sailing out of that shelter, but we were to find that out later. The first night out I had trouble staying in my bunk, but lying on my side, knees up and back tight against the panelling, I was OK, and was asleep right away.

The following morning we had a nasty surprise. We all turned up at breakfast, and the first sip of tea told us everything - the tea was salty. I didn't like it, neither did anyone else, so we had breakfast without tea. We heard the Captain didn't like salty tea either, and he ordered the Chief Officer to find out who was responsible. It was the Carpenter who took the blame.

When we left Lagos the covers had not been replaced on the water tank intakes. With the heavy seas running when we left harbour, the sea water coming over the bows had gone down the intakes and fouled the water.

For a number of days the deck crew drank salty tea or none at all.

Luckily the boiler water wasn't affected as the boiler tank covers had been replaced before we left. So in the engine room we were more fortunate as we had access to the boiler water. A sounding pipe in the engine room allowed us to lower a glass boiler gauge tube tied around with string down the sounding pipe to get enough to fill our kettle. The only thing was we had to ensure was that the water was boiled for twenty minutes before making the tea.

After almost a week, we reached the Cape Verde Islands where the tanks were pumped out and refilled. While we were at anchor children swam around the ship, shouting for pennies. The water was so clear that it was possible to see the bottom of the harbour, and when we threw the coins we could see them fluttering to the bottom like falling leaves. Most of the coins never reached the sandy bottom as the kids caught them before they got there.

We thought we were only there because of the water problem, but maybe not. Shore personnel came aboard and we all had instructions to take effect immediately.

All deck lights were removed and we quickly realised that our holiday cruise had come to an end. We were informed that there was to be no smoking on deck after dusk, and no smoking in cabins with the scuttles open. The engine room skylight was closed and covered with two layers of sandbags and the scuttles were fitted with metal covers, which had come aboard with the sandbags.

The passageway in our accommodation had dark blue lamps fitted, and the doors at each end were later fitted with switches which turned the lights off when the door was opened. The wireless sets were impounded and put in bond as almost all sets of that period transmitted slight signals from the aerial, which could be picked up allowing U-boats to home in on the target.

All this happened more than two weeks before war was declared, but we had sensed this would happen when we had refitted at Cape Town. Never again did we sail along the coast, we were always out of sight of land.

The palm oil from Singapore was to be unloaded at our first port of call in the USA, Paulsboro.[26] Left unattended palm oil turns solid in cold climes, so from Cape Town the deep tank in which this oil was transported had to be progressively heated to keep it liquid for pumping out when required. The deep tank was lined with steam pipes, and from Cape Town onwards steam was introduced through these pipes very gradually, day by day increasing in temperature. The temperature had to be raised very gradually as the palm oil would burn if the heat was too localised.

It was my job to monitor the rise in temperature twice a day, but just to make sure I took the reading three times, I didn't want to make any mistakes. The Chief never remarked on the three readings in the log book. I don't suppose he noticed.

Our next port of call was Paulsboro, which was an oil terminal with a small town nearby; here we discharged the palm oil. We didn't see much of the place as we only had about an hour ashore. But we did visit the open air war museum with various old 1914-1918 tanks and some dwellings which appeared to be right out of the Wild

[26] Paulsboro is a Borough in Gloucester County, New Jersey. Editor

West. The dirt road was lined on both sides by timber shacks, complete with porches or verandas and rocking chairs on the verandas. There was a chapel or church half way down on the right hand side, old Western style.

We had half a dozen children around us, walking with us, but they were more interested in our origin and dialects, than answering questions. It looked as if the bungalows were occupied but we weren't sure, they may have been part of the museum as is the Welsh museum at St Fagan's. But I felt that I'd seen a bit of the Wild West at last.

We reached the end of the road which disappeared into the distance, where there were purple mountains with their heads in the clouds.

We discharged our cargo of palm oil overnight and the next morning sailed for Philadelphia and New York.

Three days out from Paulsboro we had a slight accident, although it could have been serious. I was fast asleep, scuttles open, when a sixth sense woke me up, or was it the smell?

I think that I was gaining an inner instinct that you need in an engine room, a feeling that things are not quite right. I smelt first, and then listened, then slippers on and down the ladders. I can't remember putting my trousers on, just dashing down the ladders, shouting for the Fourth whose watch it was.

I ran to the pump, which was pumping oil into the settling tank and closed it down. I'd just shut it down when the Fourth came over wiping his hands, wanting to know what all the fuss was about. When I told him he turned a deathly white, he was in a state of shock, 'What do I do now?' he said.

'Well, you'll never hide it,' I replied. 'There must be a couple of tons of oil flowing down the deck. Best bet is to get on the voice pipe to the Chief and put yourself in his hands. I don't know anything about it. I'm going back to bed.'

There was nothing that I could do to help him, if they found out that I had stopped the oil pump it would be even worse for the Fourth. So I went to sleep and forgot everything about it until an hour later, when dozens of lascar seamen began to clear up the tons of oil on the deck and down the side of the ship. No one around our area had any more sleep that night.

When I crept out of my bunk the ship was a hive of industry. Through the scuttle came the noise of both deck and engine room crews scrabbling about the deck. The crew were out there cleaning up, mopping up the oil with coir and cotton waste. Some of the crew were over the side, sitting on boards, cleaning the hull which had black oil everywhere. The coir and oil soaked waste was stored down below ready for burning at night. It couldn't be burned during the day as it would make so much black smoke, and smoke was a come-on for any U-boat. War was in the offing and the Captain was taking no chances.

The Chief wasn't satisfied until all traces of the oil were removed from the ship. Even in those days pollution was followed by a heavy fine, especially near port. The Fourth had a dressing down from the Second and the Chief, but these things happen and who knows, if whatever had attracted his attention had not been attended to it may have been much more serious.

When we reached New York on September the third, 1939, we heard officially on the Chief's radio that we were at war with Germany. Things would never be the same again.

From New York we sailed to Boston, the most English city in the States, then on to Halifax, Nova Scotia.

As we sailed north from Boston the weather deteriorated, masses of fog rolled down and surrounded us. To a degree we were pleased, we could see no one but then no one could see us. At night the ship's fog horn would blare out. Not very often as we had no wish to attract attention, but although it was loud and just a few yards from our accommodation, it never woke me up or prevented me from sleeping.

Indeed it was a most nostalgic sound as it took me back to my childhood days as I lay in my bed at Low Fell. Where, if the wind was blowing from the north, I could hear the ships in the Tyne sounding their fog horns to inform the man to open the swing bridge and let them through.

A slight mist still prevailed as we arrived off Halifax. We were turning to enter the channel when a loud hailer ordered us to stop, and we were asked for the code of the day. The Officer on the bridge replied that he didn't know the code of the day, and had never heard of it. 'What's it all about? Please explain.'

Apparently there was a naval vessel waiting outside the harbour to escort us in, so we had to turn and go back and find our escort. After half an hour we found a destroyer so that he could escort us into harbour, but what an arrangement. I have a photograph of this destroyer but one can barely make it out in the mist.

Halifax was the main meeting place for convoys across the Atlantic, and here the switches were fitted for

304

the previously installed blue lights.

The Chiefs and Captains had lectures and when they came back we were told how to coal the fires without making smoke, the importance of not making smoke, and that cleaning the fires had to be done during the hours of daylight so that sparks were less likely to be seen.

As we sailed north from Halifax up the St Lawrence River and on to Montreal, we could feel it getting colder. As the ship was making its way up the river with all the engineers down below, the Second spoke from the corner of his mouth, 'Fiver, slip up top and see where we are.'

This time we were just passing Quebec and it was the Heights of Abraham. I had just rushed out on deck and as all I was wearing was a sweat soaked T-shirt, the bitter cold took my breath away. I sheltered behind the corner of the accommodation and had a good view as we passed.

History, I'm afraid, is not my strong point, so I may be mistaken, but I'm sure it was these heights that General Wolfe stormed with his troops to take Quebec. Here again I suspect that the Second knew where we were and gave me the opportunity to see a piece of history, a sight that most people will never have a chance to see.

When I slid down the ladders he asked me if it was worth seeing. I had him to thank for so many opportunities for seeing places of real interest as we passed through. As I thanked him, he told me to take the rest of the day off as I would be working all night, which. I already knew as we were still burning oil.

When two boilers were shut down at Montreal, we guessed we would be staying a while. I spent the night writing letters and clambering up and down the ladders to ensure that everything was OK in the engine room.

Before breakfast the next morning the third boiler was shut down. The ship laid silent, no lights, no sound from the pumps, it was uncanny.

At breakfast we were told that the ship was to be fumigated, so everyone had to be off the ship by 9:00am and no one would be allowed back on board before 6:30pm. This was bad news in Montreal as it was very religious and everywhere was closed on Sundays. Cafes, shops, pictures and pubs were all closed, no place to go at all, or so I thought. I'd been up all night, and I was tired.

As I sat writing in my cabin I heard the Second and someone else having a good argument as they passed by my porthole. Then came a knock on my door, it was the Second. He told me to stay put until he came back. A quarter of an hour later when he returned he explained that no arrangements had been made about a bed for me.

As I had been on duty all last night and would be on duty all that night the Second insisted I had to have a bed for the day, to get my head down. The entire slanging match had been with the ship's agent who had forgotten to make the necessary arrangements with a local hotel. Finally the agent made arrangements on the phone. Oh yes, the Captain had a phone on board, that was the first thing that came aboard as we came alongside the dock.

After a short while the agent came along with a piece of paper with the name of the Hotel Plaza where a room was booked in my name for the day.

This hotel turned out to be rather posh. I couldn't remember staying at one before, a B&B yes, but not in a grand place such as this. I soon learned to like it.

When I presented myself at the desk the man behind gave the key to a little page boy. I had borrowed a small case, as I only had my two big expanders, and he grabbed this and was off at a run, I followed. He put my case on the small table at the bottom of the bed, opened it, gave me the keys and hoped that I would enjoy my stay, and then off he went. He didn't wait for a tip as they do in the films. He would have been disappointed if he had, as I had no money. I looked around and said to myself, this is living.

It was a big room, a very big room, and it held two beds, a double and a single. But better than the two beds was the fact that with the room came a bath and toilet. This was real luxury, a nice hot fresh water bath, the first since leaving home. It was all there the scented soap, warm bath towels and talcum powder. Oh yes, a real treat.

As I lay in the bath I wondered how all the others were faring. If I'd known that I was going to be so lucky, the Second could have had the other bed, but there was no knowing where they were and I didn't know Montreal sufficiently well to go looking for them. So after a good long soak, warm as toast, I slipped between the sheets. It wasn't long before I was fast asleep.

I awoke at 6:00pm, dinner was to be late, but I didn't want to miss it with all the eating places closed. I'd been asleep from about 11.00am, so time to make a move, out of bed and a quick wash. I contemplated another nice soak in the bath, seeing that it would only be my second fresh water bath in six months, but I'd left it too late. I should have been up earlier and now I had to get moving.

I guessed the rest of the crew would not have done as well as I had fared and I knew that they were going to be envious.

Later over the dinner table, I learned that the Second and Chief had spent the afternoon in a warehouse sleeping on sacks of potatoes, which were not very comfortable. While the Third and Fourth had spent the afternoon in the local park and walking around Montreal, although they did find seats and shelter in the park. I was rather unpopular when I told them how I'd spent my afternoon. I explained they all would have been welcome to use the bath and the spare bed, if I had known where to find any of them.

No rats were found after the fumigation and the miserable ones in the crew thought that this was a bad omen. The rats had already abandoned the ship. However we found several buckets full of the ubiquitous cockroaches. This was good because they would eat the gum off our envelopes unless they were kept in a tin box - the envelopes, not the cockroaches.

It was cold that night and being Sunday there was no work for me, so I shivered and wrote letters to post before we left. One to Edith, with a little piece of hotel soap inside, and a letter to Mam and Dad.

After dinner the Second and I started one of the boilers up, but it takes time to get a full head of steam up. Our accommodation was over the engine room but the fires had been out all day. The warmest place was in the engine room so I stayed down there, and at 6:00am I was straight into my bunk.

Washed and dressed and up for lunch at 1:00pm, I decided I'd pop out to see Montreal and post my letters. This I did but the weather wasn't very kind, it was cold and wet. Still it was a new experience in the Post Office to say 'Merci' instead of 'Thank you'. As I walked, getting wetter by the minute, I passed the theatre. Why not? I asked myself. It's been a long time since I was in any theatre. The afternoon matinee was just starting when I walked in through the foyer.

As I walked down the aisle to take my seat the chorus girls came dancing across the stage. I had to open my eyes wide as they came dancing on, kicking high just as the Television Toppers did later in 1952. Only these girls only wore briefs, no tops. I said to myself, how can it be that every place is shut on Sundays, cinemas, cafes and shops, yet one can go to the theatre the next day and see topless females parading on the stage?

Now don't think that I am protesting. Being a young lad of twenty-two it was a most enjoyable experience, another first in fact. Even though I was the brother of five sisters I hadn't seen anything like this before. So much for my education!

After a week, we left Montreal and made our way down the St Lawrence on the way to New York. This was not too soon as I didn't like the bitter cold up there; it was much more pleasant in southern climes, and maybe I had become accustomed to the tropical weather.

We all preferred the sun, and the disappearance of the fog, so prevalent there at that time of year, was welcome. New York appeared like home as we sailed up the Hudson River, it was much warmer than northerly Montreal and a new attraction was the 1939 World Fair. This we had to attend, as it was one of those 'once in a lifetime' things.

We paid our visit on a Sunday, the two cadets, the Third Engineer and me. I'd been awake all night looking after the engine room, but managed two hours sleep before breakfast.

We left Brooklyn and travelled the underground, although to tell the truth it was dangerous on the underground station. For our own safety we stood together with our arms around a pillar on the platform, and by the time the train arrived we were hanging on to each other and as well as the pillar to prevent ourselves being pushed onto the railway lines. The train came slowly into the station and stopped, only then did we let go of the pillar.

Immediately we were carried off our feet and bundled into the nearest door and down the corridor, eventually ending up on our hands and knees on the floor of the carriage. Not content with using the doors people were climbing in through the windows, until no one could move an inch. The doors were shut, how we didn't know, but the train pulled out of the station and shortly we were on the surface seeing the countryside on our way to the exhibition.

To me, this was a king-sized treat. I thought of all the people, from all over America, travelling to this one spot. I supposed to a degree fewer people would attend from abroad because of the war. However, there must have been thousands of overseas folk who had visited already as the exhibition was opened on April 31st 1939, five months before war was declared.

The exhibition was located about nine miles from Manhattan on the site of an old rubbish dump. It took six months to completely remodel the area to make a park which was three times the size of Hyde Park in London. More than three thousand trees were planted and two large lakes excavated.

The entrance fee to the exhibition would be considered ridiculous these days, a mere dollar, and with the then rate of four dollars to the pound, we were through the gate for the equivalent of twenty five new pence.

The theme building was a huge sphere which, at a guess, I would say was about two hundred feet in diameter. The approach was a long walkway, which went from ground level to a door in the sphere's circumference.

The sphere held a most unusual exhibition which alone was worth more than the entrance fee. We walked up the approach road, well out of breath at the top, and entered the door. Inside we stepped onto a balcony which ran all around the inside circumference of the globe. This balcony moved slowly around, so there was no need to walk. We leant on the rail and gazed upon the scene below, then raised our eyes and gazed upwards.

Down below was a model of New York, the streets with the cars stopping at the traffic lights, and then moving on again as the lights changed. The ships in the harbour were sailing up and down the Hudson River, then docking at the various jetties, some sailing downstream, some arriving. As night fell the lights were switched on in the buildings, the street lights lit up, and the city slowed down.

Looking up we noticed that the sky was darkening, the stars appeared, twinkling overhead, and the moon cast an eerie glow over the whole scene. Then the sun rose and the whole city come to life again. One by one the lights went out, the sky became lighter and the river traffic came to life again.

311

Slowly the balcony moved around until we were back at the beginning, a new day had started and we were at the exit. I couldn't say how long it took for the balcony to complete its journey, I was so entranced that time was forgotten, it was another unforgettable experience.

Next to this large ball was the needle. This was a huge, slim, seven-hundred-foot high, three-sided tower, tapering to a sharp point.

By this time we were hungry and it was at a restaurant here that I tasted tuna fish for the first time. I'd never seen it in the UK, salmon yes, but not tuna. The restaurant had a glass roof and glass walls, and a menu that lacked nothing. I chose to have the tuna salad, peach pie and a pot of tea. There were six varieties of tea alone, so I had Russian tea. All three choices were new to me. We would have liked to lash out but we had to watch our budget. I enjoyed my lunch, even though I couldn't finish all the salad, it only cost one dollar fifty cents. It was very cheap to eat ashore here and a change from ship's food.

We never had salad on ship at sea as it doesn't keep well in an ice box. We only had this sort of meal in port and in season, as in South Africa where we had salad served up with an enormous crayfish. In Cape Town these crayfish were like big lobsters and were really delicious.

Most of the pavilions at the exhibition were advertising their country's products, but really there were so many more interesting things to see, and this was our only opportunity to see as much as we could. There were talking typewriters and computers in the experimental stages, and talks on the future of computers.

The British pavilion was disappointing, however I

312

think one could understand this as war was imminent when all this was put together. Rolls Royce and Bentley were represented, Sheffield cutlery and some good china, but we were disappointed by this part of the show.

The artificial lakes and waterfalls were spectacular, as were the fountains, rising and falling to music and changing colour as they bobbed up and down. There was a huge funfair in full swing but we had so much more to see it was a no go, in fact there was too much to take in, in the time available. Probably that is why everything I saw then is so hazy now. It would have taken three or four visits to see everything.

We had our cameras with us, but out of the three of us one had a lens that was better by far to the others so he was voted cameraman for the day; all the prints we had were taken from his negatives. We had already decided to buy new cameras in Hong Kong, when we got there.

However another five cents on the train got us back to Brooklyn and the short walk to the ship. It had been a cheap day out and a memorable one.

It would have been nice to have a diary[27] to refer to, but that was something I failed to do and have always regretted. During war time no one was supposed to keep a diary, but many did. Later, during the war, searches at the convoy assembly ports were carried out and any diaries were confiscated. The reason given was that any records falling into enemy hands would help the submarines to locate ships and convoys by giving them

---

[27] All my father's photos were dated which allowed him to write his travels in sequence. However, as he visited the same cities several times, I am not sure how he remembered what happened on which visit. Editor

clues of their movements.

Captains of merchant ships always had weighted bags in which to put code books and ship's papers, which were to be thrown overboard if they were apprehended by the enemy.

In New York we stocked up with fags and other essentials like toothpaste. I preferred English cigarettes but the American ones were so much cheaper, and one can get used to almost everything given a good reason.

From Brooklyn we sailed down the coast to Newport News, the American naval base, and then across to Norfolk (Virginia) where we loaded coal, much to my delight as I was getting fed up with night work.

While at Norfolk I had a chance to walk around the harbour before we sailed, and was lucky to see a goods train coming across the ferry from Newport. I stood six feet away and watched the train drive off the ferry and onto the rails ashore. I hadn't realised just how huge these engines were. It was twice the size of an English express loco, it was gigantic.

Once the coal was aboard we were off to Colon and the Panama Canal. We had changed the furnace doors to coal burning while at Norfolk and as we sailed I thought to myself, no night work for quite a while. I lay in my bunk with thoughts racing through my head, wondering what was in store for tomorrow and the future.

We stopped off Colon, standing by waiting for the dawn. In some aspects the dawns were as beautiful as the sunsets; in these regions the dawns had a wonderful calm and balmy atmosphere, cool and invigorating. With the spicy smell from the land, and just a hint of new cut grass, it was so unlike the usual daytime heat and humidity.

This time I didn't stay on deck as we sailed through the canal, the time was spent on the starting platform with the other engineers. We did get on deck for a while when we stopped for an hour at Gatun Lake waiting for the eastbound traffic to pass through. There was another stop at Balboa for an hour or two; I suppose the Captain was getting instructions from the owners via the ship's agent. No captain used the wireless telegraph now to radio information, as transmissions could so easily be picked up by the enemy.

We found other changes too. The temperature in the engine room had shot up another eight degrees whilst we were stopped. The ship was still sitting in the water and with the skylights closed and covered with sandbags, there was no cooling draught coming down the big ventilators. I therefore had an extra job of keeping the big ventilators turned to the wind at all times.

During war time the watertight door between the engine room and the tunnel, where the shaft from the engine goes through to the propeller, had to be kept shut at all times. Yet the bearings still had to be inspected at least once every watch, so this inspection was included in the taking over of the watch.

The door would be opened to allow the engineer to get through, and then closed by the other engineer. After the bearings had all been inspected the engineer rapped on the door with a hammer, then the door was opened allowing the engineer to come out, after which the door was immediately closed again. This was repeated at the takeover of every watch.

If the engine room telegraph gave two full quick rings

then that was the signal to get one's skates on for an emergency. Up to that time we hadn't had an emergency, but later on we did, and as it happened it was during my watch on the next voyage.

Since the third of September, while at sea the lifeboats were slung outboard, that is overhanging the sea ready to be dropped or launched at a moment's notice. During peacetime or in port they were slung inboard. With the lifeboats slung outboard there was a lot more space on the boat deck and a better view, however we only had the sea to watch as ships tended to avoid each other and keep away from land.

There were practically no submarines in the Indian Ocean, Pacific or South Atlantic during the first twelve months of the war, but there were German surface raiders. These were German or captured merchant ships mounted with hidden guns on the lookout for victims. While lounging on the boat deck, I always kept both eyes open.

Sundays and Wednesdays were special days for lunch and dinner. My favourite being beef olives followed by banana soufflé, but roast chicken or pork chops, maybe braised steak were also really enjoyed. There is an old saying 'At sea, a good cook is more important than a good captain.' I think we were lucky to have both.

Auckland came up again after an uneventful three weeks, during which we never saw land or another ship. Our hair was growing again after the shearing at Balboa, and soon we'd all been queuing up at the barber's chair again, and he would ask the same question, 'Who in God's name cut your hair last?'

We always replied, 'The same guy as last time.' I

wonder if he asked the same question of all his customers.

When we arrived at Auckland and Finished with Engines was rung down on the telegraph, we closed down two boilers and then came on deck. The first thing we saw was a sailing ship lying at anchor. One of the old quartermasters was gazing across, probably remembering bygone days when he sailed in such vessels. This one, he said, was a three masted barque.

I've learned since that this ship was called *Killoran*, built in 1933 at Troon in Ayrshire. She was a steel ship of one-thousand eight-hundred and seventeen tons, two-hundred and sixty-one feet six inches long, with a thirty-nine foot two inch beam, and registered at Mariehamn in the Baltic. She was originally built for the grain trade.

As she stood in the water she was a beautiful sight, just waiting for a fair wind to get her on her way. She may have had a cargo on board or passengers on a cruise, or maybe she was a rich man's toy. She sailed two days later, no one shouted to us below to tell us she was leaving. I would have loved to have seen her sails set free as she left, we were so near.

The following day the three of us, the Third, Fourth and I went ashore together. A rare day, as usually one of us would be aboard looking after the shop. That day however the Second was staying aboard and sent us off.

There was a fair at the end of the road. I didn't much care for fairs but it was a chance to stretch my legs, and it was more interesting than walking around the deck. I hoped that there would be no trouble, because trouble and punch-ups seemed to follow the Third and Fourth around when they were together.

Passing a shooting gallery, we thought it would be a bit of fun to decide who the best marksman between the three of us was. Then up strolled three American soldiers who suggested that they join in. I thought to myself, shades of Surabaya! Both the Third and Fourth had short fuses, but as they'd had nothing to drink yet I hoped that all would go well; although I didn't know how much the Yanks had had.

As it happened I had nothing to worry about, we won a dollar each. I got a maximum score, so I was pleased, the Third and Fourth were pleased to have won, there was no punch-up, and the Yanks were happy. Me, I was relieved to get back to the ship in one piece.

As we were in Auckland over the weekend we knew that we would be spending the next three weekends in New Zealand, and the next stop would be Lyttelton in five day's time. I don't know how our Captain managed it, probably he liked being in port at the weekends just as we did, but he did it every time.

On Friday we arrived at my favourite New Zealand port, Lyttelton, where a letter from Edith was waiting. The next weekend was spent in Wellington and the one after in Dunedin.

I was looking forward to my favourite part of the trip, up the east coast of the continent along the Great Barrier Reef, among the hundreds of small islands. I was hoping for calm sunny weather so that I'd be able to work on deck for the entire trip.

I'd been to Sydney before and I wasn't one to go drinking, also I had letters to write. So when the Third came along and asked me to take his night aboard, I was quite agreeable. I'd rather have a night ashore in

Singapore later and spend it playing billiards with the Second.

The Third and Fourth wished to visit a night club. I cannot remember the name of this club, something like The Ten Ten Club, but no matter, they were off. There were four altogether, the two young Quartermasters and the Third and Fourth. We had a run-down of the evening's entertainment at breakfast next morning.

This is how I remember it. The four were seated at a table and the floor show was about to begin, when a clumsy individual tripped over a chair leg bringing one of the Quartermasters to the floor. Now this Quartermaster was all of five foot five, and the guy who tripped was about six foot two. They had all had their full ration of drinks, the little fellow more than enough, so he was up and was going to make someone pay.

The Fourth, who was around six foot tall, told the little one to sit down, he would take care of things and proceeded to take his jacket off. However the clumsy one was with three mates, all well over six feet, and they approached the table apologising profusely. They told the waiter to renew all the drinks, asked if the little fellow was hurt, and apologised again before disappearing through a side door.

After breakfast the paperboy came aboard with the local daily newspapers. The headlines stood out 'Gangland killing in night club'. Someone had knocked on the door of the night club, and when the identifying flap in the door was opened, had fired a sawn-off shotgun through the aperture. It must have happened after our crowd left, as they said they'd heard nothing.

The faces of the men wanted by the police were on the

front page, they were the faces of the men our lads had their incident with. Our crew members reckoned that they may have had a very fortunate escape.

We stayed at Sydney longer than usual to have a gun platform and gun fitted; even so we never learned if there were any arrests as a the result of the shooting.

The platform was built on the poop deck, which was reinforced to take the extra weight. The gun was a four-inch calibre Japanese naval gun, built in 1917. We also inherited three Australian naval personnel to look after it and to train a gun crew from the deck officers. Nevertheless, we all hoped that there'd be no need to use it. Two of the Aussie gunners were Jack and Cyril, unfortunately the name of the third escapes me.

After the gun deck had been built and the gun mounted, we sailed north along my favourite seaway, from Sydney to Thursday Island between the coast and the Barrier Reef. Here was another chance to feast on the beauty of the scenery, the coral islands, the glassy sea in which swam the multicoloured sea snakes. Poisonous? Some of them were, but all were beautiful.

This was always a chance to work on the winches and there was enough work to do on them. There were fourteen winches and the windlass and we had a wee hoist for bringing up the bags of ash from the stokehold. We had all manner of spares for these winches; the Company was very generous in that respect and it was left to my discretion as to their use. All that mattered was that the winches were ready and in good repair when needed.

I had a helper whilst working on the winches. I called him Rangi, only because his name was so long that I could never remember it, but he didn't mind. He enjoyed his job out of the engine room. He was old, seventy years as I learned later, and he spoke English well which was why he was assigned to work with me in the first place

Rangi was a strange man, but he was always there wherever I worked and he was a wonderful help. As I lay on my back I only had to put out my hand to find the particular tool I needed placed there..

When we sailed from the USA, two of the deck crew didn't wish to sail any further with us. They were afraid of being torpedoed and wished to return to India right away. The American authorities weren't very sympathetic; they insisted the two men had to leave on the vessel on which they had arrived. By the time we had reached the Panama Canal they were both unconscious, with a fever and low heart rate.

The doctor came aboard, but couldn't say what was wrong. He travelled through the canal with them and at Balboa decided they would be safer in hospital, so to hospital they went. Enquiries were made when we reached Auckland, but they had made a rapid recovery as soon as our ship left. We never found out what was wrong with them, and indeed we heard nothing more of either of them.

However, Rangi told me that self hypnosis is quite easy and commonly practised in India. As he said there were many wonderful things in India and no one knows all.

While we were working Rangi asked me if I was married. I told him that, no I wasn't married but had a girl friend who I was hoping to marry when I had saved enough money. He told me that he had been married but his wife had died of cholera before they had any children. That was when he went to sea.

The ship was now his home, and when I asked him if he was looking forward to seeing India again, he told me that he would never see his homeland again. He didn't say why, so I never asked, but he gave me some advice. He told me that as soon as I had enough money, I should go home and marry my girl, have babies and stay at home. The sea was no life for a man with a wife and babies. He was adamant 'You will be married *Sahib*, this is very lucky ship. Family needs man.' Oddly enough the *City of Kimberley* finished the war unscathed.

Rangi never saw India again. A couple of days before we reached Columbo, he died peacefully in his sleep. He was a lovely old man and regarded very highly by everyone who knew him which was everyone on the ship. He wasn't buried at sea, his body was taken ashore and I believe cremated.

The trip up the east coast of Australia was, to my mind, the most enchanting part of our voyage. Of course there must be other parts of the East that compare, but the routes of the merchant ships are trade routes, different from the leisure cruises of the great liners. As a cruise I wasn't complaining, this was a great experience and I was being paid to enjoy it. But again, it would have been perfect if Edith had been with me, enjoying it as well.

Tomorrow we'd be in Victoria harbour, Hong Kong, and the winches were ready for operation. I always tried to have them ready a few days before they'd be needed.

We would be lying at anchor in the harbour and the cargo would be unloaded into barges by our own winches. Delay in getting the cargo unloaded could cost the Company thousands of pounds and everyone had to accept their responsibilities. Mine was to have those winches ready for when they were needed, and they must not break down.

Hong Kong, a romantic name: I was becoming used to these romantic places but I hadn't been there before and was looking forward to going ashore. We shut two boilers down, a good indication that we would be there some time. Then we learned that we would be there for three weeks, well over the Christmas and New Year period.

That night I leaned on the ship's rail. It was a black night, a half-moon shining, and stars twinkling overhead. The moon and stars reflected in the black water, glistening on the ripples, no noise at all except for the rhythmical bump of the circulating pump. I reflected on the fact, it was Christmas Day in two day's time, and then Boxing Day, the day that I first met Edith.

Hong Kong had a large open harbour, ships, large and small dotted about all over. Victoria Peak was right ahead, and on top was the hospital. The Peak was a small mountain overlooking the city, dotted with luxurious houses and bungalows, landscaped among the trees, and owned by the richest of the population. There were roads to these beautiful places, but the local folk used the funicular railway that ran from the town to the hospital.

The usual traders were aboard the *City* every day touting for business. The other lads were wearing their uniforms, and as here was the quickest and cheapest place to be kitted out, I decided to have one made up. I didn't do it on my own; luckily I had the Second in to help. In four days and three fittings I was wearing my new uniform. With the haggling it cost me seven pounds, and this included cap, cap badge, white top for the cap, and white cotton scarf.

I was surprised at the number of merchant navy officers in uniform, as prior to the third of September 1939 one rarely saw a MN officer in uniform. Certainly the officers on the *City* never went ashore in uniform before that date. However when passers-by saw young men walking about without uniforms they asked questions with their eyes, so it was much easier going ashore in uniform, especially in Commonwealth ports.

Nowadays one recognises Hong Kong by the high-rise buildings, offices and so forth on the shore line, but in 1939 none of these skyscrapers existed. Then it was the mysterious orient, very unlike the city appears today.

We were anchored in the bay, and during the day the cargo was unloaded by our own winches into lighters alongside. There was no night work here and this was more civilised, as we could get a good night's sleep.

Many of the local families lived on sampans, which were long, light boats, mostly oared over the stern but they could put up a sail if needed. Live chickens lived in a cage at one end of the sampan ready for the pot, and at dinner time there was a fireplace at the other end with cooking pots and pans. The owners only charged a few coppers for a ride ashore. If we wished to go ashore we hailed a sampan, like hailing a taxi, they would come to the gangway and we would step aboard. When we wished to return we did the same thing at the quayside.

The great problem was finding one's ship, there were so many to choose from and they looked very much alike. The fact that all the names had been blacked out on account of the war didn't help matters, but it made things very difficult.

I thought it very unfair to have Sikh police, they were all about six feet tall and the Chinese were so small. The police turbans accentuated the difference in height, and to see one of these policemen hurrying the little Chinese along by hitting them with their long canes didn't seem fair. The Sikhs certainly had no sympathy with any Chinese that dawdled.

We saw old women carrying huge loads. I wondered if they were delivering furniture as I saw one old lady, very wrinkled, trotting along with a long pole on her shoulder and a large armchair on each end. The chairs hung at the end of the poles bobbing up and down as she trotted along.

We also saw funeral processions with everyone dressed in white, the opposite of the custom in England, and there fireworks and joss sticks everywhere.

The Third and I bought our new cameras here, they were similar models with consecutive numbers, and were much superior to the Agfa. Our new cameras were half frame, that is, they took sixteen pictures on a one hundred and twenty film, which usually took eight pictures.

In fact this camera served me as a main camera for years, and I still have it. They cost us four pounds each and with duty of fifty percent, would cost us a further two pounds when we returned home.

I also bought a small carved camphor wood box, which I still have,[28] as well as a miniature ivory scull

---

[28] I inherited this box, which is beautifully carved, and it still retains a faint perfume of cedar wood. Editor

which had a small ring, so it could be attached to a watch albert. It was only half an inch across and a perfect likeness. I bought it when we visited an ivory carver's workshop, I couldn't afford anything bigger.

Shopping was very easy here. All the camera shops were in one street, leather goods in another and carved wooden boxes, including coffins in a third. The Second bought a big blanket chest for the equivalent of four pounds fifty. He had the pull to instruct the carpenter to box it up for him and cover it with canvas, so that it would arrive home in prime condition.

But the main occupation was walking and taking snaps. We had a wonderful subject as the place itself was so different to any other place we'd been ashore. We rode to the hospital on the funicular railway to visit a chappie, an engineer from another ship of our line, who had been injured and was waiting for a company ship to take him home.

There was a special lunch the following day, Christmas Day. The Captain had sent down a bottle of wine and another of whisky, the Chief Steward sent a bottle of port, but just as we were getting into the feast we heard a loud commotion outside. The Second got up and went out and we all followed. What-a-to-do.

The youngest of the Aussie gun crew, Jack, was as drunk as a skunk. He was drilling a bunch of terrified Chinese in the art of presenting arms. The Chinese had sticks, Jack had a .303 rifle fitted with a bayonet. We could see the poor Chinese shaking with fear and something had to be done. We tried talking to Jack that did no good, so all six of us rushed him, picked him up, and tied him in his bunk. He couldn't move a finger. We persuaded the Chinese to say nothing and to just carry on by telling them that if the Captain found out he'd order them off the ship. Jack had his Christmas dinner fed to him with a spoon as he lay trussed up like the turkey.

I was unfortunate. When the gong sounded for lunch I had been in the process of receiving a bottle of whisky from the Mess Boy that I'd asked him to get for me from the Steward so I could offer a drink to anyone who called in at my cabin. We were just outside Jack's cabin at the time, and I had handed the bottle to the senior Aussie, Cyril, asking him to look after it for me until after lunch. Unfortunately Jack had found it on one of the bunks and had drunk the whole bottle, my bottle.

After all the excitement had died down we resumed our lunch and enjoyed it, pleased that no one had been hurt. Jack's two mates had to look after their companion until he sobered up, but we heard nothing from Jack for quite a while. It cost me another bottle of whisky, as I needed a replacement to offer callers a drink over Christmas.

Although I don't think that anyone went ashore that day, Christmas Day was my day aboard and it was my turn to keep an eye on things in the engine room. Every half-hour I paid a visit down below to see that everything was as it should be. Reading and dozing passed the afternoon away until the gong sounded for dinner, and then we had another four course meal to demolish. Oddly enough in those days it was no problem. I had a great appetite, but then I was a growing lad.

After dinner I lay down to let my food settle, but as I was looking after things below I daren't risk going to sleep, so out came the pen and ink and I became interested in writing a letter or two.

Time passes quickly when writing, and about 7:00pm there was a knock on my cabin door. There was a party in the Quartermasters' cabin, and my presence was requested. I explained that I was on duty and would they please excuse me. However my four visitors insisted that I attend even though I was very loath to go to their sort of parties. These started with booze, carried on with booze and ended with booze, but they wouldn't take no for an answer. They picked me up and carried me along the corridor to the Quartermasters' cabin, and sat me on the top bunk.

The Quartermasters' cabin was furnished with two bunks, one over the other, a writing table with drawers, a large settee against the bulkhead and a washbasin and stand, with the usual book shelf on the wall. When I was dropped in the cabin there were ten of us, four on the settee, one on the table, three on the lower bunk, and two on the top bunk, including me. Present were the Third mate, four Quartermasters, three Aussies gunners, one apprentice and myself.

The party, which had started at 6:30pm, took the form of story-telling recounting the various adventures of the crew, a few drinks, a joke, another drink, more adventures, another round of drinks, and then more drinks. Every thirty minutes I had to climb down from the bunk, and walk across the bottles on the floor, (there were no cans then) however by 10:00pm there were so many bottles on the floor that it became quite easy to walk on them. Then down the metal ladders and catwalks to inspect the engine room and then clamber back to my seat on the top bunk for another rendering of the First

Noel.

Unfortunately I couldn't afford to get drunk, so I did my best to stay sober. As soon as a glass showed signs of being half-full, or what the pessimists thought was half-empty, it was immediately filled. No one asked what the recipient was drinking; his glass was filled from the nearest bottle which could have been beer, gin or whisky, or even rum.

Every time I visited the engine room I took the precaution of calling in to the toilet, it saved a double journey. I managed to get hold of another glass, keeping one for myself which I tried to use sparingly and another that I kept holding out to get filled up, but this one was emptied into someone else's, so it kept my consumption down. Even so it was a very easy way to get drunk.

While I thought I stayed sober, I may have been too drunk to notice. However, I never missed my half-hourly trip down those ladders and I was always capable of climbing to my seat on the top bunk without fail. We retired to our bunks at 2:00am knowing that we could lie in next morning.

Next morning, Boxing Day, a steam launch came alongside and the Padre of the Mission to Seamen wanted to know if anyone aboard would like a conducted tour of the island. Seven of us put our names down and were told that we would be picked up after lunch. The launch duly arrived and we trooped down the gangplank to be taken to the Seaman's Mission, me resplendent in my new uniform.

There we had a game of billiards whilst the Padre was organising things. After a short while we had at our disposal three taxis, the drivers of which had received instructions to take us to all the places of interest and to stop and start as requested. But, like Cinderella, we had to be back in four hours.

We had a wonderful afternoon, stopping at various places, such as Aberdeen with its population of boat people. Some of the elders had been born on a boat and had never stepped ashore in their lives. We called at the Repulse Bay Hotel, the most famous hotel on the island where we had a drink, as the old Quartermaster couldn't pass a pub.

It was here that the Canadians made their famous last stand against the Japanese before the fall of Hong Kong, where they were almost wiped out.

Our cameras were kept busy during the afternoon, and when we arrived back at the mission at six we all sat down to tea with the Padre and his wife. After tea five of us were left to our own devices, but the Padre and his wife were taking no chances with the morals of our two cadets. The men were left on their own, but the two lads went to the pictures with the Padre and his good wife, and were safely returned to the *City*.

It was dark now and the lights, neon signs and fireworks with jumping jacks being thrown everywhere, were a wonderful sight. It was Boxing Day, of course I thought of how much Edith would have enjoyed this.

The shops were a revelation, all lit up like Aladdin's caves. We went back to the old ivory carver's shop where I had bought the small skull earlier. There we had a longer look at the artist, and his work. We saw three balls, one inside the other, carved out of a solid piece of ivory, and rows of elephants, with six descending in size to half an inch tall. Unfortunately the carvings were too expensive for our pockets, and as is usual when consorting with old sailors and Australian naval types, we were drawn to a place of liquid refreshment. This time it was to the Army, Navy and Air Force Club down on the quay.

There was a concert in progress when we arrived and soon we were sat at a table with pint pots in our hands, joining in the revelry. As two of the five weren't members of the armed forces we were guests, and therefore were not allowed to buy drinks. We didn't object to this arrangement, we were on to a good thing, free beer for the night.

As it was Christmas time, a long way from home, everybody had someone to remember. The married men remembered their wives and families, their friends and relations, the single men thought of their girl-friends. Christmas carols were the favourite feature of the program and as the beer went down *Danny Boy* came up, and then as the Irish songs continued, even more joined in. And so it continued until 10.00 pm when we decided to call it a day and head for home.

The heavy beer had taken the legs of the Aussies, but it didn't affect the old man at all, he seemed impervious to alcohol. Me, I didn't like the heavy, flat beer they were drinking, and I had stopped drinking when the bitter ran out.

The three Aussies were well away, but with the Quartermaster's help we set out for the landing stage to find a boat to get us to the ship. I didn't know if we'd find it, it was so dark. The landing stage that we normally used was along by the town, a good walk from the Forces club, and as we didn't need a long walk we decided to find another one. This proved more difficult than we thought, but we stumbled on and found a wooden staging leading to the water.

We walked along this staging, on and on, until we started to wonder if we were on the right road. It was a black night, not a light anywhere. We stopped, straining our eyes, just trying to see anything. What we saw looked like submarines. We thought at the time that it wasn't the thing to leave submarines lying about like that, unattended, in wartime.

We looked again. They were subs, and we were walking over the decks of eight submarines. It didn't take us long to retrace our steps and we decided to walk along to our usual landing place, it would probably be safer. Eventually we arrived there.

Hailing a boat we thought that we'd made it, but we still had to find the ship in the dark, and while there were lights at the landing place there were none out on the water. We all piled into a small boat which had at least got a motor aboard. We were well crushed together as we moved over the dark water, keeping our eyes open trying to recognise the ship; those of us who were sober anyway.

There was usually a man on gangway duty but this was Christmas, so we moved from ship to ship asking, 'What ship?' We asked that question many, many times that night.

We were moving from ship to ship when suddenly a silent projectile passed us within six feet, the bow wave throwing us about like a cork, we just hung on and hoped. Our boatman saved the boat by turning into the wash, if he hadn't we could have been swamped.

The cruiser or destroyer ghosted past, silent except for the sound of the pumps. Jingle Bells was still going strong however. After asking the names from another half a dozen or so ships, we finally found our own, got the two carol singers up the gangway and dropped them on the floor of their cabins. They were home and could look after themselves now. The hatch cover adjacent to our cabins was covered with empty bottles; it looked as if somebody other than us had had a good party.

At breakfast the next morning the Third asked if I knew anybody out there. Apparently a party had come aboard looking for me, they'd brought all the booze with them and the empty bottles were still all over the deck. I asked him if they said who they were, were there any names mentioned. No they had come aboard and asked who the Fifth was, and had he served his time at Clarke Chapman's?

They were definitely looking for me, but I never found out who they were. Maybe it was John Henderson, or Bert Moderate, but Bert would have asked for me by name.

Bert was serving on the cruiser H. M. S. Cornwall which may have been the ship that almost ran us down, but the answer to this one, I'm afraid I will never know. Bert was killed with his ship a few years later.

Hong Kong was a wonderful place. We crossed the harbour on the ferry and visited Kowloon, a walk around the streets and a visit to the holy temple. We climbed about five hundred steps to get there and then had to come down those same steps afterwards. We were exhausted when we reached the street again. We tried to take photographs of everywhere we went, but became so engrossed that we forgot that we had our cameras with us.

We were walking back from the ferry when I was reminded by Cyril, one of the Australians, that I was in uniform and had to return salutes when they were given. I hadn't noticed anyone saluting me so I kept my eyes open. Sure enough a sailor came along and saluted. I returned the salute. Why I don't know, we don't salute in the Merchant Navy. The Aussies had an answer; they reckoned that the sailors couldn't tell the difference between the single gold rings on the two uniforms.

I believed differently. The difference of a 'v' on the MN's gold stripe could not be noticed readily, and it was simply safer to salute. As I didn't wish to embarrass anyone I always returned a salute.

I don't think that I would enjoy Hong Kong today in the same way as yesteryear. I was young then, everything was new, and as the saying goes, the world was my oyster. It was really romantic in 1939.

33. One way traffic, Kolambugan, 1940

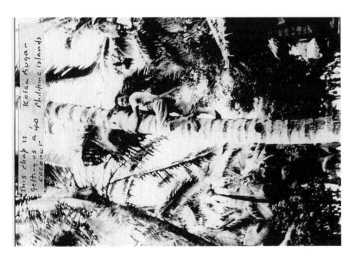

34. Climbing for coconuts

35. Manila, Philippine Islands, 1940

CHAPTER TWELVE
Hong Kong to Home
January – March 1940

After three weeks in Hong Kong, on the 10th of January, we sailed for Cebu, the capital of the island of the same name. We arrived three days later at a most fortunate time, it was festival time. That was the good news. The bad news was that we only staying overnight and we were leaving at 5:30am the following day, Sunday. As we were only staying a short while no boilers were shut down and watches were still being kept. This meant that I was free to go ashore until dinner, so I gathered up the Aussie gunners and we walked around the dock area.

Behind the docks was a village of Spanish design, we didn't go far as the village was so interesting. All the streets were decorated with flowers and fruit, and just as in this country we have the harvest festival, they had theirs in the streets. The cul-de-sacs were decorated on three sides and up to the eaves of the houses there were a mass of flowers. A large bonfire was ablaze, with men, women and children dancing around. We were invited to take part, but we wanted to see as much as possible in the one day we had.

The streets of trodden earth were lined with wooden houses with overhead balconies, and the streets were so narrow that two people on opposite balconies could lean over and shake hands. Through a hole in a fence we saw two sumo wrestlers practising. It was first time I'd seen one in the flesh, and there was plenty of that, they were huge.

The folk dancers and promenaders were all dressed in their Sunday best. The girls wore their bright dresses, while the married women were dressed in black to the ankles with white trimmings and lace mantillas on their heads. The men were dressed Spanish-style with tight trousers, red cummerbunds and fitted jackets. Everyone seemed to be in their best outfits and having a whale of a time.

On the way back to the ship we called at the dockside pub. In my inexperience it could have been a brothel but we only looked in. We had no money, not even enough to buy half a pint of lager between us, but the old lady behind the bar waved us in. We pulled out our empty pockets, thinking that she didn't understand. However she still put a pint each in front of us, intimating that they were on the house. It must have been on account of the festivities.

We regretted that we were to sail next morning as there was so much to see. The light was fading and we had no fast film. I have only one picture of Cebu, a snap of the pub from the ship.

We sat down to dinner, and as it was my night aboard I supposed that that was all I was going to see of the place.

We learned the next morning that we weren't sailing until Monday at 5.30 am. However, this was my day aboard and none of the engineers were going to swap, especially as I'd been ashore on Saturday, but as it was Sunday I could lean on the rail and watch events on the dock.

Boys some as young as six years old, and perhaps even

younger, sat on the dock and played guitars and mandolins. Money didn't appear to be problem with these kids as they had instruments for sale or barter. We found that bright-coloured clothes were great substitutes for cash, and a bright blue sports jacket, well past its best, was swapped for a mandolin. I had my mouth organ with me but a stringed instrument was something different with which to pass the time. Years later George Lamb, my future brother-in-law, accepted it.

After dinner everyone, with the exception of the Chief, the Second and me went ashore. I was busy writing letters and every half hour slipping down the ladders, but about 9.00am my wrists were getting tired and I wandered out on deck. The night was still and warm, the crickets were gently chirping. In contrast, with the noise and the lights flashing on and off, the pub seemed to be jumping.

I saw the Chief and the Second over by the rail. They'd taken their armchairs out on the deck and were enjoying the music. I went over to join them and we watched the merriment from the ship's rails. I don't know where the lads got the money for the booze, but it was flowing, one only had to listen. I found out later that the Chief Steward had funded them.

I must have looked rather wistful standing there by the rails because the Chief put his hand in his pocket and pushing a dollar note in my hand, told me to get over there and have a drink with the lads. I reminded him that I was looking after things down below, but he said that the Second would see to all that until I got back. I didn't need telling twice.

I ordered my beer; however the noise was terrific and I

knew that I wouldn't be able to stand it for any length of time. I finished my first pint and thought that I had time for another. It was quite a big dance floor so it took some time to get to the bar, and on the way over a commotion broke out. One of the local lads had taken offence when someone asked his girl for a dance, and had pulled a gun. Before he could do anything with it the Third and Fourth jumped on him, grabbed the gun, and handed it over to the old lady behind the bar.

Trouble always seemed to follow those two around, wherever they went. They told me later that they had free beer for the rest of the night.

After my second pint I thought that I'd better be getting back as the noise had really given me a bad headache. If we were sailing at 5:30am we'd have to be up at 4:00am. The Second would want to get to bed as he too would be on duty at 4:00am, so I left the party and made tracks for my bunk.

We sailed from Cebu on time, and you may not believe it, but the entire staff of the club was on the quayside waving us off.

We expected to dock at Kolambugan[29] about 5:00pm. As I was working nights I had the day off, but I would be on standby when we arrived, on duty at 6:00pm, and working at 8:00pm. I decided to have a few hours sleep before we got there.

As expected the Stand By sounded at 4:30pm and we came alongside a ramshackle timber jetty, stretching out into the sea. That night I completed the jobs that had

---

[29] Kolambugan is a municipality in the province of Lanao del Norte, Philippines and is located along the Panguil Bay facing Ozamiz City. Editor

been set out for me and retired to my bunk at 6:00am, to be awakened by the Aussies just before lunch.

After lunch we went ashore and found that Kolambugan was a village built around a saw mill. The mahogany trees in the forest surrounded the village, and these were cut and brought to Koolambugan to be sawn into planks, dressed and planed, then shipped all over the world. The loading place, to which we were tied up, was about ten foot wide with a narrow gauge railway stretching out along the jetty. It was about four to eight feet from the water, depending on the tide.

The saw mill was the only source of employment. There was however a school for the workers' children and a picture hall. Coconut palms lined the narrow streets; there was no paving only the packed earth, with a banana tree here and there. This was rather strange. I always thought that bananas grew pointing downwards, but the opposite is true, they point upwards. I had to wait twenty two years to find that out.

From the local people we found out that there were no sharks in this area, so there was the possibility of a swim whilst we were here. As we walked through the village we were kept busy answering the children's questions. We never found out why the children weren't in class, and why there were so many running around the village. Some walked alongside asking where we came from and where we were going to. One asked if we'd like a coconut. We were thirsty, and said yes we would.

The boy must only have been seven or eight years old but he seemed to walk up the tree, with this big machete on his belt. I was pretty good at climbing when young, but no way as good as those kids.

He threw three coconuts down, then came down and opened them. He was a real expert. The fluid wasn't milk as we'd supposed it would be, it was like still fruit juice, but coconut flavour. We were told that these weren't ripe and naturally there was very little coconut inside.

The local bus had no windows, probably it would have been too hot inside if it had, and it would never have passed an M.O.T. The tyres had no tread, it was running on the canvas, and have you ever seen a bus with bandages round the tyres? There were holes in the body work where the bus had scraped against the trees, and the mudguards and bumpers were tied on with wire. The driver just drove it as if it was quite normal; I suppose to him it was.

As we returned to the ship I didn't have my camera at the ready in time to catch the snap of the day A hundred feet from the beach a war canoe sped along, heading straight for the pier. It carried twenty men paddling whilst standing. With the prow of the boat being five feet tall we thought that they would never get underneath, but as the boat reached the pier, every man in turn went down on one knee and rose as he came from under. They must have really practised this manoeuvre to have been so expert.

I never thought to ask if there were other crews on the island and did they race these boats. However I saw them on TV quite recently, and yes, they do race other teams.

We loaded timber overnight. I was on duty and remembering Saigon, I muffled myself up against the mozzies, however here I wasn't troubled.

Before we sailed for Manila we had our swim but found it hard work. There was no gangway out so we dived off the ship's side and climbed back on board with the aid of a rope ladder. Once was enough. After swimming for ten minutes in water of eighty degrees and climbing up a rope ladder I was exhausted.

This was Thursday the 18th of January 1940 and we learned that we were on our way home via Colombo. We were only a couple of days at Manila, but there were letters waiting for us and we had letters to post. We didn't know which would reach England first, the letters or us, but we took the chance, it didn't matter if the letters followed us.

At this time we were still burning oil and I was working when in port. Colombo was the only place left to look for small presents to take home. Up to then all my efforts had been to save, but I would have to take back a small present or two. I managed to get some jewellery and a couple of very heavy black elephants[30] at Colombo and there was the carved box and ivory skull from Hong Kong.

We were only calling at Colombo to pick up anything available to take back to wartime Britain. During the war no ship returned to Britain with any empty cargo space and every Captain made sure that his oil tanks were full. Britain had no North Sea oil in 1939/1940, and all oil, petrol and diesel fuel had to come from abroad. The RAF, Navy and Army depended on it, it was vital to the

---

[30] As a very young child I recall these as a family of three elephants, which stood on the very top of the dresser in the dining room. The largest one fell off, hitting my mother as she passed, and the two largest were promptly consigned to the bin as too dangerous. They were very heavy and could have seriously injured her, never mind a small child. I have no idea where the smaller one went. Editor

343

war effort.

While burning oil abroad even our soot was saved, bagged up and brought home as a source of radium, which was short in wartime.

We stopped at Aden just to fill our oil tanks to the brim, and then sailed on our way through the Red Sea. It was about four days to Port Tewfik[31] where we put in to make arrangements to go through the Suez Canal.

I was looking forward to going through the canal, but I was to be disappointed as we went through at night. A great floodlight was fixed on the foredeck, pointing straight ahead it only lit up the canal and a yard or two of land on each side. As we slowly sailed on the Pilot kept the same amount of light on each bank ensuring that we kept in the centre of the canal. I had hoped to stay on deck as we went through, but the intensity of the floodlight destroyed my night sight. I couldn't see anything on either side so took to my bunk and woke at Port Said.

Altogether it took fifteen hours and twenty minutes to go through the Suez, a large portion of which was spent going through the lakes. The canal is built up of various lakes, as is the Panama, joined up by sections that have been dug out.

From Suez we went to Port Tewfik, then into the Little Bitter Lake, the Great Bitter Lake, Lake Timsah, Balah Lakes, and then the canal proper, with Port Said at the end. We were only at Port Said for an hour or so, and then off into the blue Mediterranean.

---

[31] Port Tewfik or Bur Tawfiq as it is also known, amongst other spellings, lies on the Red Sea whereas Port Said lies at the entrance to the Suez Canal on the Mediterranean. Editor

Did I say blue Mediterranean? Black it was. The clouds hung low, the rain fell in torrents, the wind was blowing a gale, and the waves heaved in all directions. It was not pleasant. The weather didn't improve until we reached Gibraltar where we were pleased to come to rest in a still harbour.

As we came into harbour the gun crew was taking the standby ammunition down to the magazine so I gave them a hand. The standby ammo is the ammunition ranged around the gun platform ready for use when needed, and has to be taken to a safe place while in port. It is the gun layer's responsibility to see that the gun is not loaded. As an extra precaution the gun is trained, or pointed, in a safe direction, for example out to sea.

At Gibraltar all the ships gathered together and the convoy was planned and formed. The respective captains were lectured, given their instructions, and expected to remember all they'd been told.

Convoys were formed of ships of approximately the same speed. The *City of Kimberley* with an economical speed of twelve knots would usually be in a ten knot convoy. On the occasion of this convoy to London, the *City* carried the Commodore who was in charge of the whole proceedings, that is the whole convoy, until it reached London.

While we were having breakfast one morning we heard a gun fired, and at lunch we heard the story. The gun layer of one of the ships had not unloaded his gun when they had entered port. A member of the crew, not the gun crew, had been examining the gun, running his hands over it, and thought, what's this? And then pulled - a four-inch shell went screaming overhead into the

Atlantic. An unfortunate gun layer had some explaining to do.

While in port no one was allowed ashore for security reasons, and we didn't know what was happening from day to day. We did know that we were going home and from our point of view that was everything.

After a few days things began to happen. Instead of taking things to pieces in the engine room, we were putting things together, a sure sign that we were getting ready to sail. The day came and the Stand By was rung down from the bridge bringing everyone to their post, just waiting for the next order. Everyone knew that the next stop was London.

Then the movements started, Slow Ahead, Stop, Slow Ahead, Stop and so on for fifteen minutes or so, always with a pause in between each ring, Slow Astern, Stop. Eventually the signal Full Ahead rang down and ten minutes later the double ring of Full Ahead.

Anyone on deck would be able to see the fifty or so ships getting into their allotted positions.

At this stage we got busy, changing from auxiliary to main condenser, the oil pump started for the turbine, feed pumps synchronised and the turbine started up. We were about ready. Whoever was on watch would go round the engine, feeling the temperatures, checking the water in the boilers, then when he was satisfied that everything was to his liking, he would accept the watch and be left on his own.

Until the convoy got itself sorted out and into the correct pattern, the engineer on watch would have a difficult hour. It took a long time to get the feed system correct and constant, a small adjustment on the port boiler, another on the other two. Once they were settled they would stay constant for half an hour or so.

The officer on the bridge had to keep in line with all the other ships and keep his station; if not, the Commodore would give him a rocket by signal.

In bad weather, fog, or even at night, keeping station is a difficult exercise. On the stern of each ship is an object like a witch's hat with a blue electric bulb inside. This shines a faint light on the water below and, beside the ship itself, is the only guide for the officer on the bridge of the following vessel. This and direct vision were the only aids to preventing collisions. Consequently one has to be on full alert at all times so as not to run into the ship in front.

If a ship was gaining on the others, the officer would ring the engineer on watch and ask him to reduce speed by one or two revs per minute, or if he was dropping behind, speed up by the necessary revs. In practice the officer would ring and just say, 'Up one', or 'Up two', 'Down one', or 'Down two'.

This is easy if there is a rev counter but, we didn't have such a refinement. We had to count the revolutions looking at the clock, turning the steam valve a minute amount, and then count again until we got it right. The engine normally ran at seventy-eight revs per minute, getting it to run at seventy-seven revs per minute was rather difficult.

It always reminded me of taking someone's pulse, indeed I suppose we were checking the engine's pulse. We found it very difficult at first to judge the engine revolutions but in time became quite expert, just listening to the engine.

Another awkward thing was that if the steam pressure dropped slightly the revolutions dropped as well, so a lot depended on the stokers. With oil fuel we didn't have that problem.

We sailed right out into the Atlantic, well away from land, hiding ourselves from prying eyes. It was quite a sight, row after row of ships just like us, sailing along together. It was not quite the same as being on one's own, but the powers that be said it was safer.

It was extremely important not to make any smoke in convoy. We had a lot of ships here, and one careless fireman or engineer could put us all in danger. Smoke from the funnel can be seen by a submarine even when the ship is hull down[32] and invisible.

As I said, there must have been forty to fifty ships in this convoy and our escort was two French destroyers. It was a new experience sailing along in the company of so many ships. Since the third of September we'd avoided other ships like the plague, one could never tell if they were friendly or not. But after an uneventful voyage we came within sight of the Lizard lighthouse.

It must have been about six bells of the afternoon watch, 3:00pm; the Second was in the engine room. I was on deck at the time enjoying the peculiar feeling of coming home after twelve months abroad. I never thought that I would come up the Channel with tears in my eyes. Standing beside me the Chief Engineer was enjoying it just as I was. It was a most peculiar feeling which I can't describe - it was a very emotional moment.

As we stood together the engine revs increased. 'Ah, the Second's opening her up,' the Chief said as he turned

---

[32] Below the hoizon. Editor

to me. 'Now we'll see what the old girl can do.'

The dispersal signal had been hoisted and every ship was on its own, hurrying to get into port as quickly as they could. The engines speeded up and we began to overtake the other ships one by one, soon all were behind us. The Chief stood with a little smile on his face, turning to look at every ship as we passed.

We passed sunken ships, our first evidence of the war, some with only their masts above water, others with the bridge high and dry.

As we neared Gravesend the Stand By sounded from below, time to get down there. As I slid down the rails, the turbine began to slow down and the telegraph spoke again. We slowed down to pick the Pilot up, and when he was safely aboard, we started again to be first into the Thames. We docked at Tilbury.

There were German raiders loose in the Indian Ocean and submarines in the north and south Atlantic. We had been very lucky not to have seen anything of the enemy, all we had to defend ourselves with was an old four-inch naval gun and three .303 rifles. Yes, we'd been very lucky.

The events of the last twelve months were behind us, and I think the only thought was getting home and seeing our loved ones. As soon as Finished with Engines was rung down on the telegraph, two of the boilers were closed and fires drawn, and all the preparations were made for at least a week's stay.

The Second was making a list of all jobs that needed doing. He'd already compiled lists of spares he needed during the last six months and given them to the Chief whose job it was to order them in.

The news went around that we were to be paid off the next day, so whose replacement would be the first to arrive? Most couldn't go on leave until their replacement arrived. Not so the Fifth. He's of less importance; that is, the work he does is necessary but not as important as that of the other engineers.

The following day, after lunch, I was leaning on the rail looking at the filthy water below, when the Chief came alongside. Resting his arms on the rail he said, 'Fiver, do you think that you could look after the engine room?'

I turned to him and said, 'Chief, I really hadn't considered it, I've only been aboard twelve months.'

He said, 'That wasn't the question I asked. Could you look after the engine room?'

I replied, 'I'm sure I could, Chief.'

He said, 'That's better my lad, because when you come back off leave you'll be coming back as Fourth. Well done. The Second and you will be able to go on leave in the morning, so you'd better get packing.'

I was working that night until 6.00am, so I missed breakfast and after making arrangements with the Second, I slept until 10:00am. I was asleep when the Customs Officer called. He saw me asleep and apologised saying he would call later, but I was awake now so asked him to carry on. He asked me if I had anything to declare, there was only my camera, which I showed him. He apologised again for waking me, and as he left told me to take anything I thought could be dutiable to the saloon when I got up.

After an early lunch with the Second, I visited the saloon to clear things with the customs. I'd already packed my bags so they could be checked and cleared, and there were only the presents and the camera. Fifty percent duty on the camera cost me two pounds, the box and everything else were duty free. I came out better than the Third.

He tried to tell the customs that he'd had his camera over twelve months. What a wally! Our cameras were identical, even the numbers were consecutive. He lost the camera, three times the duty and three bottles of whisky to keep it quiet. It was only the whisky that saved him from being charged.

We were paid off that morning and so as soon as we were cleared by the customs, the Second and I made tracks for the 11:30am train from King's Cross Station. He was off to Middlesborough, me to Newcastle Central. We managed to get there in time due to a kindly old man who knew all the short cuts on the underground. He insisted he saw us on the train, possibly because we were both in uniform, even though he wasn't leaving from King's Cross.

I arrived at Central Station at 6:30am. I didn't have much time to catch Edith before she reached work because she started at 7:30am. I put my cases in the left luggage and ran for the tram. When I offered the fare, I was told by the conductress that she didn't take money from strange men, there was a smile on her face but apparently service personnel travelled free on the trams.

I was hopping up and down on my seat trying to urge that tram to speed up, but I reached Edith's workplace before she did. Her face lit up like a beacon. 'Come on lass,' I said. 'You're not going to work today.' Taking her arm I steered her towards home.

Back home we were met by Edith's mother, 'What are you doing back here?' she said.

Edith didn't reply, but I told her mother that Edith wasn't going in to work today. She was having the day off and over the next two weeks she'd be having a few more days off. Edith had already spoken to her employer and he had told her that she had his permission. I think that her mother was thinking of passing out. She may have done so if she thought that we would sympathise.

I had managed to get a few presents together. While my sisters shared the necklaces and bracelets, Mam had an embroidered cloth from Hong Kong; however Dad was unfortunate. I bought him some duty-frees but fags were hard to get in the UK and he had given up smoking, so I offered him the ivory skull to hang on his watch chain. He smilingly declined, saying that he would look like that some day and he didn't want to be reminded of the fact.

Edith took a number of days off during the next two weeks, but her mother never complained. I made Edith's wages up at the end of the week, so no one was out of pocket. After all, Edith still had to live at home after I'd returned to sea.

Our first day was a busy one. We opened our first bank account; I wanted to put both of our names on that account, but Edith insisted that it should go in my name only. After we were married, that was a different matter. Next we had to collect my ration books. These were the days of the so-called phoney war with the only action taking place at sea. Edith knew all about ration books, gas masks, and all the paraphernalia of wartime Britain.

The following day we met in town, and became

officially engaged. Oh yes, we did everything right, I even asked her dad for her hand in marriage. He was delighted, not so Edith's mother, she was going to lose Edith's wages and her housemaid and cook.

We became officially engaged on the 16th of March, 1940. We bought the ring at Summerfield's in Newcastle, and Edith bought me a watch to mark the occasion.

The next day, Sunday, we spent at my home in Low Fell, and I the evening we went to church together. I can't remember which church, probably Christ Church where I was confirmed at the age of seventeen years. Edith enjoyed being escorted by me in my uniform, although she said she was embarrassed when sailors saluted me as they passed. Quietly, I think she got quite a kick out of it.

Edith couldn't have too much time off work; she had to have her job when I went back after my leave. Edith took as much time off as her boss would allow, and he was quite generous understanding our position. But we had the evenings together, during which we walked and visited mutual friends, and Saturdays and Sundays were special.

Easter fell early in 1940 and we spent Easter Monday at Walkworth, a seaside resort which Edith loved so much. We walked along the river bank and watched the sea from the sand dunes. We took a picnic lunch and tea, very romantic as well as economical - Edith's words. We had a lovely time together.

We caught the bus back to Newcastle at 6:20pm and attended the Paramount cinema[33], to see *The Stars Look Down*. In those days the picture house was every courting

---

[33] The Paramount was renamed the Odeon, but this has since been demolished. Editor

couple's dream. Two seats in the back row for a kiss and a cuddle was heaven, and in those far-off days it only cost the equivalent of two and a half new pence each.

The second week was spent in similar fashion as the first, visiting our friends, cinemas and theatres, and walking. On occasions we visited our favourite cafe in Newcastle, Dickens Tea Rooms. No way could we have afforded dinner out, we were like the proverbial church mice and our pockets were very thin.

After tea one day we walked along to the Queen's Theatre where we stood in the queue waiting for the next performance. The queue moved very slowly, it was tiring standing, and were just about to move off when the commissionaire came alongside and whispered in my ear, 'Wait two or three minutes chum, then saunter down to the side door and see me inside.'

Edith and I did just that, and the doorman was waiting. 'Can't see a laddie in uniform standing outside with that lot,' he said. He'd found us two seats in the back row - he must have remembered his own courting days.

The following day I would need to entrain for Liverpool, but next time I came home it would be to be married. We had enjoyed our holiday in the way we wished, we'd had a lot of time together, we'd visited our friends and made a lot of plans for the future.

It was a tearful goodbye, but I knew that my father would see that Edith fared well until I returned, he had promised. We would rather have married there and then, but finances wouldn't permit. As I was going back as Fourth Engineer the money would be better, and perhaps in another six months we could afford to get married. Not to have a large wedding but at least to get married and be together.

As I thought of the promotion the old butterflies started to flutter, just as they had twelve months ago. I hoped that whoever had been watching over me would continue to do so.

I talked it through with myself and decided that I'd gone through this before; after all, I was going back as Fourth, and I'd been promoted after only twelve months. I'd known men at Clarke Chapman's who had been Fifth Engineers for three years without being promoted. I must have done something right, why not again?

Edith and I had talked long and seriously during the last two weeks. We'd had a good time together, but things were spoiled to a certain degree by her mother's attitude.

I'm glad that I was blessed with the parents I had. I couldn't understand Edith's parents. Edith did most of the heavy work at home, and she wasn't allowed out at night until she had completed the housework. Her mother had trouble with her hands, although I do think she traded on the fact. We were both hoping that we would be able to marry next time.

36. Rough Weather 1, Pacific Ocean, 1940

37. Rough Weather 2, Pacific Ocean, 1940

CHAPTER THIRTEEN
Liverpool to New Zealand
March 1940 – June 1940

The next morning I caught the train to Liverpool. It was a lonely journey. I was informed that the ship was lying at Huskisson dock, but I'd been caught out before and left my bags at Lime Street Station. Then I called at the dock only to be informed that the *City* had sailed for Glasgow. I had been told to join the ship in Liverpool and was rather annoyed that she wasn't there, so I decided to visit the shipping office. Why should I pay the extra fare to Glasgow? I was to learn another lesson when I found the place.

At the office I complained that I'd been told to join my ship here, now I had to get to Glasgow, what could they do about it? I was asked if I'd received a telegram. I was told that I would have received a telegram in a couple of day with all information and a rail warrant to cover the fare. In my ignorance I had done myself out of two days leave, what a wally!

I told him that I didn't have enough money to get to Glasgow so he was obliged to make out a warrant, which he handed over with bad grace. All he had to do was cancel the other one. After all I'd already paid half of the fare and I honestly did not have the fare to Glasgow. I'd expected to meet my ship at Liverpool and I hardly had enough to buy something to eat. For the record, I left Liverpool on the 30th March 1940, and caught the train

357

to Glasgow.

It was a terrible journey. I was wearing my uniform but had no chance to shave. I must have looked as if I was trying to grow a beard, but my shaving gear was in the bottom of my big case. I'd been travelling all day and now all night, and I felt scruffy and hungry. We didn't stop very often, and when we did the only places open were the forces' canteens.

Twice I hopped out to get something to eat. The first time I stood in a queue and had to leave in a hurry as the train began to pull out; the next time I managed a couple of sandwiches and a cup of tea. The third time when I reached the counter I asked for a cup of tea and a bun and was told right away, 'We only serve members of the armed forces.'

I knew that we were classed as civilians, but I didn't think that anyone would take it so literally. But a number sympathised with me and the sailor behind me gave her a real dressing down. He asked for tea and sandwiches, and then presented me with them at the counter, refusing to accept any payment. I was extremely grateful, I was starving. I hadn't expected my journey to last so long.

I arrived at Glasgow about 7:30am; I was cold and still hungry. The shops were all shut, and I was as miserable as I could be. I didn't know where the ship was, and the shipping office wouldn't be open yet. I had a cup of tea at the station although there was nothing to eat.

As I drank my tea I thought things over, and after careful deliberations decided to try to find the *City*. The shipping office probably didn't open until 9:00am and it was now only 8:00am. If I was unsuccessful I could contact the office at 9:00am. I took the tram to the top of the dock road and decided to work backwards. I'd learned my lesson well, and my luggage was still at the station.

I called at the first dock that I came to, asking if the *City of Kimberley* was there. The reply came, 'Sorry sir, I'm not allowed to give out information of that nature.' I told him that I was supposed to join my ship here and that I knew it was here, I just wanted to know which dock. But he still wasn't helping. I tried three more docks, with the same result.

I boarded the tram and made my way to the next dock, but the thought arose that the ship may have been in one of the docks I'd already visited. I began to wonder how many docks there were in Glasgow.

When I reached the next dock I was really down, and asked the gateman if he minded me sitting in his office for a while. While sitting I told him of my movements during the last twenty four hours and asked him a favour. Would he phone the shipping office, which would now be open, and ask them if he was allowed to tell me?

He spoke into the telephone, explained the situation, listened, and then told me that the dock I wanted was York Hill Quay. I thanked him, took the next tram and walked back to the dock, thankful that I'd left my cases at the station. I found the ship at last and was ready to fall into my bunk.

As I climbed to the deck the first person I saw was Cyril, he looked at me and wanted to know what had happened. I must have looked a mess, I felt like one. 'Nothing has happened,' I said, 'you know I always look like this. Do me a favour, I haven't arrived yet, I'm going to get my head down.'

He gave me a good looking-over and asked me where

my bags were, I told him they were still at the station. 'Give me the tickets, Jack and I will pick your bags up.' he said, 'You go and get into your bunk.'

I thanked him and made my way along the corridor and, just in time, remembered that I had a new cabin. As I opened the door I noticed right away that the cabin had been redecorated; instead of the red upholstery there was a royal blue settee, with the gold feathers of the Prince of Wales. I had a new job, a new cabin and now a new decor. I flopped out on the bunk, and when I woke someone had placed my bags in the centre of my cabin without waking me. What it is to have good friends.

When I awoke about 10:30am, the first thing I wanted was a good wash and shave. So it was round to the mess-room to see Raj who welcomed me back. Whilst waiting for the water I changed into my patrol suit and elastic sided boots. Raj wasn't long with the water. 'Ah, I see you found right cabin. *Cha Sahib*, hot water *Sahib*, OK?'

After a wash and shave and the two hour kip, I felt much better and descended into the depths below to find the Second. I didn't find the Second, but I did find the new Third and Fifth. I've long forgotten the Third's name, only that he was Australian and big, about six feet two. The new Fifth was Tony Mulholland, he was Irish from County Cork and a wonderful story teller he was.

The previous Fourth wasn't available when I left the ship in London, so I wasn't able to say goodbye and thank him for all the help he'd given me. I had thought, wrongly as it turned out, that the Third and Fourth were coming back. The Fourth had left the ship to sit his exam for his Second's ticket, the Third for his Chief's. I was sorry to have missed them both.

But the new lads and I introduced ourselves and now instead of two Scots, two English and a Welshman; we had two English, one Scot, one Irishman and an Australian. Still a good mixture I think, although I never found out why a man from southern Ireland with a wife, a business and two children should want to go to sea in an English ship during wartime.

The Second hadn't arrived back from leave. He knew the ropes and waited for his telegram, so he had two extra days holiday at home.

While we were at Glasgow I broached the idea of Edith coming up on a visit, she always said that she'd love to see over the ship. I'd seen the Captain, who would arrange permission to enter the dock and accommodation on board, but her mother vetoed the idea unless she was accompanied. My mother was consulted and was interested, but somehow it all fell through so Edith never saw the City.

While we were loading at York Hill Quay the entertainment was of a high order, our cargo being whisky. Nowadays it would be packed in big steel containers, but then the whisky went into the hold in cases. There were thirty or forty cases on a big platform lifted by slings at each corner. The cases were individually stacked by the dockers and there were quite a number of breakages down below. One could get drunk from the fumes emanating from the hold, and at frequent intervals two or three dockers were lifted from the hold in nets and laid out on the dock to sober up. They were a very happy set of dockers who really enjoyed their work.

What amazed me was the number of different brands of whisky, there were well over seventy, and I only saw part of the loading. Most of the time loading was taking place I was working in the engine room and a new Fiver was attending to the winches. I don't know how many bottles we had aboard, or even cases, but we learned later that the cargo was worth a million pounds. I'm sure every Scotsman's heart was with us when we sailed. The vision of all that lovely stuff lying at the bottom of the sea would have sorely wounded them.

The cargo was stowed, hatches closed, and three days later on Wednesday 3rd of April we signed articles ready to sail the following day.

While in Glasgow I'd spent nearly all of my time aboard the ship, only leaving once to go to the pictures and once for a trip to Glasgow's Rouken Glen, a local park. There was a letter box near the dock so there was no necessity to go far to post our letters. I had no wish to explore Glasgow. As we were sailing during the morning watch, which was mine, I think the nervous tension kept my thoughts on the start of the voyage.

For the last twenty four hours the engine had been warming through, steam hissing at every drain cock and around the piston rods, but now the hissing had stopped and we were ready to go. However, we had to wait another day. Our Navy had located an enemy sub just north of Ireland, on our route, so we were advised to sail on Friday. The elder seamen didn't like it, to them sailing on a Friday was worse than unlucky, it was suicidal, but we sailed on Friday the 5th of April 1940. As I mentioned previously, we had a new Fourth (me), a new Third, and a new Fifth as well as a new Carpenter and two new Wireless Operators because in wartime the radio had to be manned twenty four hours a day.

Friday morning the Stand By was rung down and soon we were manoeuvring out of the dock and into the Clyde, moving down to the sea and the start of our journey. This time the Second didn't ask me to pop up and see where we were, he asked the new Fifth.

I was now a senior partner, unproven. As the Pilot was dropped, the turbine was cut in and running, the condensers were changed over, and we'd received the double ring on the telegraph. I was on my own. The Second did have a word before he went on deck, 'You'll be OK Fiver, er sorry, Fourth, I know just how you feel.' I was left alone with the *Tail Wallah* walking around oiling the engine.

The *Tail Wallah* or 'oil man', plied his oil can to every bearing, and it was the duty of the watch keeper to ensure that he did so regularly and correctly. You had to learn to drop oil from the oilcan into a moving one inch-square box, but only as it was moving away from the can to ensure that the oil reached the right place.

As the other engineers disappeared up the ladders the butterflies started fluttering inside, but not as they did twelve months ago when I first joined the ship. Now I was alone, and in charge of the engine room of a six thousand ton cargo liner with a cargo of a million pounds. And oddly enough I was at home there; the Sunday morning watches with the Second had given me more confidence than I had realised. I was beginning to like this new job.

I was sorry not to have been able to say goodbye to the previous Third and Fourth, but it was too late now. I thanked them both in my mind for what they had taught me and silently wished them luck.

So now I had other things to learn. As Fourth Engineer I had different responsibilities - instead of looking after the winches I was responsible for the pumps. I had to work on them and overhaul them when we were in port, and in a ship there are numerous pumps doing different sorts of work.

On the *City* there were two circulating pumps, one centrifugal and one reciprocating, three boiler feed pumps, twin oil feed pumps, a turbine-lubricating pump, and three pumps for taking on board fuel oil, filling the settling tank and moving oil from one tank to another. Then there's the air pump, a deck water pump, and two bilge pumps. So I had quite an assortment to look after.

I had the morning watch which was 8:00am to 12 noon and the evening watch 8:00pm to 12 midnight. These are traditionally the Chief's watches. He was responsible for the running of them and if anything went wrong we were both in trouble. The other engineers were certificated, I wasn't. They could hang me but they couldn't take my ticket from me, I didn't have one. I learnt too that normally eight to twelve bells were four hours, but not in my case, I had five hours to do.

At 9:30am every day the telephone rang from the bridge, a signal to synchronise the clocks on the bridge with ours in the engine room. The difference in time sailing westwards meant that the clocks went back half an hour each day, so my watch lasted four and a half hours. Then the Third Engineer came on duty at 12 noon; with lunch at 12:30pm I was down there whilst he had lunch which was another half an hour, making my watch five hours instead of four. Still, if you can't stand a laugh you shouldn't have joined.

You might say that since the clocks go back when one sails west, then when one sails east that should put things right. The point was that we very rarely sailed east, and if we did the clock change took place during the Second's early watch from 4:00am to 8:00am.

While on watch there was everything to look out for. Steam pressure was important because if this was allowed to fall, revolutions dropped, and then the officer on the bridge would complain that he couldn't keep station in the convoy. Every time I walked past the boilers it became a habit to glance up at the gauges to see if the water level was OK.

There was sometimes a note in the log book, 'Do not pump bilges clear until six bells.' This was to ensure that the ship was well away from land as pumping bilges leaves a residue of oil on the water. Near land we only pumped out some of the bilge-water, without oil floating on top, in this way the oil stayed behind in the bilges.

Half an hour before the end of the watch I went around and took the temperatures, checking the water in the hotwell, the sea temperature and then the dials, steam pressure, vacuum, boiler fan mercury level, and so forth. Jotting them down in the log book, and then with a last look at everything at 11:45pm, I would ring one bell to remind the Third that he was due to take over the watch. He came down the ladders, sliding down the handrails, elbows locked, and the takeover was carried through.

As I reached the deck the cold wind would strike through my saturated boiler suit, underneath I would only be wearing a vest and underpants, and it was often cold up on deck. The sea was rough, the ship heaving and rolling, it felt more noticeable up on deck than it did down below.

I was pleased that I had joined the Merchant Navy rather than the royal counterpart. Our escorts, the little corvettes, were bobbing about like corks and the destroyer astern was going through the waves with water breaking over her bows continually. However, I had another half hour to do and as soon as one bell sounded at 12:30pm I slid down into the warm again while the Third had lunch.

During that half hour I totted up all the entries and divided by six, to take an average of the readings for the last twenty four hours. When the Third came down to continue his watch I took the log and handed it in to the Chief.

At 13.00pm the Third and I changed places, he came back down from lunch and I headed for mine. The Second was usually still sitting there having a last cup of tea, so while eating my lunch we discussed any matter that either of us wanted to raise. I had a good teacher in the art of watch keeping. He impressed on me to be my own man, to make my own mind up and once it was made up, stick to it, and certainly not to let someone else make it up for me.

One occasion, much later, when I was taking over the watch from him one of the small end bearings was over heated. He told me it was cooling down, had been for twenty minutes and it would be OK very shortly. I didn't know if he was testing me or not, so I decided to play safe. I told him that as I'd only been down a few minutes I couldn't form an opinion on the matter, and that I'd wait a while and see how it progressed. After thirty minutes I decided that it was cooling down and accepted the watch.

The Second wasn't too pleased to be kept down an extra half hour; he wasn't testing me, but after all it was he who had taught me.

One thing I noticed when I joined the ship, no one cracked jokes in the engine room, at least not while the ship was on watch stations. Everyone was dead serious. I supposed that one couldn't afford to make even one mistake, concentration was everything and concentrating is tiring. The watch only lasted four hours but that was long enough. The watch keeper was on his feet every minute of those four hours, with the temperature often one hundred degrees. In the tropics this could be one hundred and twenty degrees with the humidity in the nineties.

We had a *chatti* hanging under the big ventilator that was bringing the cool air down into the engine room. This *chatti* was a large, unglazed earthenware bottle containing about a gallon of water, and as it was porous the constant evaporation kept the contents cool. This bottle was our life saver, keeping us refreshed. When it was half empty the *Cassop* would top it up so that we always had a cool drink. Of course, there were times when the wind was behind us and the sun really hot, then even the water in the *chatti* would be warm.

The bad weather continued, for which we gave thanks as heavy weather kept the U-boats down. We didn't mind this weather across the Atlantic and our ship could cope with this. It usually took us nine days to cross the Atlantic to New York, but because we were in convoy and could only steam as fast as the slowest ship this time we would take longer. We reached New York in eleven days with no sign of enemy action, and I suppose everyone heaved sighs of relief.

No one, in my hearing at least, had admitted to being afraid. Indeed at that time all of them appeared to be in the same frame of mind that they had been in during the last twelve months. Although I guess that we all would have thought differently if the convoy had been attacked and ships sunk.

We sailed up the Hudson River and passed the Statue of Liberty to a berth at Staten Island, not in Brooklyn as before. In those days it took a week to discharge our cargo, and the whisky came out of the hold with the same aplomb as it went in at Glasgow.

Tony informed us that he had an elder brother living in New York and could we look him up?

Tony rang his brother, who lived in the Bronx, a suburb of New York, and arranged to call on the Saturday. None of us had had much experience of the city, except for the famous Broadway, but that Saturday afternoon we set out to find this place.

Clad in our Sunday-best we caught the ferry to Manhattan then the underground to the appropriate station looking for the house, or flat as it turned out to be. As the four of us walked the streets we envisaged being mugged at every corner, believe me it was like an American gangster film. We didn't like this district one little bit. When we found the door and pressed the bell, the door opened and we found ourselves in a little palace. It didn't belong to the mean streets outside.

There were introductions, followed by drinks, then steak, fried tomatoes and chips. The walk-in fridge was the size of our larder at home, stacked up with grub, bottles of beer and lager. His wife had asked a couple of friends in who wanted to meet Tony. We had a great night and with thanks to a gigantic radiogram, music and dance as well as conversation. The two friends left at midnight, and at two in the morning we thought we had better to be getting back to the ship. Only to be told it was impossible, there was no ferry until 5:00am.

However our host and hostess were able to cope. We were bedded down for the night with mattresses and blankets and awakened at 5:30am to bacon and eggs all round, with toast and coffee. We queued up for the bathroom, and after goodbyes and sincere thanks to our hosts, we hurried off to the ferry to get back to the ship in time to get changed and down to work for 7:00am.

Tony's brother was the manager of a food store, a big one in Manhattan, and by the look of his flat and life-style he was doing quite well for himself. They were a very warm-hearted generous couple, and that night was special.

Tony came from County Cork, a small village called Ballyhornan, where he and his wife ran a small cafe with B&B. He never volunteered any reason as to why he'd left home and taken a job at sea, and no one pressed him to do so, that was his own personal business. He told me that if ever I was in Ireland I could have a free holiday with him and his family, and 'Don't forget to bring your wife,' he said.

After all the whisky had been unloaded, we moved over the water from Staten Island to a wharf in Manhattan, where the passenger liners berth. Here we loaded cargo for Australia and New Zealand. It was while we were tied up there that the Chief knocked on my cabin door, it was my night aboard and I was lying on the settee reading.

He didn't look very happy, and said, 'Will you run ashore and get me some Aspros, but they must be Aspros.' I asked him if he was trying to get me into trouble as it was my night aboard. It raised a little smile.

'Sure I'll go Chief, right now,' I said. I walked ashore, and spent two hours searching Manhattan for Aspros until I eventually found a drug store which stocked them. But the Chief was like Old King Cole, a dear old soul. When I got the Aspros back to him, his headache had disappeared and he'd forgotten he'd sent me.

After we'd finished loading we gladly sailed for Panama, it was cold in New York. We were looking forward to a little sunshine and as we sailed south we could feel it getting warmer every day.

When on watch the Fourth's work, compared to that of the Fifth, was much less physical. Though it wasn't boring to me yet, I could see that in time it might get boring to some extent. As I have said before, the 8:00pm to midnight watch is traditionally the Chief's watch, so every now and again it was no surprise to see him descending the ladders for a look around during the watch. He'd come down, ask if everything was all right, and then with a, 'Goodnight, Fourth,' he'd return to his cabin.

Maybe he was a little unsure about the new boy as he did this quite often during the first month. I think that I would have done so too, if the positions had been reversed. After all, before I was Fifth, I'd never been to sea, and now after only twelve months I was in charge of the lot. No, I think that if I'd been the Chief, I'd never have left the engine room.

But something always has to happen, and it did. Everything was going along fine when I heard a loud crack and the generator slowed down, and then stopped. Of course all the lights went out, there was no emergency lighting, but we did carry a torch on our belts. The generator also fed the field coils of the turbine generator, so when the current was cut off the turbine began to race and then cut out. I dashed to cut the steam off to the generator, however without lights everything was in darkness, and it was awkward holding a torch and operating steam valves at the same time.

The next thing to do was to start the circulating pump for the auxiliary condenser and the auxiliary oil pump for the turbine, and then change over from main to auxiliary condenser. After which the boiler water pre-heater had to be switched and therefore the boiler feed pumps had to be de-synchronised. After all this, I had to find out what had gone wrong with the generator.

It was at this point that the Chief came down, perhaps he'd been reading when the lights went out or he may have noticed the beat of the engine had changed. He came rushing down the ladders shouting, 'What's up?'

I told him that I thought it was the governor on the generator, and that I'd heard something hit the side of the ship and was just off to look for it. Torch in hand, and not a bead of light other than this, I made my way across the engine room with the Chief behind, asking if I'd done this and done that. I replied yes to all his queries as I clambered down into the bilges, which fortunately were all pumped and dry. With luck I found the pin within a few minutes, and after getting a new split pin and washer I soon had the lights on again. I suggested to the Chief that since I'd had no time to contact the bridge to let them know what was going on he might do that, and at the same time inform them that they would have full speed within twenty minutes.

Now everything that I'd done had to be reversed, but I had the Chief helping and we had lights. The turbine was started up, condensers changed over, pumps synchronised again and so back to normal. A quick look round to check water levels in the boilers, a feel all round the engine, then over to the log book to enter all particulars. After I'd finished writing the Chief had a good look at the log, walked round the engine room, said 'Goodnight Fourth,' and disappeared up the ladders.

I think that he was satisfied that I could handle the job because after that he never came down again during the night watch. I wondered if he was accustomed to staying awake until midnight, just in case. I was surprised that I was able to do everything by instinct, as at no time did I have to think of what to do next. I put this down to the Second's training over the last twelve months. Another result of this incident was that the butterflies in my tum never made another appearance.

I liked the new routine, working from 8.00am till noon, a leisurely lunch at 12:30pm, every afternoon off and dinner at 4:30pm, and then work again from 8:00pm until midnight. When the Third took over it was a pleasant moment. After being on watch for four hours in hot conditions, coming up on deck into the balmy evening air was an experience in itself.

Some nights with a moon, or even only the stars, one could see their reflections shining on the ripples and the white bow wave tumbling past. The bows being bluff didn't cut through the water, rather just pushed it aside to tumble over itself, until it joined the wake behind. The beauty of such a night was unforgettable.

However to fully appreciate such a night, one had to forget that out there enjoying the same experience as ones self were enemy submarines on the surface, charging their batteries or silently watching, waiting for a victim.

My first job after the evening watch was to attend to the inner man, a cup of tea for myself and one to take down to the Third. Then it was into my bunk, sometimes to read for a while, sometimes to add to a letter for Edith or Mum and Dad. It was easy to sleep with the slow roll of the ship and the gentle rhythm of the ship's heart beating below so unlike the vibrations of a diesel engine, these supplied all the sleeping tablets anyone would need.

The likelihood of anything happening to the *City of Kimberley* never entered our heads, but I speak for myself. Probably like all kids I had had so many narrow squeaks in the past I thought myself immortal. Morbid thoughts never disturbed me, I really believed that I would save enough money to marry Edith and live happily ever after. I could always sleep like a log from 1:00am to 7:00am, and an hour or two during the afternoon.

But one thing that always woke me was if the engines stopped, or if the beat of the engines varied. On such occasions I woke immediately. After I'd left the sea and married, there were quite frequent occasions when I would sit up with a start in bed and Edith would ask, 'What's the matter?'

I would reply, 'The engines have stopped,' still half-asleep, then lie back realising that I'd been dreaming.

Other members of the crew all had their respective duties to attend to, so at sea we didn't have a full social life. During the afternoon the Third was on watch, the Second in his bunk sleeping before he took over the watch at 4:00pm, and of the wireless operators one would be on watch, the other sleeping ready for his stint later on. The Fifth of course would be working on the winches, or if it was raining, working down below. The only time we all got together was when we were in port.

If the weather was kind, a favourite spot of mine was on the boat deck. As this was on the top of our accommodation, I had to tread very quietly because the crew could be sleeping in the cabins below. I kept to the middle which was over the engine room and walked on tiptoe.

I was surprised that I was the only crew member who had a deckchair. There was no room for the deckchair in my cabin so Cyril stored it in his, his cabin was the nearest one to the ladder up to the boat deck so Cyril was privileged to use the deckchair while I was on watch.

Up there I had a wonderful view from horizon to horizon, and here it was that a great many of my letters were written, and ones from home were re-read. Here I snoozed on warm afternoons or just sat and admired the scenery around me.

Scenery, I hear you say, only miles of sea. But in the warmer climes of the Pacific there were dolphins racing the ship, criss-crossing the bows, one could imagine them enjoying the fun. I saw whales spouting in the distance, and flying fish skimming the tops of the waves, trying to escape their predators beneath the surface. It's said that turtles are solitary creatures, yet on one occasion in the Pacific I saw ten or more swimming in a small group.

At that moment we had a little way to go before we reached the canal and there were U-boats about in that part of the Atlantic. From my deck chair I used to wonder how I would feel if I saw a periscope. I was glad that I didn't.

Up there on the boat deck I'd often close my eyes and drift from one memory to another. With the steady beat of the engine, the rhythm rather than the sound, past experiences went one by one through my mind.

There were so many memories floating in and out of my mind. They say that a cat has nine lives but I must have had more than that. Apart from the narrow escapes already mentioned there were two when I really thought all was over.

Coming home from Edith's house one night, the traffic lights had changed to green. I thought that if I put a spurt on I would just be in time before they turned back to red, but I didn't see the pot hole and over the handlebars I flew. I landed on my chest then continued to roll across the junction, hitting the footpath on the other side of the road. Getting to my feet I looked up and down, this was the A1, the main road from London to Edinburgh and there wasn't a vehicle in sight. Never before had I seen it so deserted.

I also thought of the time I was at Sanderson's working with Harry the electrician when I should have been electrocuted. The bacon factory pump house was a small brick building in the yard, at the foot of the four storey factory. In this little building was a brick pedestal on which stood the electric pump. Around this pedestal was an eighteen-inch gap inside the walls, and at the far end on the wall, low down, was the electric starter for the pump.

Harry was at the third floor window shouting down instructions, and he asked me to look at the starter to see if there was any movement when he switched on. It took me ten minutes to crawl into this eighteen-inch wide space between the wall, which was running with water, and the pedestal. Harry shouted down but there was no movement so I put my hand on it, just to give it a little help. Two minutes later I was out of the door, wondering what had hit me. I had the full four hundred and eighty volts from that starter. I never told Harry, I was too ashamed. I knew that I shouldn't have touched it. I did it without thinking, but I learnt the lesson. I also learned that my heart was in good condition.

Yes, and during those dreams of the past there were also dreams of the future or should I say thoughts of the future? Such as returning home, getting married and seeing all my friends again. Writing and receiving letters is no substitute for talking face to face and being within touching distance of loved ones.

We arrived off Colon about four bells, 6:00am; the Second was on watch and needed no help, so there was nothing to do except to stand by until the engines were needed again.

The morning was warm, just turning light, no breeze, and with the lights of Colon shimmering across the water, it was just the same as the last time and the time before that. It was getting lighter now so we could smoke on deck. It was very pleasant sitting on the forward hatch watching the day become lighter by the minute.

When we started to go through the canal however, we found it very different from the last time. The canal authorities were now on a wartime footing. No crowds of vendors aboard this time, instead we had armed guards with prominent side arms. They didn't trust the telegraph, so we had one officer on the bridge, another by the starting platform in the engine room, and in between an armed sailor every six foot, relaying the order from bridge to engine room and vice versa.

On one occasion the engine stopped on Top Dead Centre (TDC) and when Slow Ahead was rung down, the engine of course wouldn't start. So the Second reversed half a revolution to take the engine off TDC to enable us to go Slow Ahead. The American officer was off his seat like a shot, pulling his revolver from the holster as he rose. He wanted to know what was going on, as he wasn't familiar with triple expansion steam engines. It took ten minutes to explain to him the necessity of taking the engine off TDC before we could reverse, or vice versa.

The Lascar crew thought it was hilarious, and to have the Lascars laughing at him made things worse. We were trying to hide a giggle ourselves, even the American sailors in the relay were openly grinning at their officer's action, but he was only doing his job.

At Gatun Lake we had to drop anchor while other traffic came through the canal from the Pacific end. Some bright spark suggested a swim, and as we would be there six hours or so we had plenty of time. The Second didn't swim so he elected to look after the engine room; in the meanwhile we donned our swimming trunks. The deck crew kindly put the gangway down for us, so there was no need to climb up that exhausting rope ladder to get back on board. The water was grand, and swimming in the Panama Canal would be something to write home about.

As we disported ourselves in the water, who should come by but the Skipper, with a smile on his face, 'Bloody fools,' he said. 'You wouldn't catch me swimming in there.'

When we asked why, he said, 'Crocodiles,' but we kept on swimming. If there had been any danger of that sort he wouldn't have said crocodiles, he would have blown his top. If the Third, Fourth and Fifth were eaten by crocs, who would look after the engine room?

Somebody must have taken him seriously though, as two Aussies lay on the boat deck with .303 rifles to the end of our swim. Soon everyone had had enough. The next hour was spent looking for crocodiles, not that we saw any. As soon as we came out of the water we changed into our working clothes, and when the Stand By rang we were ready to carry on to Balboa and from there across the Pacific to Auckland.

We had taken on a new Indian crew at Glasgow, the other crew had transhipped to a vessel going direct to India. The new crew weren't as experienced as the original crew; neither did they seem so pleasant. Possibly the atmosphere would change when we got to know each other, however I had no complaints about my *Tail Wallah*, he was conscientious and never missed a turn around the engine.

The first Sunday out of Balboa the old rituals were observed, and round about lunchtime the barber's 'shop' was open and we had our haircut. Things went along quietly for a few days. The sun beat down and the engine room temperature rose to a new record. The deckchair on the boat deck was forgotten, the sun was too fierce.

Then one day at dinner the Second announced during the conversation that he had had a premonition, there was trouble about. As we ate we hoped that he was wrong. We didn't like trouble, but whether we liked it or not, it came a few days later.

During the Second's watch, at four bells, the engine stopped. We all woke immediately and within three minutes were down below. The Chief was in animated conversation with the Second, the rest of us trying to find out what was wrong. Soon we could smell it, hot brass, an over-heated bearing. The Second was practically jumping up and down, really blowing his top. One of the main bearings had over-heated and the white metal had run.

The bearings are bronze with a soft white metal lining, and it was this metal that had got too hot through lack of oil, and melted. The *Tail Wallah* should have noticed the temperature rising, so should the engineer on watch, but it was no good apportioning blame. It had happened and the bearing had to be changed. This was not a pleasant job.

The sea was choppy and the ship was bobbing about like a cork, but there were no big waves so things could have been worse, however, it was going to be a nasty twenty four hours.

Looking at it from the Second's point of view, this mishap or disaster reflected on him because he was on watch at the time. This made the Third and I look across at each other. I know that he was thinking the same as I was, thanking the good Lord above that it hadn't happened on either of our watches.

But one good point, it was a main bearing, an easier job than a big end bearing, and we carried spares. We all set to work to get the job done as quickly as possible under the direction of the Second.

A ship under power is a steady platform on which to work, but dead in the water it is a different proposition. She was bobbing about, pitching and rolling, slipping and sliding, still one second, and dropping suddenly the next.

The large holding-down bolts were really tight, requiring a big spanner which hung on a rope to take the weight. The bolts holding the bearing were two and a half to three inches in diameter, so you can visualise the size of the spanner. It took two men to carry it and a seven pound sledge hammer to use on the spanner to turn the nuts; this with the ship moving about all the time.

The man with the hammer was held steady by another man behind him, and the hanging spanner was held by another two men. Any one falling at this point could have had serious consequences, we had no doctor aboard, neither could we use the wireless to get help.

Block and tackle was erected to lift the old bearing out, the keep on the plates being tied up to prevent it sliding about. Taking the bearing to pieces was the easy part, then the new ones were slid into place, and the process of bedding them in started.

White metal is comparatively soft and is scraped, not filed. It had to fit the shaft as near to perfect as possible. Lead wire was laid between the shaft and the bearing, tightened down hard then taken apart. The thickness of the lead wire was measured with a micrometer, then more scraping. This process was repeated until the

Second was satisfied with the result.

In twenty four hours the job was completed to the Second's satisfaction, and we began to clear up. Block and tackle taken down, spanner and hammer back in store, labels attached with all data. The old bronzes would be repaired and relined with white metal ready for the next time.

During the whole operation we had been well cared for. The Captain had sent down a bottle of rum to keep us going, and the Chief Steward sent down a bottle of whisky, tea and sandwiches. Volunteers fed us these while we worked as oil, grease and sandwiches don't mix very well.

After this experience the watch-keepers had to be ever vigilant, with this bearing particularly. I drew extra oil from the stores and attended to this myself for the next few days. As this crew had proved to be inexperienced all the watch-keepers were extra careful and did extra oiling themselves. The *Tail Wallah* on my watch was very good, so as not to hurt his feelings too much, I followed him around on occasions and explained it was on instructions from the Chief until the new bearing was properly run in.

A week later we realised we had been inordinately lucky because we ran into a hurricane. If this had come while we had the breakdown we would have sunk for sure, no way could we have carried out the repair under those conditions.

One morning, about a week before we reached New Zealand, I had a notion that we were moving about a little more than usual. In fact half an hour on, I knew we were. As the ship rolled I was sliding on the engine room plates and had to hold on at times. It wasn't difficult to slide as the plates were kept polished with kerosene and coir to prevent rust.

The movement of the ship made it difficult to see the water level in the boilers, and one could only make an educated guess. I thought of the stokers throwing coal into the fires, it was really difficult from their point of view.

During the next hour the rolling and pitching worsened. I'd never had to hang on before to prevent myself sliding, and I thought that it must really be heavy up there. I was really looking forward to seeing the waves at the end of the watch. Eight bells rang, and the Third was reading the log. I was climbing up the ladders, but as the ship rolled one way I was having to hang on to the rails, when it rolled the other way I was almost lying on the steps.

I managed to reach the deck and keeping tight hold of the rail around the accommodation, I inched towards the ship's rail. The ship was being thrown about like a toy. One second the waves were up in the air and I was looking up to them, the next I was looking down and then seeing them come up like a lift.

I crept into my cabin, wondering what sort of mess it would be in. Luckily Raj had closed the scuttles and locked all the drawers, and also cleared up all moveable objects such as the photos from the table. Good lad!

That afternoon I just watched the water. Peeping around the corner of the accommodation watching the giant waves come towards the ship, slipping under, and then carrying straight on. The ship slid down the sea-mountains sideways, standing still on the crest, then accelerating down the slope to end up digging her nose into the great trough. As her nose rose, tons of water cascaded over the foredeck.

I became quite expert in the art of holding my cup in one hand and keeping the top level whilst eating my dinner. It was a good tip to drink half of a cup of tea before putting it down on the table. I learned to carry three cups of tea down those ladders, without spilling a drop, five cups without the storm. The table was fitted with fiddles, removable strips of wood, which prevented the plates from sliding about but did nothing about the soup in those plates. I also became expert at eating soup, holding the plate to keep it level and spooning the soup into my mouth.

That afternoon the wind rose even higher and became stronger. At eight bells I took over the watch from the Second, and had four hours of sliding from one place to the next and hanging on. By this time the novelty had worn off somewhat and I was wishing for some better weather, but as yet there was no sign of that. As 11:45pm came around the Third appeared to take things over, no one was ever late to relieve the watch, and I went up topside to make us a cup of tea.

When the Third came down to take over he remarked that the sea was getting worse. At the time I thought it wouldn't make much difference, the ship was going up and down like an animated lift already, but when I arrived on deck I understood what he was talking about.

The wind was really howling, and spray was flying horizontally across the deck stinging my face. The night was so black that only the immediate surroundings could be made out as solid. It could have been someone's idea

383

of Hell.

I looked about, sheltered from the wind by the accommodation, straining my eyes just to see something, anything, when a slight movement caught my eye. Instinctively I grabbed the first thing I could. My arms went around the piston rod of a winch, and clasping my hands together I hung on while tons of water poured over me. It swept me off my feet and it seemed ages before I could breathe again, although I expect it was only fifteen or thirty seconds. I lay there, half drowned. The weight of the water had been terrific and all the breath had been knocked out of me.

The water had come over the bows, cleared the bridge over our accommodation, and down on me. I learned later that the same deluge had damaged four ventilators, the rails around the foredeck and the bridge. I was very lucky that night not to have gone over the side. At midnight no one would have heard or seen me had I done so, and no one could have survived in that sea.

If I hadn't caught a glimpse from the corner of my eye and grabbed that winch I would not have been seen again. Once again I was saying to myself, someone up there is still looking after you, Ern.

The only casualty was the watch that Edith had given me. I tried to rescue it but it rusted up inside, despite a soaking in fresh water and then kerosene. I was soaked right through when I took the Third his cup of tea. He didn't ask why I was soaked, and I never told anyone, I would only have been told that I should have known better.

All the next day we stayed at Half Ahead, just keeping the bows to the wind and waves. I took some photos but the scope was limited, it was too dangerous to walk around the deck.

It was thrilling to stand in the shelter of the deck houses, the ship stayed where it was just going up and down. The waves must have been sixty to seventy feet high, and the trough a quarter of a mile across. As I stood, peeping around the corner of the heads, or toilets, the ship tipped forward off the top of a wave. Immediately the screw left the water, the governor clanked into operation and the engine stopped momentarily, then came to life again as the prop entered the water.

The ship accelerated as it tipped forward, ran down the wall of water, hitting the bottom with a gigantic 'whumph' then coming to a dead stop, as white water covered the foredeck. Then the wave, running beneath, lifted the *City* and the whole process started again. It was a fascinating experience, as was learning to sleep in a bunk without falling out.

I took a few more photographs but the Captain swore at me from the bridge, and when the Chief caught me on the well deck he promptly put it out of bounds. The trouble was that taking pictures from above flattened the effect, taking the impact from the scene, but with that I had to be content.

I was on watch the next morning. The huge waves were still rolling and the prop was still breaking the water almost every time, with the governor still banging in and out. I knew that if the governor failed to act promptly and the engine started to race, the engine could shake itself to pieces. Then it happened, the governor failed to respond.

I rushed down to the platform and just got there when

the prop bit again, but I was ready for the next time it raced. Beside the starting platform is a hand lever. In an emergency pulling this cuts off the steam immediately, so if the prop leaves the water the engine can be stopped right away. When the prop is back in the water, pull the lever and it starts the engine again.

I couldn't spin the valve wheel fast enough to stop the engine, the propeller was leaving the water every three or four minutes and I couldn't leave the throttle to repair the governor. I had a good think for a second or two. If I couldn't get to the governor, someone else would have to do it.

The time was 10:00am. The Second would be in his bunk, having come off watch at 8:00am. Waiting for the right moment as I pulled the lever back, I leaned a little further and blew the Chief's voice pipe. He picked it up right away, but he had to wait until the prop came out of the water again before I could speak. This time I was just able to get three words out, 'Need help Chief,' before stepping away from the voice pipe as I pushed the throttle lever forward.

The Chief didn't come down, but the Second did. He saw what was wrong, got a big hammer from the stores and used it to good effect. He waved then went up top again, and I was able to leave the throttle and continue with the watch, back to seeing that the engine room was functioning correctly in all departments.

Then came the time when the clouds disappeared and the sea began to revert to normal, the sun shone again. We crossed the International Date Line on Thursday, June 6th. Edith's birthday was the 6th June. We had gone to bed on Wednesday night and as we crossed the date line, the next day was Friday, so Edith didn't have a birthday that year.

We arrived in Auckland as we had before, with the attention of the same barber and the same remarks. We were expecting the remarks so they didn't have the same impact, but they were new to the new boys. For us the remarks were like golden oldies. Even after six months we were still remembered and we introduced our new members, the Wireless Operators, the new Third and the Carpenter. The two Wireless Operators were straight out of radio school; one was twenty one years old, the other only eighteen.

At that time the big job on board was an inspection of the holding-down bolts on the engine. The heavy weather we'd experienced in the Pacific had given the engine mounting a terrific pounding and, with his experience, the Second Engineer knew that they would need attention. I hadn't even thought about them.

Under the engine room are the double bottom tanks, which carry water and these were all pumped out ready for this inspection. The tanks can be envisaged as thirty-six inch cubes with a twenty-inch diameter hole in each side. The engine is bolted down on this bed of cubes. I suppose the idea is that this is the strongest method of construction for the bottom of the engine room, and convenient for the storage of water. The holes served two purposes, they enabled us to get to the bolts holding the engine down securely, and the water has to flow to be pumped in or out.

There were about seventeen tanks from one side to the other, but I never found out how many there were fore and aft.

One of the tanks had a bolted-on cover and this was the entry to the maze. As the engine was bolted directly on to the tank tops, all the bolts had to have a waterproof seal or grommet to prevent oil from seeping through and contaminating the water in the tanks. The bolts were really studs; that is, they had no head only a square end, and the screws were about one and a half inches in diameter.

My job was to crawl through these tanks with a torch, and a rope around my waist so that I could find my way out again. First I had to find the broken screws, which were lying in the tanks where they had fallen out, and push the broken half up out of the hole so that the Second could start to replace it.

Down below I took off the nut from the broken screw, and placed a grommet and nut on the new screw that the Second pushed down, and then held it up while the Second put a nut on the top and tightened it down with the sledgehammer. It was a very awkward job twisting and turning through the twenty-inch holes, which all had sharp edges. In all we found fourteen broken bolts, and then we had to go right round the engine tightening the others.

I can't remember how many bolts there were altogether, but it took two full days to complete. I was chosen for this job, so the Second said, because he wanted someone down there who knew what he was doing. Any one can believe that, if they like, I didn't. I was the only one that could get in and out again. The Fifth was quite tubby, as the Second was himself, and the Third was all of six foot two inches tall. I don't think the Second fancied anyone getting stuck down there or having a heart attack. In those circumstances it would have been a major operation to get an unconscious man out of there. I was only too pleased that I wasn't claustrophobic.

This was the third time that I'd visited Auckland and each time the Skipper had timed it just right. Arriving on Friday or Saturday morning in Auckland ready to have the weekend off, meant that we would have a weekend again in all of our New Zealand ports. While we were renewing the holding down bolts on the engine, the deck crew had been dealing with the cargo, and so we were ready to sail off to Lyttelton, Wellington and Dunedin.

The weather was warm and sunny and I spent afternoons on the boat deck in my deckchair, sometimes writing, sometimes just lazing. We hadn't heard of any submarines operating in the neighbourhood so we had nothing to worry about on that score.

During the weekend at Lyttelton, we walked around the town and climbed the surrounding hills, although it didn't have the impact of the former visits. However, at Wellington there was something new, they were having the one hundredth anniversary of New Zealand, so we had to visit the exhibition. We spent a day there, but unlike the World Fair, I think we saw everything.

At Dunedin, we entered in style. We were manoeuvring towards the dockside with the engineers on the starting platform, Slow Ahead, Stop, Half Ahead, Stop, and then bump! This I duly noted down in the log book, together with the time. We heard nothing at the time, so thought that it couldn't have been anything serious, also the Pilot was on the bridge. We sorted things out down below then came up on deck as we were curious. We found ten feet of the quay was missing.

On my travels I'd bought a small model aircraft kit, a Spitfire. I'd been spending an odd half-hour now and again working on it. The skeleton was a little warped due to the fact that I didn't have a board to build it on, but it went together, and was duly covered with tissue paper and then painted. I only had elastic[34] to power it and, until then, no means of trying it out. The highest I could get without too much trouble was the top of the ladder on the big ventilator.

I wound the elastic up fully, and then launched it down the river. I was quite proud of that plane. Amid cheers it flew straight and true, out of sight, and then I suppose it floated. It was a sad end, but a successful flight.

---

[34] Model airplanes are typically constructed using balsa wood, so are very light, and elastic bands can be used for power. My father taught my brother how to build these airplanes, and we spent many family days out, happily testing and flying a succession of ever larger aircraft; the later ones being driven by a small engine. Editor

39. The Wedding Day, back from left to right, Win, me, Edith, Alan and Joan in front

38. Edith and me, 4 October, 1940

391

CHAPTER FOURTEEN
Australia to Home at Last
June 1940 - October 1940

After changing the furnace doors we left Sydney and were now burning oil. It was especially comfortable sitting up on the boat deck when we were burning oil as you didn't have the grit falling about your ears, as one did when burning coal. Oil was much cleaner.

Since leaving Glasgow, I'd been looking forward to the trip up the Australian coast. This time I'd be able to sit in my deckchair on the boat deck, and really appreciate the trip to Thursday Island with a clear conscience. As Fifth I was working on deck during the afternoons, but taking time off to enjoy the scenery gave me a guilty feeling, so I kept one eye open in case the Second wasn't in his bunk. This time, however, as Fourth Engineer, I could spend every afternoon in my deckchair.

The weather, for my enjoyment, couldn't be better. A clear blue sky and water so still, not a ripple until it was disturbed by the ship's bows. The sea snakes swimming near the surface, red, green and some with yellow bands could be clearly seen, and watching them swimming alongside was a sheer delight. Later, as we sailed further up the coast we could see the islands off the starboard beam not too far off; occasionally we passed one so close that we could see the individual trees just behind the beach.

I realised that this was the last time that I would come this way, in this I was mistaken as it happens, but at the time the thought left a feeling of depression,

When we reached Thursday Island we dropped the Pilot and sailed towards Malaysia, through the Indonesian Islands, past Java and Sumatra to arrive at Singapore where we berthed. Finished with Engines was rung down on the telegraph and the Second announced what he wanted doing while we were there. It was a long list, so we knew that we were there for some time.

But the Second wasn't a happy man. We'd been having trouble with the gauge on the settling tank for some time, and although the Second insisted he had repaired it, both the Third and I had had conflicting readings resulting in some puzzling entries in the log book. I always put in what I saw, as did the Third, but the Second liked the log to read evenly. He didn't like the big differences in the entries, whereas the Third and I thought that to ignore even one degree could lead to trouble.

However, the Second pounced one day, bawling me out for not reading the gauge on the settling tank, his reading didn't agree with mine. I thought that he was really out of line as this took place in front of the engine room crew down below. We had a right old barney and I'm afraid that I forgot who he was and swore right back at him. He had also had a go at the Third with the same result as he had with me. No, he wasn't a happy man.

We both told him that rather than effect the repair himself, he should have had it repaired at Sydney. He replied that there wasn't sufficient time. We both told him that as it looked as if we'd be here at Singapore for quite a while, we should fill the tank up now and get the gauge repaired at the same time, while we were running only one boiler. There would be enough oil in the tank to last a week with only one boiler.

That night I was sitting in my cabin, finishing off some letters, when there was a knock on the door, 'Come in,' I called. The Second entered and invited me out for a drink or two. I told him that it was my turn aboard that night.

'That's OK, I've seen the Third and he'll see to that, give you a chance to post your letters. Ready in twenty minutes?'

In twenty minutes I was on deck when the taxi drew up alongside. We played billiards at the Seaman's Mission and had a few beers until 10:00pm. When we were ready to go back to the ship the Second asked the Steward to call us a taxi.

He never said 'Sorry,' the gesture was his apology. I understood that, I also knew that the Third would get the same apology that I did. At sea no one can get along without each other; no quarrel can last on a cargo ship as everyone needs everyone else. Then we heard that we were going back to Sydney, and I knew that we would be going down the east coast again.

While we were there at Singapore we took aboard a load of tea, sisal, pineapple chunks and bales of raw rubber, the usual products of the area, all for the UK. We had a good three weeks there, during which the gauge on the settling tank was repaired, and for our benefit a local bigwig opened his swimming pool, which we enjoyed on a couple of afternoons.

We left Singapore for Sydney and, as usual, picked up the Pilot at Thursday Island and sailed down the coast. Now I was going to see this coast for the last time, but I'd been most fortunate to see it at all.

About two days after picking up the Pilot we reached Townsville. This was a surprise stop, particularly when the Second said we were going into dry dock. It was something new, everything was happening on this trip.

Apparently we'd sprung a leak when we hit the quay at Dunedin in New Zealand, and we were in dock for three days. The damage was slight, a few rivets loose, but enough to cause anxiety in the Captain. We never found out who was at fault, the Captain or the Pilot.

I found it very strange in dry dock. Looking over the side one appeared to be up in the sky, no water beneath us, certainly the drop looked dangerous. We continued to eat on board as the galley fires burned coal, however, to go to the toilet we had to walk the plank to get ashore and go to the office to get the key, even at night. Cables for the lights were strung across from ashore. It was difficult to remember that in dry dock we were ashore. But with the engine silent and the pumps not working, the greatest inconvenience was not being able to get to sleep at night. It was also colder, much colder. Our accommodation was over the engine room and boilers, and with them not being in commission we really felt the difference.

But there was one thing we were interested in. We could see the ship in her entirety, the shape, rudder and prop, and few seamen ever see these parts of their vessel. I cannot understand why I didn't take a photograph while she was out of the water.

After the hull was repaired, the water was let into the dock, and once again she was back in her element. The engines were warmed through and everything was ready to move over to the coaling dock. I believe it was here that we took coal on for the trip home.

Taking on coal is a filthy job especially when it's small coal, and this was almost dust. As at Liverpool the coal was loaded from chutes, but as this was so dusty water was sprayed on the stream of coal as it came down the chute into the bunker. Even so, enough escaped to cover the whole ship and the dockside, and coal dust could be seen billowing over the cargo sheds. I pitied the crew who had to clean up the mess on board. The dust penetrated the cabins even though the ventilators once again were stuffed up and the scuttles shut tight.

Every drawer in every cabin had to be taken out and cleaned, all clothes taken out and either washed or, in the case of outer garments, brushed and hung to blow in the wind. When we got moving again it took weeks to get to rights, but worst of all was the danger it caused later on.

We sailed from Townsville to Brisbane, then on to Sydney, where we docked at Woolomaloo, a suburb of Sydney. We knew this town quite well now but hadn't docked in this part before. From here to Sydney proper was a pleasant walk across what was called the Domain. This was a large park come playground, once a place of ill repute and danger where anyone with any sense walked in twos and threes.

Our old shellbacks knew it in the bad old days of their youth, and they told us of shipmates waylaid, beaten up and mugged on their way back to their ships after drinking in the town's pubs. They said that only drunks, who knew no better, passed through the Domain in those days.

In the UK in 1940 we were getting over the 1929 depression, but here in Australia they still had a good standard of living. I bought two pairs of British made

Daks trousers, good ones, which were cheaper than at home. I had no means of shortening the legs on board, so asked them to be done at the shop; they would be ready in a couple of days.

Two days later I went across the Domain to pick up my shortened trousers. During the conversation with the shop assistant he told me that he was off on his holiday for the next three weeks, he was taking his family to the U.S.A. But when I got back to the ship, the Second was waiting for me. I had completely forgotten that it was my night aboard.

I could only apologise and take a good dressing-down. I knew I was in the wrong and had to stand there and take everything he threw at me, but worse than that was the feeling that through my forgetfulness I had let the side down.

After Sydney we reached Melbourne two to three days later. We only stayed two days, just time to have a quick run ashore and purchase another plane kit. This was a Beechcraft biplane, and I think would have made a wonderful model. What surprised me was how much cheaper almost everything was there, even model aircraft.

But this model, unlike the Spitfire, was destined for an unhappy end. I kept it in one of my big drawers, with tissues around, to stop it from moving and being damaged, and there it stayed until it came out to be worked on. The plane was almost half-built and all it needed was covering with tissue. I hoped that as we were on the way home its first flight could take place in England.

From Melbourne we made our way to Adelaide and Port Pirie. I liked Port Pirie; it was different, very small but really picturesque. There appeared to be a very large number of immigrants here from the United Kingdom, and it seemed the custom that all of them visited the quayside on Sunday mornings. This custom was a thing of the past in the UK but here, away from the war zone, security wasn't an issue.

Folk walked along the quayside and shouted up to the Quartermaster standing at the top of the gangway, asking him if there were any crew members aboard from a particular town in the UK. If they received a positive reply they asked if they could talk with him. They wanted the latest news of their home town, not the sort of news that they could hear over the wireless. They were looking for someone from the street in which they used to live, and wanted to know if the street was still there, if the picture hall on the corner was still standing, and how was Mrs Baker from number four. Any sort of home news.

The whole family came down if they found anyone from where they used to live. The lucky crew members received books and magazines, fresh-baked scones and cake, and on one occasion I saw a bottle of whisky handed over to one fortunate chap. Anyone local lucky enough to find someone who knew an old neighbour would invite the member of the crew to their home for a pleasant evening. Unfortunately there were no immigrants from Gateshead.

From my point of view the main attraction of Port Pirie was the Wild West scenario. The cinema where we sat through a western and quite a large number of the houses were timber-built. Also, the railway line came up the middle of the main street and I was fortunate to see a train arrive. The conductor stepped down with a set of wooden steps, which he placed in position for the passengers to use when stepping down from the carriage. For all the world like the pictures I saw when I was seven years old.

Port Pirie was the end of the line and after waiting while all of the passengers alighted and the conductor had taken his steps aboard, it slowly moved off in the direction from which it came.

Another character from Port Pirie was the Padre from the Mission to Seamen. He would call on any ship that came in, welcoming all aboard to the mission. Describing all of the facilities, the chapel, billiard hall and the library, where any number of books could be exchanged on a basis of one for one. We knew of the library exchange system at the Missions but this one was exceptional, and we made a note to acquaint the Third Mate of this fact. We could do with some new books.

This Padre was an expert in scrounging fags. Sitting on the rail chatting with whomever, he would ask, 'Do you smoke?' The best thing to do was to say sorry. If you said yes, expecting him to get his fags out, you would be disappointed. He'd say, 'Have you one to spare? I'm gasping for a smoke.'

We were only there for a few days, but we did get the books swapped over and so had some new books to read during the rest of the journey.

Whilst we were here, the Second had a brilliant idea. He spoke to the Chief Steward and arranged with him to purchase, on our account, some tea and sugar to take home, as it was rationed at home but not here.

This he did and we divided it between us. If I remember rightly, we had seven pounds of tea and fourteen pounds of sugar each. Now, where to store it? The sack of sugar went under the seat of the settee, but just then the dinner gong sounded. I put the seven pounds of packet tea into the first drawer that I opened then dashed to the mess for dinner. Yes, that drawer had my plane in, and after a little rough weather later on it was a drawer full of matchsticks without heads.

We had changed the fire doors at Sydney ready to burn the coal loaded at Townsville, and swept the bunkers out ready for cargo to take home, but it wasn't to turn out like that. Fortunately we hadn't loaded much coal as we had trouble all the time it was being burned. Ordinarily it would have taken us a week to reach our next port, Fremantle, but it was to take us half as long again. Yes, we had trouble with that coal.

Steam pressures were falling, and the stokers were getting upset. I felt sorry for them. The ash content of the coal was three or four times the norm and they couldn't keep the pressure of two hundred and twelve pounds. In fact while cleaning fires, it often dropped to one hundred and seventy pounds per square inch. All this of course was written in the logbook, and to be honest I didn't know what to put in, so I put both, the lowest and the highest, just to be precise.

As I mentioned earlier, it was my job to monitor the temperature of the bunkers, this I did every day at noon jotting it down in the log before taking it along to the Chief. For three or four days the temperature had been rising a degree or so every day, so when I handed the log to the Chief I pointed this out. He told me to keep a close watch on it, taking the temperature every four hours instead of twenty four.

Day by day it continued to rise, very slowly, and the Chief decided to check it out during the afternoon watch, so that the Second would be available.

The hatchet cover was removed, then as the boards were raised a burst of smoke rose from the bunker. The deck hoses had already been prepared for action and as the boards came off the hoses were directed on to the coal. After a good soaking the coal looked like mud. The Chief leaning into the opening and decided that it was safe to enter. Two firemen, trimmers, were helped over the combing and into the hatch with instructions to dig towards the heat.

Smoke and fumes continued to rise, and after ten minutes the two diggers were feeling the effect of the fumes. They were lifted out and two more took their place to continue the digging, shifts of men changing places every ten minutes. The Second Engineer climbed in before the new men entered to gauge the temperature and density of gas.

This continued all afternoon, with soakings from the hose, then more digging. By now the smoke was thickening and the temperature was rising the nearer the diggers got to the centre of the fire. The men in the relay were becoming exhausted more quickly, and diggers were being lifted out amid fears that the whole bunker would burst into flames. However, continual bursts of water from the hoses managed to keep the flames at bay.

Eventually the heat inside the bunker became so intense, no one could stand in there. Then the hoses were turned full on and the core of the fire thoroughly soaked. I don't know where all the water went to, it must have drained into the bilges and been pumped overboard. The barometer was standing high, so the covers were left off the bunker and the temperature was monitored for the next week. We had no more trouble from that particular bunker, but we still had trouble with this so-called coal.

It not only affected the engineer on watch. The poor stoker had to work twice as hard as usual and the fires had to be cleaned more often, which is not a nice job. In a stokehold it's hard work and very hot.

On one occasion during a night watch the steam pressure dropped to one hundred and seventy pounds, and this time it stayed there. So much so that I had to go through to the stokehold to see why, and found one of the stokers sitting on a locker by the bulkhead.

Although I could sympathise with him, the boiler pressure was still dropping and I could hear the engine beginning to labour as it lost power. I opened one of the doors on his boiler and right away I knew why. The fire needed cleaning, badly. I took a slice, a steel bar about ten foot long and flat at one end, pushed it under the fire, and leant on the end so the whole fire lifted up. The top of the fire was one lump of clinker, or slag. I asked the stoker, when had he last cleaned this fire? All I got in reply was a shrug of his shoulders.

I told him that I wanted it cleaned right away, I couldn't afford to let the pressure drop any lower. On my way back to the engine room I thought that I'd have a word with the *Tindal* but as I walked back, out of the corner of my eye, I saw this fireman pick up a big spanner and follow me.

In the circumstances I couldn't do anything. These men worked under the *Tindal*, and I couldn't take his authority away. When I reached the *Tindal* I nodded my head in the direction of the stoker and told him, quietly, 'The *Burra Sahib*, Chief Engineer, wouldn't like that.'

The *Tindal* looked at the stoker with the spanner in his hand, walked over to him, took the spanner and then kicked him as hard as he could between the legs. The stoker collapsed on the plates, and the *Tindal*, quite unconcerned turned to me and said 'He be OK now *Char Sahib*, he be very good stoker from now, I look after him.'

I didn't want any bad feeling on my watch and thought that I'd done the right thing. After all, the foreman should look after his own charges. No one, except those in the boiler room knew anything about it. I never mentioned the incident to anyone and I think the stokers appreciated it, although I don't know whether the fireman concerned did or not.

However, I had nothing to complain about after this incident. In fact, as I learned from the log book, the 8:00pm to 12:00pm watch had less trouble with the steam pressures than either the Third or Seconds' watches.

But all were glad when we had finished that coal; the fires were difficult to fire without making smoke and smoke was a big giveaway to subs, or other ships. In a week or twos time we'd be in sub-infested waters when we neared Cape Town.

There were rumours of surface raiders in the Indian Ocean which we had to cross later going from Fremantle to the Cape. From Freetown, Sierra Leone, to the UK we'd be in convoy and then making smoke would put everyone in danger. So there was great relief when we changed over to oil before leaving Australia.

The next port of call was Fremantle, a small place in

itself, but a big name in sailing circles. In 1940 it reminded me, like so many other places around the New Zealand and Australian coasts, of the frontier towns of the Americas. The wooden buildings in the main streets gave it a different flavour.

Fremantle is situated on the south west coast, a short bus ride to the city of Perth which we decided to visit. Perth was a really beautiful place, very clean, as if it had been especially scrubbed for our visit. A further point that has always stayed in my memory was a curious lane.

Off the main shopping street was a very narrow archway opening out into a wide cobbled street lined with shops of all descriptions. The shop fronts were as they would have been built in Edwardian times, they were like pictures from an old book. On entering one had a greater shock as all the shop assistants were dressed in period costume. The women were in crinolines and the men in long jackets or coats with high collars. It was as if one had walked back in time when stepping through that archway.

The journey from Fremantle to Perth was only twenty minutes, but it was a wonderful afternoon. My only regret was I'd forgotten to take the camera.

Unfortunately we didn't spend a weekend there. Only enough time to change over to oil and undertake a few of the most urgent repairs, and then we were on our way to Cape Town. We knew that we were heading for troubled waters but we'd posted our letters home and we had received some to read, and the great thing was that we were heading for home. We had to miss any German raiders on our way to the Cape and the subs in the Atlantic, and then we would be home. But it was still a long way and anything could happen.

My sister mentioned in one of her letters that Teddy Mynott, a friend of the family had joined the MN six months earlier. I wrote back and told her to advise him not to join the tanker fleet, but I suppose that during war time one was given a ship of any company. However a few days from the Persian Gulf his ship was sunk with all hands by a German raider. I believe the raider was the *Pinquin,* which I believe in turn was sunk by *H.M.S. Cornwall*, the cruiser on which Bert Moderate served in the Royal Marines.

But a day out from Fremantle I had something else to worry about, a tooth. A niggle now and again, which developed very quickly into a continuous niggle, and a few days later another joined in. One canine tooth and a big molar in the bottom jaw.

After a couple of days I knew that I was in trouble. The molar wasn't too bad, but the other ached continually so I took it for granted there was an abscess there. Our Chief Steward was our first-aid man but I learned that he'd never had to pull teeth. I wasn't going to be the first. I would have to bear it using toothache tincture and whisky, although the latter could only be rubbed on the gums. I suffered with those teeth for over fourteen days from Fremantle to Cape Town.

The Second had made representations to the Captain via the Chief so that I was assured of treatment when we reached port. But keeping my watch was a great trial. The heat in the engine room intensified the throbbing, which was keeping time with the engine's turn over of seventy-eight revs per minute, almost the same as my pulse.

When we docked at Cape Town, the agent came aboard and arrangements were made to have my teeth seen to. One of the cadets was also booked in for treatment and we made our way to our dentist. We were only at Cape Town for a few hours, just sufficient time to fill any empty oil tanks and take on board a load of tinned pineapple while pumping the oil across.

The cadet and I walked off together, talking light-heartedly to hide our nervousness from each other. The dentist's surgery was only twenty minutes walk from the docks, and appeared even shorter because the road was lined with lawns and flower beds. There were seats where one could sit and enjoy the sun. Only we had appointments and yes, we wanted to get things over and done with. My teeth were still reminding me why I was there.

We presented ourselves at the dentist's reception desk. While the cadet had his tooth out there and then, I had to wait another hour. I waited until he came out, saw him on his way back to the ship, and then spent the time sitting on the park bench enjoying the sunshine and flowers. I thought how odd it is that while waiting ones turn to sit in a dentist's chair, the toothache disappears.

The hour soon passed and I was back in with the dentist, a huge man, his arms covered with black hair right down to his finger nails. I remember thinking that he'd be strong enough to pull teeth out two at a time. He inspected my teeth.

I explained my position, how I'd put up with it for over two weeks and couldn't carry on like this for another five or six. So after another look and some more persuasion, he decided to get to work and pull. The front one came out as clean as a whistle and he showed me the abscess right at the root. I was glad to get rid of that one.

The big one at the back was another story. It was hollow, and when he got hold of it the top broke off and left the roots behind, for which he had to dig. This he did after two more injections, but he got every bit out. I knew that I had had a hard time, but he must have had a hard time too because he asked his assistant to go to the cupboard and bring the whisky and three glasses.

Another first, this was the first time that I'd been treated to a glass of whisky at a dentist's surgery or in the dentist's chair. I resolved to tell my local dentist at home of this local custom.

For the next half hour we chatted and drank his whisky. I suppose he was making sure that I was capable of getting back to the ship on my own, but with the whisky, the extra injections and the relief of getting rid of those two teeth, I was beginning to wonder if I could walk that far.

So rather light-headed I set out. I had no idea what time it was and I was on watch at 8:00pm. I reached the ship unaided, but when the Second saw me I don't think he wanted to look too closely. He told me to get into my bunk and he'd call me at 7:45pm in time for my watch.

I certainly must have looked under the weather as there wasn't a lot of sentiment in our Second, but on the other hand it was decent of him to give me an hour in my bunk. He knew nothing of the whisky though, unless he had smelt it?

However, I was awakened by the Stand By, so I got up, pulled on my boiler suit, and went below to take over the watch when we left Cape Town.

We took aboard fresh provisions at Cape Town, most notable were the fresh crayfish and for a few days they were on the menu. I'd never eaten crayfish or lobsters before. These crayfish were the size of lobsters and were delicious, reminding me very much of the crab sandwiches I had as a boy from the foreman at Sanderson's.

I'd posted my letters from Cape Town, two very special ones. One to Edith telling her that we'd be married as soon as we were together again, and another to the shipping company telling them that I wouldn't be signing articles after I was paid off at the end of this voyage.

We had entered dangerous waters now. During 1939 - 1940 the danger spots were the north Atlantic with submarines, the German navy, and the German raiders in the Indian Ocean disguised as merchant ships. Later on subs were in the South Atlantic as well as the North, laying mines in the Cape Town approaches and the trade routes round the Cape of Good Hope.

We sailed due west, so anyone seeing us leave would think that we were going in the direction of North or South America, however once out of sight of land we turned north, trying to be invisible. Burning oil fuel solved the smoke problem, it was much easier and cleaner and we could keep a full head of steam without smoke.

At 8:58 every morning the telegraph was rung down from the bridge, this was to tell me to stand by to synchronise clocks. I rang back to answer the call, then two minutes later it rang again; this time I set the engine room clock right on 9:00am to synchronise it with the bridge clock. Then I answered the ring.

Now this little ceremony took place every morning without fail, so when one morning the telegraph rang twice, one after the other, I said to myself, 'Hello, the silly sod's slipped up this morning, no two minute interval.' But when the telegraph again rang twice a minute later, I began to think. Two rings in two seconds was an emergency signal!

I rang the answer back to the bridge, opened the door to the boiler room, and shouted to the *Tindal* to change the number eight jets in the fires to number twelve's. Then I ran up the ladder to the first level on the main engine and opened up the valves on the HP and MP cylinders. The response was immediate. The engine revs increased to eighty six and the ship heeled over as it turned to port on a new course. I shouted up to the *Cassop* in the store room to tell the day workers in the engine room to get up on deck and stay there. He was also told to unlock the lubricating oil store and allow unlimited oil for the *Tail Wallah*. The *Tail Wallah* was told to concentrate on the main engine while I looked after the rest of the engine room.

The Chief, alerted by the increased revolutions of the engine, came running down the ladders, buttoning up his jacket as he did so. I was surprised that he didn't come a cropper. He said, 'What's up?'

I replied, 'I haven't the faintest idea Chief, they don't tell you anything down here.'

He asked what I'd done up to now, and when I told him he remarked, 'Good lad,' then suggested that I opened the HP valve another point. He said that he'd pop up and see what it was all about. A little later he came down and told me not to worry, it wasn't a V-boat it was an S.O.S. A tanker had been in collision with a White Star liner carrying evacuee children to South Africa. The liner was holed just above the water line and was asking for assistance.

We arrived at the scene just as the Third came down to take over the watch at noon. As soon as he was satisfied, I went on deck to see what I could do.

A number of other ships had answered the call and were all scattered about, if there had been any subs in the area they would have had a field day. There were eight ships altogether, all smaller than we were, and when a naval cruiser arrived we were told to stand by. The others were told to continue their journey.

One by one they disappeared and we were left with the liner and the cruiser. The tanker was stationary, about three miles off. I heard that the cruiser was *H.M.S Cumberland*, I suppose the officers had been in touch. A few hours later we were joined by an armed merchant cruiser and they began to take all of the children off the liner. Luckily no one was hurt in the accident. One would think it was impossible that two ships as large as these could collide in daylight with full visibility.

The weather was dull with a choppy sea and we were hoping that we'd have to tow the liner to Walvis Bay, the nearest port. A salvage claim would have run into thousands, my share might have been a lot more than I'd saved over the last eighteen months. What a thought! But the weather instead of deteriorating was improving, and the liner proceeded to Walvis Bay under her own power, escorted by the naval cruiser, while the armed merchant ship carried on to Cape Town with the children.

We had been standing by the liner for twenty-four hours and were on our way again. We were told the children were all safe, that no one was hurt in any way, and that both the liner and tanker reached port safely. We were only too pleased that the emergency hadn't been a V-boat alarm.

We continued travelling northward, doing our watches, setting the clock every morning, and getting a call from the bridge asking for fresh water to be pumped up to the fresh water tank.

This was a tank on the boat deck holding the drinking water. It was pumped full every morning, or when it was empty, so that the water would flow from the tap on deck. We only had one tap, just outside the galley, which was fitted with a lock so that in times of an acute water shortage it could be locked during certain times of the day. Yes, we had a real economy ship, and I loved it.

The weather was getting warmer every day. Soon we would be crossing the equator and nearing Lagos, capital of Nigeria. I asked the Second why we were calling at Lagos. Apparently we had only taken on a small amount of oil at Cape Town as it was too expensive, and we were to fill our tanks here at Lagos, where it was much cheaper.

I was enjoying my afternoons now on the boat deck, writing letters and keeping my eyes open for enemy shipping; the weather was ideal, blue sky and sea.

During war time letters from home were first sent to Hertzmonceau Castle where they were censored, resulting in whole passages being blotted out with blue pencil. We soon learned to write only personal stuff and not to mention any ports, route times, or war news. The letters were then sent, in batches, to the various agents throughout the world. Edith used to tell me that she hoped the censors were women, as she didn't like the thought of other men reading her love letters. I hadn't even thought of that.

A few days before we reached Lagos I learned that my good fairy was still hovering around me and keeping me out of trouble. During the morning watch I had an accident, not serious as it happened, but it could have been.

One of the gauge glasses on the starboard boiler became so discoloured that I couldn't determine the level of water. Shutting the bottom valve and opening the drain allowed the steam to blow straight through the glass tube, thereby cleaning the tube. In this case the tube exploded, and not only the tube, but also the armoured safety glass.

I was lucky in two ways, Firstly, before it broke, the safety glass absorbed the force of the glass tube exploding, and secondly my back was up against the big fan casing so that my chest was only twelve inches away from the tube when it exploded. If the same thing had happened on any of the other gauge glasses I'd have been standing further back, and my eyes would have been in the danger line.

Fortunately the steam was directed slightly downwards and very easy to turn off, but my chest was peppered with tiny glass crystals, mostly from the safety glass. I was picking tiny pieces of glass from my chest for weeks afterwards. Even after Edith and I were married I always carried tweezers with me, and at the first sign of an itch found another speck to remove.

However I collected new gauge glass and safety

guards from the stores and fitted them right away. They gave no further trouble. The Second learned of the gauge glass incident from the logbook and insisted that I had treatment from the Chief Steward. As he said, it would make things easier if by any chance I had trouble with my chest later.

At Lagos we filled the tanks up to the brim, which only took thirty six hours, and that included taking on a little cargo as well. Then we were off to our last port of call - Freetown, Sierra Leone.

The ship anchored offshore in the wide tidal river, it had taken us almost a week to get here. It would have taken us a couple of day less if we had come along the African coast, but we stood out well into the Atlantic out of sight of land, and made landfall during the day.

This place was the convoy marshalling point. The first instruction we received was to stay aboard, and then we were warned that anyone swimming or in a boat after 6:00pm would be shot on sight. What we called a real friendly welcome to Freetown.

Ships came in, but none went out. In the engine room there was no work to be done, that is apart from spit and polish, as no one knew what was to happen next. Apart from the organisers of the convoy no one had any idea when we were sailing, so there was no question of stripping machinery down as we may not have had time to put it together again. But we did have time for a swim.

Swimming time was restricted to when the tide was turning. There was only an hour of safe water, any other time and the swimmer could find himself up in the jungle or out at sea due to the strong tide. The gangway was lowered until the lower platform was at water level.

Someone must have consulted the local people, probably the company agent, to ensure that it was safe. This time I wondered about crocodiles as I always thought that African rivers were crowded with them, but maybe all African crocodiles were fresh water ones.

A good hour was spent by all of us including the native crew, until the tide became too strong. Then we learned how fast that river flowed. Not even a world champion could swim against that flood.

Being only seven degrees from the equator, it was hot and humid, very uncomfortable during the day and at night the mosquitoes made life miserable. We all did our best with the Flit spray and burned a candle in the corner of the cabin. This was not a religious thing; the candle was to encourage the mosquitoes to commit suicide.

During the day the locals came alongside in their canoes, selling whatever the ship's crew could be persuaded to buy. I bartered a hundred fags for a stalk of Canary bananas. There must have been well over a hundred bananas, all for twenty five pence worth of cigarettes.

We only stayed there a few days, but we didn't know we were leaving until the Stand By sounded in the engine room. During our stay, the boilers had remained fired and we held watches as if we were at sea, so when the telegraph rang we were all down on the starting platform. Once down there we were blind to what was happening on deck. The deck officers got all the fun.

The ships left, one by one, moving out into the Atlantic to take up positions in the convoy, forming a box of six ships in a row and six or seven rows. We never counted how many ships there were as we couldn't see the ones at the back. The deck officers knew of course; what they didn't know was that the Carpenter had bought a monkey at Freetown and smuggled it into his cabin.

The Carpenter's monkey looked quite small when sitting in the boat below, but when it was hoisted on to our deck the Carpenter was surprised to find that it was almost three feet tall. It sat on the deck, but if anyone approached it went wild so no one dare go near it. Chippy didn't know what to do with it. He got plenty of advice mind, none of it printable. He was scared the Captain would get to know, which he was bound to do on his first Sunday inspection. Somehow however the Carpenter managed to get the monkey into his cabin, but I don't think he'd realised that he was going to spend the night with a wild monkey.

Locked in the cabin, the animal really went to town; scared out of its wits, it went berserk. No one dared open the cabin door. We were looking through the portholes, watching the inside of the cabin being destroyed. It tore the bed to pieces, the settee and everything it could lay its hands on.

There was a small ventilator in the door and the stench was revolting as the monkey had defecated all over the cabin in its terror. Little pet monkeys wear nappies. This one was a big monkey, it wasn't house trained, and it certainly was no pet, believe me.

The cabin was a complete wreck. The poor Carpenter didn't know what to do, but he knew that there was no way that the Captain could be kept out of it. When the Captain did find out he carried on like the monkey, only in a more refined manner.

He put it to the Carpenter. 'Get rid of it before we

reach the UK, monkeys can carry rabies,' he said, 'and who is going to foot the quarantine bill?'

The poor Carpenter had a job on his hands, he was looking around for helpful volunteers, but they were very thin on the ground. No one wanted to be mauled by a mad monkey.

But there came a time when it ceased to be a joke. It hadn't been a joke to the Carpenter for quite a while, but now everybody except the Captain was feeling sorry for him. The death sentence was the only conclusion anyone could come to, but how? The Aussies had .303 rifles, the ship was surrounded by water, the Carpenter wanted to strangle it, but daren't. After all that it was drowned. Personally I think the kindest thing would have been to shoot it, but I wasn't consulted.

I was on watch when the execution took place, I was glad of that as I felt sorry for that monkey. Why should anyone take it from its home in the jungle? Why should the Carpenter even think of buying it? He must have known he couldn't take it back home.

The Carpenter, being a handy bloke, had the job of putting things to rights. He cleaned everything up, moving into another cabin to sleep while he did so. The carpet, walls, even the deck head was soiled. The settee he took apart and washed and cleaned the upholstery, the bulkhead and deck head were painted, and all the woodwork varnished. The sheets and bed linen were replaced by the understanding Chief Steward.

I don't think the Carpenter ever forgot the episode of the monkey, we never did. I can imagine him in the years to come recalling it to some youngster just like I have.

The convoy sailed on at ten knots. It seemed slow

compared with the usual twelve and a half knots, but we had to sail at the speed of the slowest of the others. Again, the *City* carried the Commodore of the convoy who usually sailed in the biggest ship, or the one with the most suitable accommodation.

At the end of the line there was one ship very deep in the water. When we left the shelter of the bay, it began to roll, and a week later it was still rolling. Against the other ships it looked out of place. As far as we could see, it was the only ship in the convoy that was rolling. All the other ships were sailing nicely along, while this rusty hulk was rolling from side to side.

I pointed it out to the Second as we leaned together on the rail. He told me that it was an ore carrier with a full load, and that it would still be rolling like that when we reached the UK. If it was hit with a torpedo it would take less than three minutes to sink. Not a nice ship to sail on.

This was the second convoy I'd been in while taking a watch, the first one being from Glasgow. Now after six months I was able to do everything automatically, but I had a light to work by, not so the deck officers. I wondered how they must have strained their eyes at night keeping watch in the dark, trying to see that small light of the ship ahead. We had no radar in those days, eyes and ears were all. However we had no collisions.

The only ship that came to grief in this convoy was a small tramp steamer of around three thousand tons. It developed engine trouble and dropped astern one night. No one was allowed to stay with it, cargoes were too valuable and escorts too few.

Unofficially, we heard from the wireless operator that they had received a message that it was being shadowed by a submarine. The Captain of the steamer was undecided whether it was a Q ship or not, and was waiting for the sub to surface to use his gun, not wishing to use a torpedo on such a small target. But during the next two days the Germans decided not to surface and torpedoed the little ship. We were a long way ahead by this time, and could only hope and pray that the crew got away safely in the boats.

Taking the watch was just the same, but it was easier with the experience that I had had over the last six months. Judging the revs of the engine was easier now, although the 'one up', 'two up', and 'one down' signals were a nuisance. It would have been much more convenient with a rev counter like modern ships.

It was still warm enough to enjoy the deck chair up on the boat deck, although I didn't have much longer to indulge myself. It was wonderful having the afternoons to myself, just to sit and cogitate while the ship cruised along. One incident I remember occurred a month or so after we had the gun mounted on the after deck.

I was in the engine room during the morning watch when there was a tremendous explosion. I thought we had been hit. Half the lights in the engine room went out, then the bridge telephone rang and we were told that they were having a gun exercise, which had just fired. We thought it was nice of them to tell us, but would have appreciated it even more if they had rung down before they fired.

Another time I thought we'd been hit by a torpedo. The gun crew had thrown a barrel over the side which had a weight inside, so that it floated on end with a pole sticking up so that it could be seen from some distance.

During this target practice the gun team hit the barrel with their third shot, just over half a mile distant. No one rang down to tell me what was happening. The noise it made in the engine room and the subsequent shattering of half the light bulbs gave me the biggest shock of the last eighteen months. I really did think that the stern of the ship had been blown off.

But we were nearing home. The days were getting fresher and that warm tropical sun wasn't getting through to the bones as it once did. I wondered if I would ever feel it again. I'd enjoyed my eighteen months at sea, and as the thoughts went around my head I realised that all my worries at Clarke Chapman's had been needless. I had coped, and risen from a junior to a watch keeper in twelve months. Something which later on, when I was called up for the Royal Navy, astounded the Chief Petty Officer who was conducting the interview.

But I knew that although I loved the sea and loved this ship, I would never return to the sea as long as I had Edith. I was going to have a far different life from now.

The route from Freetown took us far into the north Atlantic, away from the African coast towards France, up north and round Northern Ireland into the Irish Sea. Here the ships bound for Glasgow and Liverpool left the convoy and sailed on their way, while we carried on south for Avonmouth. The ship that started rolling when we left Freetown, the iron ore carrier, was still rolling slightly when she left us. Even though we were so near home, things could still go wrong.

We had rounded the north of Ireland entering the North Channel. Although we were bound for Avonmouth, we had to come south through the Irish Sea

420

as a large minefield was in place from Cornwall to County Cork in southern Ireland.

The weather was atrocious, with huge waves crashing over the starboard bow, and to make matters worse, the De-Gausing gear began to give trouble. This was a large coil of electric cable all round the ship in the scuppers to combat the magnetic mines, We'd had it installed at the same time as we had the gun mounted, and it had been no trouble before, but now the cable had deteriorated badly due to the salt water and tropical sun and it was shorting in a number of places.

The Second and Chief worked on the breaks, wearing rubber gloves and boots, taping the wire as it lay smouldering on the deck. I was sheltering around the corner of the accommodation with my eyes open, ready to shout a warning of waves that were coming over the deck. When they did, the Chief and Second just hung on to the rails. All afternoon we carried on trying to repair the cables. We couldn't afford to turn the current off, the anti-magnetic effect was essential for the safety of the ship.

They were still at it when I had to take over the watch at 8:00pm, but as it became darker small fires could be seen at various points around the rails. The two were fighting a losing battle; as they stopped one fire another erupted, they just couldn't cope. Eventually all they could do was to cover the small fires with sand and hope for the best. Someone was detailed to patrol the deck that night with a bucket of sand to keep down the fires, as they made us a target for any enemy planes that might have been about.

The conditions that night befriended us, a stormy sea,

with low, heavy clouds hiding us from the German air force that was on the lookout for our convoy. They passed over, we heard them, but they couldn't see us, so they dropped their bombs on Northern Ireland. We read about the raid in the newspapers when we reached Avonmouth.

The current for the De-Gausing gear was switched off when we reached Avonmouth. There was a rumour that a contact mine followed us into the dock and we were told the following day that it was towed out to sea and destroyed.

Edith and I had already decided to get married after this trip. I don't think that sea going is a suitable job for a married man, yet I don't see how the MN could manage otherwise, almost all of the senior officers were married.

As we edged into the dock and alongside the quay, my thoughts were tumbling all over the place. This was the last time that I'd be standing on the starting platform. I had stood my last watch and was now, in a sense, saying goodbye to an old friend.

It had been a very lucky ship, since the 3rd of September 1939 there had been no sign of enemy action. Every member of the crew had come home unharmed except for Ranji, who died of old age. It was a good ship.

I had a last look around during which I thought to myself of the time I had shut the wrong valve while crossing the Atlantic eighteen months ago. It seemed no time at all since I had had the ship going around in circles.

I climbed the steel ladders to the boiler tops to shut down two of the three boilers. This was a dirty job, and I thought that I would take advantage of an empty bathroom and freshen up. As I came up on deck, the old four-inch gun was there out on the stern. We never saw any U-Boats to fire at; it was only fired three times in practice. They said if you don't hit the U-Boat in three shots you may as well jump overboard.

As I ran the salt water for a bath, I was thinking of anything and everything. I just lay in that bath and soaked, making plans about going home, when all hell broke loose.

A noisy siren, screaming less than fifty yards away, nearly deafened me. We hadn't heard anything like this before and we didn't know what it was. I think that while we were away, we should have had some lessons about Britain at war. Someone banged on the bathroom door and shouted, 'Air raid!'

Unaccustomed to noises of this sort, I came to the conclusion that I couldn't go anywhere like this in a hurry, so I lay back and took it easy. Over the last eighteen months we'd had peace and quiet, except on two or three occasions. Before I was dressed the All Clear had sounded. It was a different noise than before so I presumed it was OK. I hoped that we weren't going to get too much of this. How naive could one get?

There was still work to be done. The Second had his list of repairs to cover and I couldn't go home until I'd signed off. There were pumps to be overhauled, and of course if one started to repair a pump it had to be completed as soon as possible. No one knew when it would be needed in an emergency. But apparently we were to be here for some time, the De-Gausing gear had to be replaced before the ship could leave.

During the week, the Fifth and I decided to walk to

Bristol. After all the foreign places we'd seen neither of us had been to Bristol, it was somewhere new. To recall old memories we went to the pictures, I can't remember the film, but Edward G. Robinson, I believe, starred. I replaced the watch that Edith had given me on our engagement, although I still kept the original watch.

When we reached the bus terminus on our way back to the ship, we were informed that the last bus had already departed, so we began to walk. However, a bus overtook us after we had walked a mile or so and we flagged it down as we'd both had enough of walking. To our surprise it stopped to pick us up, and on climbing aboard the conductress informed us that this was the drunks' bus, run especially to tour the bus stops after closing time to get the drunks home.

I must admit that most of the passengers seemed under the weather. One or two were still trying to get a tune from their throats. The driver only did the driving in those days, the conductor or conductress collected the fares. When we offered our fare to the conductress it was refused, 'No man in uniform pays on my bus,' she said.

We'd been at Avonmouth for a few days when the Second's wife arrived. I was introduced to Mrs Wilkinson and their eight-year-old daughter when they came aboard. Later on, the Second asked me if I minded showing his daughter over the ship, I was only too happy to do so. It had been a long time since he and his wife had seen one another, so I made it the grand tour.

But it was a pleasure and so easy. The eight-year-old was really interested in all parts and aspects of the *City*, the bridge, galley, cabins, and could she see the cargo?

This was the first time that she had been aboard,

which made it more interesting. Probably her dad had told her all about his ship, now she wanted to see it all. What is this? What is it used for? Why was this here? How do the winches work?

We had to be careful though when she insisted on seeing the engine room and into the stokehold. She had on a very pretty dress and I didn't wish to see it ruined. An engine room is not the ideal place for pretty dresses, or pretty girls, so I was glad to get her back on deck without a mark on her clothes.

She was so interested in everything it was a delight to show her around. I sincerely hoped that Edith and I would have such a beautiful spark as this when we were married. We weren't disappointed[35].

Our tour lasted over an hour, but it seemed a very short one. The time passed so quickly and to tell you the truth, it was the first and only time that I stood on the bridge.

The custom officials had already been aboard; they arrived just after the boat docked and they were back again to clear us before we left for home. But first we had to sign off. We were informed that we'd be paid on Monday 30th September and I'd be able to travel that day but this wasn't to be. I had to wait another day until the Tuesday.

That morning the Chief came up to me as I was leaning on the ship's rails, put his elbows on the rails beside me, and asked me if I would change my mind and

---

[35] This wasn't in the last draft manuscript I read before my father died, so I didn't come across this comment until some years later when I eventually found the heart to publish his book. It brought a lump to my throat then and still does each time I read it. Editor

stay with the ship. He tried to persuade me, telling me that the *City* was a good ship, and that I wouldn't get a better in the whole fleet. He paid me a great compliment. He told me that he'd had every confidence in me as a watch keeper and never doubted my ability in any way, and was sorry to see me go. I liked the Chief; one could talk to him very easily. He was fussy, but had a good sense of humour and I like to think that we got on well together.

Once he called in my cabin to borrow a book and found me playing my mouth organ. He asked me why I wasn't ashore, as it was our first visit. I told him that I was short of cash. He told me to get ready and call at his cabin in fifteen minutes. I did, and was asked how much I needed. I told him that a couple of dollars would be sufficient. 'That wasn't the question,' he said.

'Sorry Chief, five dollars will be enough thanks.' He gave me five dollars and refused it later on when I tried to repay him. At the next port of call he bought himself a mouth organ.

As we were leaning on the rail I told him how much I loved that ship, how much I'd enjoyed the job and the company on the ship. In fact I thanked him for educating me as I was a boy when I signed on at Liverpool, now I felt capable of anything. I told him about my promise to Edith, and that she was my future.

Tuesday morning everyone attended the saloon and was paid off. My discharge book was signed and stamped, and then I was unemployed. I looked at my pay slip, almost two feet long. I can't remember the total, it was more than I had expected. Most importantly, with what we had in the bank, there was enough on which to get married.

The customs had been dealt with, my bags were packed. I had my money in my pocket and my travel warrant in my hand, now there was only the train to catch to Newcastle.

There were three of us travelling together, the two cadets and myself. My travel warrant was to Newcastle and the others were to Oxford and York. The warrants had been made out from Avonmouth to the destinations. However the train service from Avonmouth to Bristol was very poor and the first train from Avonmouth would not make the connection we wanted, so we decided to cut out the local station and share a taxi to Bristol.

This we did, but when we handed our warrants to the Booking Clerk he wouldn't accept them. He said, 'These warrants are made out from Avonmouth,' as if we didn't know. We had the usual argument and off he went to see the Station Master who told us the same thing.

I asked him if he wanted us to go back to Avonmouth and start again. This rather put him on the spot, so he went into his office and lifted the phone. After ten minutes he'd sorted it out, took the warrants to the booking office and then handed us the tickets. We were just in time to dash across the platform and board the train we'd arranged to catch. And it was a dash. Carrying our luggage, six expanding suitcases full of our worldly goods, but we made it and settled back exhausted.

I like travelling by train usually, but this train was going too slow. We had to change at Reading, then on to Oxford where I thought to myself, I'll be back here next week applying for a job.

We said goodbye to one of the cadets here, wishing

him well. And then on to York where the remaining cadet collected his cases and left me to travel the rest of my journey alone. When we left York I was looking for all the familiar signs of the North Country, passing Durham Cathedral and hoping to recognise Low Fell station as we flashed through. Soon we were on the High Level Bridge over the Tyne, and slowly drawing into Newcastle Central Station.

I was tired, with only one thought in my head, to see Edith and my family. I left one case at the station in the left luggage office and grabbing the other, containing the things that I needed, I caught the tram to Walkergate.

The trains in those wartime days did not stand by the timetable and it was later than I hoped, but Edith was at home to meet me. We talked and made arrangements for the next day, this was Tuesday night. We were to marry on Friday, the fourth of October. We made decisions and then I made my way to Low Fell by bus.

I seemed to have waited ages at the bus stop when a policeman came along. He decided to cheer me up. 'Waiting for a bus?' he asked and then told me the last bus had gone. It was only 10:00pm. Asking where I was going he suggested a taxi. Feeling the weight of my case I agreed with him, but where was the taxi?

'Oh, there'll be one along in a minute,' he said and to my surprise there was, just as the air raid siren sounded. I was wearing my uniform, so the policeman knew that I was either coming or going on leave.

He stepped out into the road and held up his hand in the approved manner. The taxi stopped. The policeman spoke to the cabbie, 'Here you are cabbie, you've got a fare.' The driver told him that he couldn't pick a fare up during an air raid, but the copper wasn't having that.

He said, 'You'll take this one. Where do you want to go, son?' I told him and he turned to the taxi driver who had already put my case in the back, and said, 'Right, off you go, this lad's done a bit for you, now it's your turn to do a bit for him.'

The cabbie wasn't upset at all. I suppose he'd had his instructions from the depot, maybe something to do with the insurance. He took me the seven miles home and only charged half a crown, twelve and a half new pence, and he refused a tip.

Edith made an excuse to call at her place of work on the Wednesday, entering the works by the back door. I was requested to wait in the court yard, and for the next fifteen minutes windows at the back were opening and shutting on all floors, heads popping in and out to take a look at Edith's catch. Edith had already finished at work and served her notice, but I think that she wanted to show her future husband off to her work mates. Edith must have been very popular, and she had every reason to be.

We also visited some of the places we had found together. We visited the Dicken's Tea Rooms, had tea and cakes and said goodbye to the staff. We would probably never find our way back there again. There was shopping; the wedding ring we bought at the Northern Goldsmiths in Northumberland Street, there were presents to buy for the bridesmaids, and arrangements for flowers and taxis. Alan, my old mate, was persuaded to be best man. Winifred, my sister, and Joan, Edith's sister, were Edith's bridesmaids.

The wedding took place at Newcastle registry office at 3:15pm on October 4th 1940. Edith was very nervous, I don't think that I was any less so, and we were made one that afternoon.

When Mrs Greaves was requested to sign the register my Mam rose to the occasion, but now we had two Mrs Greaves. Edith blushingly walked over to sign her name. Neither of the fathers attended the wedding, both were working and one had to have a much bigger excuse than a wedding to get time off work then, but the mothers and sisters were all there.

Edith would have liked to have been married in church, but we couldn't afford a church wedding. Besides, a church wedding was only possible if we had the support of everybody concerned. Edith was a wage-earner and her wedding wasn't welcomed by her mother, although her father was pleased for her. I know that Edith always, to a degree, resented the fact that her parents hadn't contributed to her wedding.

After the wedding we went to number forty nine, Langley Road. The families had parted and my family went back to Low Fell, on the understanding that Edith and I would be there at 7:00pm. We had tea at number forty nine; Edith, her mother and father, sisters Joan and Audrey, brother George, Doris, a friend of Edith's, and myself, but it was a very dull affair. Edith's mother sat and never said a word. At 6:30pm Edith's dad took me to one side and told me to get Edith, George and Joan over to Low Fell and have a party, he would look after Edith's mother.

So we said goodbye all round and taxied over to Beaconsfield Road, where Edith was welcomed with 'Here comes the bride' on violin and piano. We had a good party and supper with family and friends.

Next morning after breakfast, we caught the train to Oxford, my sisters seeing us off. We were happy, we had all we wanted, each other.

Epilogue

Edith and I enjoyed our married life of fifty-nine years. In 1942 our son Ernest Arthur was born, and six and a half years later a daughter, Enid Mary.

Ernest was killed in a car crash on the 8th of May 1969, a year after Enid was married to Mr Bruce Philip Moulder, on the 23rd of March 1968.

In 1973 Suzanne Amy was born, and two years later Enid had another baby girl, Christina Eve.

On the 10th of December 1999 Edith, aged eighty years, died of cancer of the colon, aggravated by Parkinsonism and Alzheimer's disease. She died at home under the care of her family, as she had always wished, loved by all.

40. Edith Greaves c.1941

EPILOGUE

Ernest John Greaves
15 October 1917 – 9 July 2004

Ernest's history is a simple one; born into a large, loving family on the 15 October 1917, in a small colliery village called the Lintz, in County Durham. A choir boy for many years, he left school at fourteen for an engineering apprenticeship, and started work at a local engineering firm, Sanderson Brothers.

On Boxing Day 1937 he fell in love at first sight when he saw Edith Lamb, a Newcastle 'Geordie' lass at a friend's party. They married in October 1940, after Ernie had spent eighteen months in the Merchant Navy sailing across most of the southern hemisphere, earning enough for them to marry. The day following the wedding they moved from Newcastle to Oxford to look for work, and as there was no property to rent, ended up 'squatting', as so many did in those times. Over the following sixty four years, he devoted himself to supporting and loving Edith, and his family, until he died on the 9 July 2004.

And yet the story of the exceptional human being and the love story behind that simple history are far more complex.

In the eighteen months Ernie was in the Merchant Navy he was made up from fifth officer to fourth officer, and became the youngest fourth officer in his fleet. After he and Edith were married, Ernest turned an old army hut in the middle of an Oxford forest into a home for her, where their son, Ernest Arthur, was born in January 1942.

Ernie started work at Pressed Steel in 1940 being taken on as a craftsman toolmaker, although he had never been trained in that field, and spent his working life at the same company, largely on the prestigious Rolls Royce lines.

Eight years after moving to Oxford, by this time living in council accommodation, their only daughter, Enid, was born in September 1948. Shortly after that Edith suffered a nervous breakdown, a condition that was to cause concern throughout their lives. Some years later Ernie suffered a back injury which was to plague him for the rest of his life.

In 1962 the now Pressed Steel Fisher Company was asked to set up a production line in Milan, Italy, for Alpha Romeo's new model, the 'Guilietta', as the exacting tolerance required by Alpha Romeo for this model was beyond the capacity of Alpha's own craftsmen.

Pressed Steel Fisher asked Ernie to set up the production line tools, this is the part of the process that determines exactly how well everything fits together. To the delight of Pressed Steel and his workmates, and the chagrin of the Italian craftsmen, Ernie brought the job in from bonnet to boot well within the tolerance required. During this two-month period Ernie wrote every day to Edith, and twice weekly to his son and daughter.

Enid married Bruce Moulder on the 23 March 1968, and they had two daughters, Suzanne Amy and Christina Eve, born in July 1973 and 1975 respectively.

In 1969 Ernie and Edith supported each other through the tragic death of their only son, Ernest Arthur, in a car accident at the age of twenty seven.

On his retirement in 1982, while their daughter went back to work, Ernie and Edith were frequent babysitters, forgetting the household chores to become 'creative playmates' with their grand-daughters, Suzanne and Chrissie. Every day was a holiday, with trips to the swimming baths, to the seaside, to the park, and picnics. With Ernie playing games and telling stories as his own father had done for him.

Both girls adored visiting their grandparents at the 'Towers', where Ernie and Edith then lived, and they adored having the girls to stay!

In 1994 Ernie was diagnosed with prostrate cancer and went through a month of daily radiotherapy treatment. Edith went to the Churchill Hospital with him every day, supporting and loving him through a difficult period. Ernie was often in pain but rarely complained, preferring not to 'worry' his family if he were ill.

He loved Edith in sickness and in health, nursing her through another mental breakdown, Parkinson's and in the final four years, the hell of Alzheimer's, until she died in 1999. She had been the only woman for him since he first saw her, and he was devastated following her death.

His own health had suffered as a result of caring for Edith and he took some time to recover his strength, although he never fully recovered from losing her.

During Edith's last illness Ernie taught himself to type so he could record the story of his first twenty two years. After Edith died, he kept himself busy completing his autobiography, building bird-boxes for his family and remote controlled boats for his grand-daughters, putting together photograph albums of Edith and their son Ernie, and helping and caring for his family, friends and neighbours.

For example, shopping for Francis, a neighbour who had called in to talk with Edith when she was ill, and who had been a true friend when he needed help following Edith's death, and helping Francis and her daughter, Lynne, during Francis' last illness. He welcomed new neighbours Ruth and Alex, and helped them with shopping and odds and ends around the house; they in turn provided him with friendship, good company and Ruth's splendid home-made cakes!

Ernie never lost his love of the North, often talking about cycling the highways and byways of Durham and Northumberland, his childhood adventures with his brothers and sisters, his time in the Merchant Navy, and his courtship of Edith.

He managed to keep in touch with his northern roots, his sisters, and his extended family of nieces and nephews, and he delighted in their children too.

These are all simple, quiet things. Ernie was not a person to shout about his concerns, pains or accomplishments. His friends and family knew him as a real gentleman, a true friend and a craftsman; not a saint, but a gentle, caring person who loved children.

Throughout his life he was able to give that very rare thing, unconditional love to those he cared for; his adored wife, daughter, son-in-law Bruce, grand-daughters, Suzanne's partner Tony, and great-grandson Matthew, who adored him in return. Indeed since Matthew's birth in 2001, he was Ernie's second favourite topic of conversation!

In the final few weeks before he died Ernie often reminisced about his life, and repeatedly said that he had no regrets and would live his life over again, even the painful parts, because he had been so lucky and because he had had Edith with him.

He will be sorely missed, a scrabble and canasta companion, an enjoyer of silly jokes, a solver of life and engineering problems, a shoulder to cry on, a rock, one of life's true gentlemen, a real friend, and an exceptional human being in every sense of the word.

Angel of the North

With arms of steel and hands so kind,
A gentle man and a canny find,
He's a secret soul from an ancient time.
My angel of the northland,
My angel of the north.

By Derek Greenacre and Louise Matthews.
Copyrighted 2003

41. Dad and Daughter Oxford c. 1957